DECISION-MAKING FOR SPACE

DECISION-MAKING FOR SPACE:

LAW AND POLITICS IN AIR, SEA, AND OUTER SPACE

BY IRVIN L. WHITE

1970

Purdue University Studies
West Lafayette, Indiana

To Pat, Randy, and David

ACKNOWLEDGMENTS

I wish to acknowledge the support and assistance of at least some of those who have contributed in various ways to this study. Specifically I wish to express my appreciation to:

the National Aeronautics and Space Administration for financial support provided through an institutional grant to the University of Arizona;

the Numerical Analysis Laboratory, University of Arizona, and the Inter-University Consortium for Political Research, University of Michigan, for assistance in data processing;

the Institute of Government, University of Utah, and Wayne State University Press for permission to use materials which appeared originally in *Western Political Quarterly* and *International Studies Quarterly;*

Professor Clifton E. Wilson, University of Arizona, and Charles O. Jones, Falk Professor of Politics, University of Pittsburgh, for guidance and assistance throughout the duration of the project;

Professors Myres S. McDougal, Sterling Professor of Law, Yale Law School, and Harold V. Rhodes, University of New Mexico, for thoughtful and perceptive comments and suggestions which were particularly useful when the manuscript was being revised for publication;

Mrs. Diane R. Dubiel, Purdue University Studies, for her judicious editing;

my sisters Frances W. Mickey and Katherine M. White and my brother-in-law Delbert L. Mickey for support and encouragement;

and finally, I especially wish to acknowledge my multi-faceted debt and appreciation to those to whom this book is dedicated, my wife Patricia and our sons Randy and David. They make the race worth running.

Irvin L. White
West Lafayette, Indiana

November 28, 1969

CONTENTS

ILLUSTRATIONS

TABLES

APPENDIXES

PART I: THE INTERNATIONAL

LAW-IN-ACTION

AND A DETERMINATION

OF THE LEGAL PROBLEMS

IN OUTER SPACE

1: THE INTERNATIONAL LAW-IN-ACTION

To many students of international politics, the title of this study may imply a "legal" analysis of international air, sea, and space law; "legal," that is, in the sense that international law is separate analytically from international politics. This is not such a legal study; this is a decision-making study which focuses on that aspect of international politics traditionally called international law.

For far too long scholars and professors concerned with international law have isolated themselves from international politics. An unfortunate consequence has been that they have largely succeeded in convincing most students of politics that international law is a deadly dull and largely irrelevant academic pursuit. Fortunately in recent years, at least in part as an effort to give international law greater relevance to contemporary international politics, there has been an increasing emphasis on introducing more social science into the study of international law.

In fact, the study of international law, particularly in the United States, has been undergoing a period of rapid evolutionary if not revolutionary change. There has been a general shift away from the kinds of legalistic and moralistic studies which characterized much past international legal lit-

3

erature. The shift has been from legalism and moralism to a focus on the dynamics of international legal and political processes. Increasingly students focus on the international *law-in-action*, the law which is observed and used, rather than on the international *law-in-books*, the law stated by publicists but not necessarily observed in practice.[1]

In the United States and Canada, this has been a part of the development of a school of North American realism and of a policy-oriented approach in international law.[2] Both are rooted in a sociological interpretation of law,[3] and both explicitly recognize the essentially political character of international law.

In large part, the change in the study of international law is an attempt to clarify what the subject matter of international law is. Scholarly concern is with *how international law is used* rather than, as in the classical tradition, with *the meaning of international law* or with what legal scholars say international law is.[4] This change in focus generally has occurred following the recognition of basic structural changes within international society. One obvious change is a proliferation of new nation-states. Much of this expansion has been a consequence of former colonial areas and dependent peoples achieving political independence. Equally important, however, has been an expansion of the subject matter of international law. The latter is largely a consequence of the heterogeneity of the contemporary international system and of the impact of science and technology on world affairs. The importance of both is, of course, widely recognized.

Several scholars, including B.V.A. Röling and Wolfgang Friedmann,[5] for example, have discussed at length the changing structure of the system which international law serves. From a small number of relatively homogeneous western European "Christian Nations,"[6] the system has been extended to include culturally, linguistically, politically, and socially diverse members.

In their *A Cross-Polity Survey*,[7] Arthur S. Banks and Robert B. Textor record this increasing heterogeneity. They require, for example, fourteen separate codes to identify the "character of legal system" of entities participating in the contemporary international political system.[8] In addition, they record significant differences among participants on such relevant factors as "international financial status," "economic development status," "ideological orientation," and "system style."

As for science and technology, it seems that their impact has been and is twofold: first, there are the accumulative effects of the scientific and technological revolution itself; and second, there is the impact of the exponential rate of contemporary scientific and technological change. Take, for example, the international legal and political questions attendant to man's venturing into outer space as well as numerous problems which arise as a consequence of a rapidly developing technology for liberating the riches of the sea and the seabed.[9]

The very need for a study such as the one undertaken here arises as a consequence of the changes briefly outlined above. This is an undertaking which explicitly recognizes the changes taking place in the study of international law and attempts to advance these changes by the introduction of social science analysis techniques. The focus here is on a systematic study of the international *law-in-action* employing a specific analytical framework.[10]

A GENERAL DESCRIPTION OF THE STUDY

As has been indicated, this is a study of legal and political decision-making in the international air, sea, and space environments. The general research interest is to determine if there exists a core of generally agreed-upon principles in international law which are applicable or relevant to certain legal and political problems either already encountered or likely to be encountered in outer space. There are three principal parts to the study: (1) a determination of the legal and political problems of outer space; (2) a determination of selected legal rules and principles in international air and sea law; and (3) an analysis of *why* the decision-makers of states accept or reject the specific rules and principles determined in Part II, and whether or not these rules and principles are likely to be applicable or relevant in resolving legal and political problems in outer space.

There are several reasons why a study such as this is needed. One of the principal ones is that it seems unlikely that participation in major space exploration programs will continue indefinitely to be limited to the United States and the Soviet Union. In fact, a number of other states already have undertaken comparatively modest space exploration projects, and a number of inter-state organizations have been established as a means of facilitating cooperative space research.[11]

There is merit to the argument that the community should be forewarned by consequences which in the past have resulted from the failure of national decision-makers to agree on ordering rules and prescriptions in areas such as controls for atomic energy, for example. It is reasonable to assume that similar consequences can arise with regard to outer space; therefore, it does seem desirable to establish early agreement on legal rules for outer space. Past experience indicates that the likelihood of achieving agreement on rules ordering any activity or environment seems to be related directly to the number of governments actively involved. When a large number of nation-states become directly involved, agreement on a comprehensive legal order becomes difficult if not practically impossible to achieve.

A core of terrestrial legal principles and political experiences should not be ignored as a possible basis for dealing with the legal and political problems of outer space. However, there has been no adequate comprehensive, empirical analysis conducted to determine whether such a core of applicable legal principles and political experience does exist. International air and sea law seem to be particularly promising bodies of law within which such a core of applicable principles might be located.

Pressed too far, all analogies eventually are made to reveal a basic weakness. Situations and circumstances simply are too variable for specific analogies to be more than generally suggestive. Although many legal writers suggest a direct application of specific analogies, most legal writers warn against such mechanical application. The general position here, and one widely accepted by legal scholars studying space, is summarized in a quotation from a paper which Colonel Martin Menter, judge advocate, United States Air Force, presented before the Sixth Colloquium on the Law of Outer Space in Paris in 1963. Colonel Menter said:

> The law governing space activities cannot be established independently of principles of law developed to govern man's activities on earth. This does not mean that all laws on earth automatically apply to space, but that in determining the law that should apply to space activities — we must reexamine analogous related laws, such as the Law of the Sea and Air Law, among others, to determine whether the underlying rationale of such law may also be applicable to the new environment of outer space.[12]

Leon Lipson and Nicholas deB. Katzenbach make the point even more succinctly. In referring to the applicability of analogies, they say:

> The futility of mechanical adoption does not mean that the experience of decades or centuries in these other fields is irrelevant to the control of space. On the contrary, reflection on that experience *mutatis mutandis* will help to anticipate problems of space and suggest ways of dealing with them. Particular solutions or devices may commend themselves for adaptation; historical failures may enable us to guard against repetition.[13]

Legal analogies are useful because all international laws are the product of a political process. Decisions within nation-states and other involved actors represent an accommodation of numerous interests. When a decision is consciously made as a part of an international decision, various interests at this inter-state level consciously are reconciled. It is assumed that decision-makers do consciously attempt to protect certain basic interests and to maximize certain goals, acting always within the context of perceived environmental factors and conditions which affect particular decisions. While, as most scholars will agree, the interests and goals remain reasonably stable, the environmental factors and conditions are subject to rather drastic fluctuations or changes over relatively brief time periods.[14] It is not possible, given the state of development of social science research methods, to isolate, much less measure these factors and conditions. However, it is possible to identify and even to quantify certain capability indicators which, it may be assumed, affect the decisions and the behavior of national decision-makers in their international political roles. For example, it is reasonable to assume that there is some relationship between such variables as a state's own defense capabilities, its dependence upon alliances for defense, the percentage of its budget devoted to defense, and that state's acceptance or rejection of certain international laws and claims which are perceived to affect national security such as extent of jurisdiction over superjacent air space and adjacent seas.

Consider also an example of an economic interest. On the one hand, it seems reasonable to assume that a state whose economy is heavily dependent upon fishing on the high seas will oppose attempts to decrease the extent of these high sea fishing grounds by other states. On the other hand, an underdeveloped state whose economy and national diet are heavily dependent upon the resources of the adjacent sea will likely strongly advocate extending the degree of its control over adjacent sea areas.

Analogies, then, potentially are a prime source in two respects: first, as a body of political experience which may offer general guidelines for anticipating and resolving certain kinds of legal and political problems in all environments; and second, as a body of existing law within which capabilities may be analyzed in relation to nation-states' acceptance or rejection of certain rules affecting identifiable interests such as security, conservation, economy, and prestige.

In summary, the justification for examining analogies is that simply changing the environment logically should not change the basic reasons for which the decision-makers of nation-states accept or reject rules, norms, and principles. Explaining or clarifying *why* decision-makers accept or reject legal rules and principles in one environment should provide a basis for better informed rule-making and problem-solving in other environments.

The remainder of this chapter is devoted to a discussion of the analytical framework which will be used in the analysis of legal and political experience in international ari and sea law. In Chapter 2, the results of a canvass of space law literature are reported. While the canvass is not intended to be a sophisticated content analysis, an attempt is made to arrive at some consensus as to what the legal problems in outer space are or are likely to be. A taxonomy of legal problems is established, priorities noted, and sources categorized. The details of this analysis, both as to method and findings, are left for Chapter 2.

In Part II selected legal rules and principles in international air and sea law are determined using the analytical framework spelled out below.

Two major analytic goals are set for Part III. First, an explanation or clarification of why decision-makers of states accept or reject particular legal rules and principles in international air and sea law is attempted. And second, the applicability or relevance of particular legal rules, principles, and political experience in international air and sea environments to particular kinds of legal and political problems in outer space is analyzed. The underlying assumption is that if one knows what interests national decision-makers seek to protect, promote, or enhance, what goals they seek to maximize, and generally why they accept particular legal rules and principles in one environment, one should be able to predict with some reasonable accuracy what legal rules and principles these same national decision-makers are likely to accept in new environments.

FRAMEWORK FOR ANALYSIS

It is evident to any student of international law that there are various *kinds* of international law. In large part the kinds seem to vary on the basis of political content. For example, international law in certain functional areas is different in kind from the rules and principles purported to regulate the use of force in international affairs. On the one hand, governments can agree relatively easily on detailed legal rules; on the other hand, the stakes are perceived to be higher, and those agreements which can be reached at all are less detailed and are much more subject to reinterpretation in terms of particular situations and circumstances.[15]

A beginning assumption, then, is that in much of what is generally called international law there is no clear distinction between international law and international politics. In fact, it seems that there is no international legal system apart from the international political system; international legal rules and principles are simply particular *forms* of decisions of the international political system.[16]

The international political system is characterized by a high degree of decentralization of authority. As a matter of form, governments voluntarily consent to accept ordering rules and principles of international law.[17] However, at least two caveats must be added to this interpretation of the essentially consensual and voluntaristic nature of international law. First, almost without exception, scholars maintain that there is, in fact, economic, political, and social interdependence or linkage among nation-states. Second, it is obvious that some nation-states have more freedom in choosing voluntarily to grant or withhold consent than do some other nation-states.[18]

In the decentralized international political system, authority is generally exercised through decentralized decision-making processes.[19] With some exceptions, principally regional and/or functional organizations, meaningful decisions concerning the exercise of authority in the international political system are made in its subsystems. Of course, nation-states are the most numerous and most easily identifiable political subsystems. While at times other subsystems are obviously involved in international decision-making, for the most part it is the decisions made in nation-states which constitute the bases for authoritative international decisions. For example, an international convention is a tangible international legal decision when the requisite number of governments and/or specific governments have ratified or otherwise accepted the convention.

There are, of course, less tangible international decision-making processes; specific laws determined to be based on general principles of international law or custom are examples of decisions from such less tangible processes. But even in these less tangible decision-making processes, decisions are made within the subsystem which indicate acceptance or rejection of particular rules and principles.

Some international decisions are made in international and regional organizations; however, the legal character of decisions made in such organizations is not settled.[20] At times *ad hoc* international and regional conferences function as forums for making international legal decisions.[21]

In every case, whatever the decision-making process, the resulting decisions seem always to be determined through some process involving quantification. International legal rules or principles generally are considered to exist when a majority of some kind accepts them, such as a majority of all nation-states, a majority of the major users, or a majority of the nation-states having a relevant special interest. Except for the case of multilateral conventions, no specific formula or calculus is explicitly stated; moreover, as has been noted, some nation-states have more freedom in deciding whether to accept or reject rules than do some other nation-states.

In order to determine what the international law in a particular problem area is at any given time, claims and counterclaims concerning what the law is are examined and the results are submitted to the test of nation-state practice. The legal rule or principle may be determined at that point.[22]

As indicated above, the calculating procedure for determining international legal rules and principles seems always to involve quantification. How obvious and explicit the quantification and calculating procedures are depends upon which particular decision-making process is used.

International legal decision-making processes involving custom and general principles are much less explicit and obvious than is the international conventions process. But in any case, regardless of the decision-making process used, it is possible, even probable, that there will not be perfect congruence between the rules and principles thus established and the law which is observed in practice.

Custom and General Principles. Legal publicists generally agree that when a practice or usage commands general assent it may be invoked as a rule of conduct. When determining a customary rule the emphasis has traditionally been on generality, not on universality. This traditional emphasis is made clear by Myres S. McDougal, one of the most eminent and influential contemporary legal scholars.

> It may bear emphasis, so much confusion enshrouds the literature, that the uniformities in past behavior and subjectivities required for the establishment of customary prescriptions in the world arena are those of generality, not of universality. The explicit consent of every particular state is not a prerequisite to the authority of a particular prescription, else the onerous necessities of comprehensive agreement would replace the flexible potentialities of step-by-step customary development.[23]

Sir Herschel Lauterpacht argues that customary rules are established by common consent, and that:

> "Common Consent" can . . . only mean the express or tacit consent of such an overwhelming majority of the members that those who dissent are of no importance whatever and disappear totally from the view of one who looks for the will of the community in contradistinction to the will of its single members.[24]

It seems, however, that the "overwhelming majority" in some cases may be a majority of the nation-states which are the major users, the major participants, or which otherwise have a special interest in the particular rule. This interpretation is implicit in the often-cited decision of the United States Supreme Court in *The Scotia,* a case dealing with a collision of two vessels on the high seas.[25] The Court stated in its opinion that:

> . . . law is of universal obligation, and no statute of one or two nations can create obligations for the world. Like all the laws of nations, it rests

upon the common consent of civilized communities. It is of force, not because it was prescribed by any superior power, but because it has been *generally* accepted as a rule of conduct. *Whatever may have been its origin,* whether in the usages of navigation or in the ordinances of maritime states, or in both, *it has become the law of the sea only by the concurrent sanction of those nations who may be said to constitute the commercial world.*[26]

The Court noted that the rules of navigation had been accepted by more than thirty of the principal commercial nation-states of the world. This number included almost all of those engaged in shipping on the Atlantic Ocean. As a consequence, it seems that the Court concluded that the rules of navigation in question were the laws-in-action by common consent of a majority of the *major users or nation-states with a relevant special interest.*[27]

In the *Asylum Case (Colombia v. Peru)*,[28] the International Court of Justice considered the question of how one determines the existence of a rule of customary international law. In its opinion, the court said:

> In trying to ascertain whether a practice has become a rule of customary international law, one must ask how many states follow the practice, which states these are, whether they follow it because of a feeling of obligation to do so, and whether there is any competing or contrary practice.[29]

It seems reasonable, based on this analysis, to assert that international legal rules and principles formulated through the customary decision-making process are based on general acceptance by some kind of a majority of the subjects of international law. *Both publicists and courts have made this implicit if not explicit for years.*

On the other hand, much less is written about general principles of international law, and courts have seldom if ever relied upon them.[30] In part, this seems to be the case because custom and convention have been adequate sources: that is, until recently the international legal rules which were developed within these two decision-making processes have met the needs of the subjects of international law — at least as well as the subjects have generally wanted their needs met. But in large part the reason has been the lack of any widespread consensus on what the general principles of international law are. Legal analogies, natural law, general principles of justice, customary international law, and general principles of positive national and comparative law have been suggested as sources of general principles by some writers.[31]

Sir Humphrey Waldock suggests that "the phrase [the general principles of international law] is a wide one; it includes, though it is not limited to, the principles of private law administered in national courts when these are applicable to international relations."[32] However, as Freidmann argues, the traditional distinctions between private and public international law are no longer clear since in an increasing number of nation-states governments have assumed many of the roles and functions which in the past have been considered private.[33] Friedmann concludes that to apply general principles of law is in essence to apply the results of a comparative study of legal principles found within domestic systems.[34] Presumably, then, if legal principles are found in a majority of domestic systems, they are *general* principles and may be considered universally applicable.[35]

Conventions. On the surface there is no ambiguity concerning the conventional decision-making process. A fundamental international legal principle is that conventional rules are applicable only to parties.[36] While it is correct that conventional law is usually considered to be applicable only between parties, it seems that if conventional law is widely accepted, it becomes acceptable as a statement of general principles, a codification of custom, or the progressive development of international law.[37]

International Organizations. As for the decision-making processes of international organizations, there is not yet widespread agreement on the binding legal character of certain kinds of decisions made therein. For example, it seems clear that resolutions passed by a simple majority vote in the General Assembly of the United Nations are not law. And when such a resolution is passed over the opposition of one or more of the "major powers," its binding legal character seems even more questionable.[38] But what of resolutions which are passed by unanimous vote in the General Assembly?[39] And what is the status of the General Assembly's "declarations"?[40]

In international law, the line separating norms which are binding from those which are not is not always distinct. Recent practice may indicate a trend towards reliance upon consensus rather than the formal binding or nonbinding character of the prescription in assessing the reality of international obligations.[41]

In summary, it seems that decisions are made within all the major identifiable international legal decision-making processes on the basis of general rather than universal acceptance. It is reasonable, then, to propose a majority rule formula for making an empirical determination of the international law-in-action. However, as the decision in *The Scotia* illustrates, certain nation-states may have a special interest, be major users, or be major participants in a particular international legal problem area; although there obviously are also problem areas, such as human rights, for example, within which all states appear to have an equal interest.

The analytic framework proposed here is based, therefore, on a modified majority rule principle. A basic assumption is that such an analysis, on the basis of the best available evidence, will provide the best possible answer to the question of what the international law-in-action on any particular international legal problem is at any particular time.[42] Three questions comprise the rules in their operational form:

1. Does a majority of the nation-states comprising the international political system accept the particular international legal rule or principle?

2. Does the majority which accepts the particular international legal rule or principle include a majority of the major users, participants, or other nation-states which might have a relevant special interest?

3. Is there evidence that the particular international legal rule or principle is observed by the subjects of international law in practice? Or, alternatively, is there a lack of evidence that the rule or principle is not regularly observed by the subjects of international law in practice?

Of course, not all international legal rules and principles are universally applicable. That is, the *extent* of applicability can range from only two nation-states (in the case of a bilateral agreement which establishes rules and principles between the two signatory nation-states) to universal applicability (in those instances in which rules and principles are sufficiently widely accepted). While analyses using the framework proposed here are designed primarily to determine which international legal rules and principles are universally applicable, a by-product of these analyses will be the determination of less widely-applicable rules and principles.

At least one additional problem remains to be solved before demonstrating the use of the proposed framework in an analysis of international law-in-action; the problem of making operational the various investigative steps stated in the modified majority rule.

There is nothing particularly new in the first step of the analysis, determining acceptance or rejection of particular international legal rules and principles by the nation-states comprising the international political system. However, there is at least one basic problem involved in making this determination: the problem concerning the character of the evidence.

Increasingly the records of international conferences are the best sources of explicit evidence of acceptance or rejection of particular rules and principles. However, the contemporary use of majority rather than unanimous vote in adopting specific provisions and even whole multilateral conventions leads at times to ambiguities. For example, a government's delegate to an international conference may speak and vote for specific provisions and may even sign the convention on behalf of his government; but his goverment may fail subsequently to ratify or otherwise to adhere to the convention. At a minimum, the delegate's statements, votes, and signature indicate an implicit if not formal acceptance of the international legal rules and principles embodied in the convention. However, it would be more satisfactory to have a ratification or some other form of adherence as evidence. Reservations also are a problem, as are conflicting public statements by government officials. Of course there are numerous other situations in which it is difficult to determine positively either acceptance or rejection.[43]

When the available evidence is explicit acceptance or rejection of a conventional rule or principle, statements concerning the binding character and the extent of applicability can reasonably be made. Signing a convention can, barring evidence to the contrary, be considered evidence of tacit consent. Positive acceptance also may be established on the basis of provisions included within domestic legislation, official policy statements, or customary practice.

In the second stage of the analysis, one must first operationally define relevant special interest, major user, or major participant. There are two primary alternatives: to identify special interest in broad problem areas of international law, such as the law of the sea, or the law of exploration and discovery, for example; or to identify special interests in particular problem areas, such as the breadth of territorial waters or innocent passage through territorial airspace.

As an example of how these interests may be made operational, consider the law of the sea. There are several alternative ways in which to identify and define this interest objectively. A major interest in the sea as a means of communications may be indicated by the intensity of shipping activity in a nation-state's ports and by the size of its merchant marine fleet.[44] Another indicator of an economic interest in the law of the sea might be the intensity of fishing activity. An economic dependence upon the sea also may be indicated in fishery products as a proportion of total exports. Net food supplies available might be used to indicate dependence or potential dependence on the sea as a food source, particularly in those nation-states where diets are deficient in animal protein. And the size of military naval forces might be used as an indication of the perceived importance of the sea to the national security of coastal nation-states.

In the third stage of the analysis the results of the preceding studies are compared in practice, and unless there is evidence that the rules determined in stages one and two are not observed in practice, the rules and principles thus determined can be accepted as a reasonable statement of international law at a particular time.

SUMMARY

This is a study in international politics, for international law is but one decisional output of an international political system. The international political system is subsystems-dominant. Consequently, international decision-making is highly decentralized and international decision-makers function also as national decision-makers. In this latter role, they seek to protect certain perceived national interests and to maximize certain national goals. This is the case even when the decisions of these decision-makers consciously are a part of an international decision, as in the case of an international convention.

International decisions, then, including international laws, are the product of decisions made largely in the political subsytems. There are three major decisional processes generally recognized as relevant to establishing international legal rules and principles: international conventions, international custom, and the general principles of international law. Some international legal scholars argue that there is now a fourth decisional process relevant to international law, that is, the process by which decisions are made in international organizations.

To determine what international law is at any given point in time, one examines claims, counterclaims, and nation-state practice, and using the appropriate algorithm determines the "law-in-action." The calculating procedure always seems to involve quantification; the quantification procedure and the algorithm vary with the particular rule and principle and with the particular decision-making process used.

This study is comprised of three main parts: (1) a determination of the legal and political problems in outer space; (2) a determination of selected legal rules and principles within international air and sea law; and (3) an analysis of *why* the decision-makers of states accept or reject the specific rules and principles determined in Part II, and *whether* these rules and principles are likely to be applicable or relevant to legal and political problems in outer space.

The justification for examining analogies is based upon the assumption that merely changing the environment should not change the basic reasons for which national decision-makers accept or reject specific legal rules and principles. Knowing why rules and principles are accepted or rejected in one environment should help in predicting which rules and principles will be acceptable in another environment.

It is intended that this be a systematic investigation and analysis. Quantitative methods and statistical data analytic techniques are used, as are traditional methods such as historical description and informed insightful speculation. It is primarily the empirical nature of the study and the use of quantitative methods and statistical analysis which sets this study apart from other studies of space law.

NOTES

1. Cf. Edward McWhinney, *"Peaceful Coexistence" and Soviet Western International Law* (Leyden: A. W. Sythoff, 1964).

2. See, for example: Anthony D'Amato, "Classical Theories of Jurisprudence and Their Relevance to World Politics," (unpublished paper delivered at the 1967 Annual Meeting of the American Political Science Association, Pick-Congress Hotel, Chicago, Illinois, September 9, 1967); Judge Alejandro Alvarez' opinions in *The Competence of the General Assembly for the Admission of a State* (International Court of Justice, *Reports,* 1950), pp. 12-21, and *The International Status of South West Africa* (I.C.J. *Reports,* 1950), pp. 174-85; Wolfgang Friedmann, *The Changing Structure of International Law* (New York: Columbia University Press, 1964); C. Wilfred Jenks, especially his *The Common Law of Mankind* (New York: Frederick A. Praeger, 1958); Myres S. McDougal and his various collaborators, particularly in his Law and Public Order Series; Edward McWhinney, op. cit.; B.V.A. Röling, *International Law in an Expanded World* (Amsterdam: Djambatan N.V., 1960); Lawrence Scheinman and David Wilkinson, eds., *International Law and Political Crisis: An Analytic Casebook* (Boston: Little, Brown and Co., 1968); Peter H. Rohn, "The United Nations Treaty Series Project," *International Studies Quarterly,* 12 (June 1968), pp. 174-95, and the work of his various associates in the project including Juris A. Lejnieks, William M. Vaughn, and Robert V. Edington; and my "A Framework for Analyzing International Law-in-Action: A Preliminary Proposal," *International Studies Quarterly,* 13 (March 1969), pp. 46-69.

3. Laws are the rules and norms which order the pursuit and realization of values. Law originates, develops, and functions within a community, which is defined as a common belief-value system founded upon group relations. Cf. Morton A. Kaplan and Nicholas deB. Katzenbach, *The Political Foundations of International Law* (New York: John Wiley and Sons, Inc., 1961); Sebastian De Grazia, *The Political Community: A Study of Anomie* (Chicago: The University of Chicago Press, 1948); Carl J. Friedrich, ed., *Community* (New York: The Liberal Arts Press, 1959); and Werner Levi, *Fundamentals of World Organization* (Minneapolis: The University of Minnesota Press, 1950).

Clearly the scope of shared values and beliefs within the international system is limited.

4. Cf. D'Amato, op. cit. He contends that "what counts is not what some scholar in a book or article says the law 'really is,' but what national decision-makers and their advisers think the law is. International law is a phenomenological datum at the national level" (p. 12).

5. Röling and Friedmann, op. cit.

6. Röling describes the evolution of the international legal system by adopting three descriptive labels for selected time spans. He uses the label "Christian Nations" for the years 1648-1856. When Turkey was invited into the system in 1856,

the system became the "Civilized Nations." This label, according to Röling, describes the system until 1945. The period beginning in 1945 he calls the "Peace-Loving Nations."

7. (Cambridge: The M.I.T. Press, 1963).

8. The fourteen codes are: civil; mixed civil-indigenous; common; mixed common-indigenous; mixed civil-common; mixed civil-common indigenous; Muslim; mixed civil-Muslim; mixed common-Muslim; mixed civil-Muslin-indigenous; mixed common-Muslim-indigenous; Scandinavian; Communist, and other.

9. It is also evident that the pace and volume of international trade between governments, corporations, and individuals constantly are increasing. Moreover, in the past several decades, governments generally have acted to provide positively for their citizens' well-being, and to ensure to all men certain fundamental human rights. In fact, some governments are beginning to accept similar responsibilities for peoples other than their own, typically through collective action within international and regional organizations.

10. At base my analytic goals are policy-related; that is, my hope is that the type of analysis undertaken here will contribute to the accumulation of a body of knowledge which eventually will provide a basis for rationally comprehensive decision-making.

11. A number of countries in addition to the United States and the Soviet Union have research programs involving earth satellites. These include the United Kingdom, France, Canada, and Italy. The French launched an all-French satellite with a French booster rocket from a French launching pad in February 1966 and since have launched several more. Most of the other launchings by these states have been with a United States booster rocket from a United States launching pad or as a part of cooperative programs in which these states participate. And now Red China has launched an earth satellite.

Numerous other states carry on even more modest programs, typically with sounding rockets. Spain, India, Japan, Brazil, and West Germany are among those so engaged.

The inter-state organizations are principally European, although Australia participates as well. The convention establishing the European Organization for the Development and Construction of Space Vehicle Launchers was opened for signature in 1964, for Australia, Belgium, the Federal Republic of Germany, France, Italy, and the United Kingdom. Twelve countries — Austria, Belgium, Denmark, the Federal Republic of Germany, France, Italy, Netherlands, Norway, Spain, Sweden, Switzerland, the United Kingdom — made plans to form the European Space Research Organization (ESRO) as early as 1960. Nine countries — Australia, Belgium, Denmark, the Federal Republic of Germany, France, Italy, Netherlands, Spain, and the United Kingdom — joined together to establish the European Launcher Development Organization (ELDO) in 1961. The first of several successful ELDO rocket launchings took place in May 1966 at Australia's Woomera facility. Apparently the existence of both ESRO and ELDO are threatened now due to a cutback in support by the United Kingdom and Italy. On April 17, 1968, the United Kingdom announced that it was withdrawing from participation in a proposed experimental European television satellite and that it intended to level off its contribution to ELDO (*New York Times,* 17 April 1968, p. 95). Italy's withdrawal of its support is reported to be the main reason that ESRO cancelled its two most ambitious satellites on April 25, 1968 (*New York Times,* 28 April 1968, p. 24).

Private industrialists also have joined together to maximize benefits from space exploration. More than 130 companies and trade associations are now participants in the non-profit-making association EUROSPACE which was established in 1961. Cf. C. Wilfred Jenks, *Space Law* (New York and Washington: Frederick A. Praeger, 1965), especially pages 74-81, and Leonard S. Silk, "Values and Goals of Space Exploration," in *Space and Society* (Dobbs Ferry, New York: Oceana Publications, Inc., 1964), ed. Howard J. Taubenfeld, pp. 43-72.

As for other international cooperation in space exploration, the United Nations sponsors a rocket facility at Thumba, India, which is open to all United Nations members. By the end of 1968, more than 60 rockets had been launched from Thumba. Forty-seven of these were supplied by the National Aeronautics and Space Administration; others have been supplied by Japan, Australia, and France (Indianapolis *Star,* 21 October 1968, p. 33).

A Centre for Research and Training on the Use of Satellite Communications has been established at Ahmedabad, India, with the assistance of the United Nations Development Programme and the International Telecommunication Union. This center ". . . was initially set up to provide training and research facilities in satellite communications for scientists, engineers and advanced technicians" (United Nations Development Programme, *Pre-Investment News,* April 1969, p. 1). Forty-two trainees from India and neighboring countries have undergone specialized training and now form a ". . . core of specialists on which the development of satellite communications networks in the Indian region depend at the present time" (Idem).

12. "Formulation of Space Law," *Proceedings of the Sixth Colloquium on Outer Space* (Washington: International Astronautical Federation, 1964), ed. Andrew C. Haley, p. 2.

13. *Report to the National Aeronautics and Space Administration on the Law of Outer Space* (Chicago: American Bar Foundation, 1961), p. 23. See also Senator Albert Gore's comments on the United Nations in U.N. Document A/C/1/PV, p. 1289; Eliene Galloway, "The United Nations *Ad Hoc* Committee on the Peaceful Uses of Outer Space," in *Proceedings of the Second Colloquium on the Law of Outer Space,* ed. Andrew G. Haley and Welf Heinrich, Prince of Hanover (Wein: Springer-Verlag, 1960), pp. 30-41; and the *Trail Smelter Arbitration, American Journal of International Law,* 35 (October 1941), p. 684.

14.   These statements concerning stability are, of course, statements of relative stability. It is possible to make a case that the so-called revolution of rising expec-

tations represents a rather drastic change in interests and goals for newly independent nation-states.

The change in status of the United Kingdom as a "world power" since World War II, and similar changes for other former colonial "powers" such as Belgium, Netherlands, and France illustrate the point that environmental factors and conditions generally are subject to rather drastic fluctuations over relatively brief time periods.

15. Of course, it is not at all clear how one makes the differences in kind operational. One possible measure of political content is to establish a continuum of the *degree* of acceptance of the particular rules in an international legal problem area. The two poles of the continuum are relatively easy to establish: a well-defined, detailed legal rule and a loosely-defined general legal principle. It is not at all easy, however, to specify the points in between the two poles.

16. This conclusion is logically consistent with the policy-oriented interpretation of international law; in fact, if in this approach there is to be something which can be called international law as distinct from policy generally, it seems imperative that the distinction be based on form.

17. Although individuals, corporations, and international organizations are becoming subjects of international law to a limited extent, nation-states are still the principal subjects.

18. Nation-states dependent upon other nation-states for economic development aid, and raw material-producing nation-states heavily dependent upon international trade are obvious examples. But which particular nation-states are more or less free to choose among rules and principles varies over time.

19. The degree of decentralization varies, however, depending upon the subject matter of individual decisions. For example, authority apparently is more centralized in inter-nation-state organizations such as the International Labor Organization and in functional international organizations generally than it is in non-functional areas.

20. Cf.: Richard A. Falk's "On the Quasi-Legislative Competence of the General Assembly," *American Journal of International Law*, 60 (October 1966), pp. 782-91; and Rosalyn Higgins, *The Development of International Law through the Political Organs of the United Nations* (London and New York: Oxford University Press, 1963).

21. Most analyses of the international political system make it clear that certain unofficial actors function as subsystems. These subsystems need to be identified when determining the inputs into the decision-making process for each particular legal rule or principle being determined. However, if one is interested only in the output, the process itself, including the various inputs, can be treated as a black box operation.

22. To many international legal scholars, this will appear to be an excessively positivistic conception of international law. However, it is contended that such is

not the case, for morality and idealism together with self-interest are all potential inputs into the decision-making processes within the international political subsystems. Surely the rules and principles which are the collective international decisional output reflect these inputs since, like all systems, the international political system is subsystems-dominant.

On establishing the existence of a rule of international law, see F. K. Nielson, American Commissioner on the Mexican-American General Claims Commission, in his dissenting opinion in the *International Fisheries Co. Case* (*General Claims Commission, 1926, Opinions 207,* 1931) as cited by William W. Bishop, Jr., *International Law: Cases and Materials* (Boston and Toronto: Little, Brown and Co. 1962), pp. 716-20.

> The existence or non-existence of a rule of international law is established by a process of inductive reasoning; by marshalling the various forms of evidence of the law to determine whether or not such evidence reveals the general assent that is the foundation of the law (p. 225).

23. Myres S. McDougal, Harold D. Lasswell, and Ivan A. Vlasic, *Law and Public Order in Space* (New Haven and London: Yale University Press, 1963), p. 118.

24. H. Lauterpacht, ed., *L. Oppenheim, International Law: A Treatise,* Vol. 1, 7th ed. (London, New York, and Toronto: Longmans Green and Co., Ltd., 1948), p. 17.

25. *The Scotia,* 14 Wallace 170 (U. S., 1871), cited in Herbert W. Briggs, *The Laws of Nations: Cases, Documents and Notes,* 2d ed. (New York: Appleton-Century-Crofts, Inc., 1952), pp. 25-30.

26. Ibid., p. 29. Emphasis added.

27. On custom generally, see, for example: Lauterpacht, op. cit.; Pitt Cobbett, *Cases on International Law,* 6th ed. (London: Sweet and Maxwell, 1947); Sir Humphrey Waldock, ed. *J. L. Brierly, The Law of Nations: An Introduction to the International Law of Peace,* 6th ed. (New York and Oxford; Oxford University Press, 1963); Briggs, *The Law of Nations,* op. cit.; Herbert W. Briggs, "The Columbia-Peruvian Asylum Case and Proof of Customary International Law," *American Journal of International Law,* 45 (October 1951), pp. 723-31; and McDougal, Lasswell, and Vlasic, op. cit.

28. I.C.J., *Reports,* 1950, cited by Bishop, op. cit., pp. 29-30.

29. Ibid., p. 30.

30. See, for example, Briggs, *The Law of Nations,* op. cit.; and Wolfgang Friedmann, "The Uses of 'General Principles' in the Development of International Law," *American Journal of International Law,* 57 (April 1963), pp. 270-99.

31. Briggs, loc. cit.

32. Waldock, op. cit., p. 62.

33. Friedmann, "*The Uses of 'General Principles'*," op. cit., p. 281.

34. Ibid., p. 282.

35. In addition to the sources cited, see Bishop, op. cit., pp. 38-40, and Briggs, op. cit., p. 48, for discussions and bibliographies. See also D. F. O'Connell, *International Law*, 1 (London: Stevens and Sons Ltd.; Dobbs Ferry: Oceana Publications, Inc., 1965).

36. However, there is some question as to the applicability between parties when reservations are made by some of the parties. See, for example, the I.C.J. decision in the *Reservations Case* (I.C.J., *Reports*, 1951, p. 15ff). Recall also that the United Nations Charter purports to bind non-members.

37. Cf. Georg Schwarzenberger, *The Inductive Approach to International Law* (London: Stevens and Sons: Dobbs Ferry: Oceana Publications, Inc., 1965), especially Chapter 2, "The Province of the Doctrine of International Law."

38. The point is sometimes made that with the changing membership of the United Nations it is possible for a General Assembly resolution to be passed by a majority vote of member nation-states which represent a small proportion of the world's population, wealth, or military power. Perhaps this demonstrates the absurdity of perpetuating the myth of sovereign equality — which of course is not merely perpetuated in the United Nations but is also institutionalized. However, this consequence has not yet materialized as these nation-states have not been able to develop the voting unity which would be required. But the records of the General Assembly make the impact of the newer and underdeveloped nation-states clear. Consider, for example, the large amount of time devoted to anti-colonialist and economic development issues.

39. One answer is that of Abram Chayes, legal adviser in the Department of State, who in an address made before a Conference on the Law of Space and Satellite Communications at the Northwestern University School of Law on May 1, 1963, stated that "the United States recognizes the principles announced in Resolution 1721 [a General Assembly resolution on certain legal problems of outer space] as stating existing law. And I believe it would so regard any principles that came from the legal subcommittee [of the Committee on the Peaceful Uses of Outer Space] and were unanimously approved by the Assembly." *Department of State Bulletin*, 48 (May 27, 1963), p. 837.

40. A 1962 memorandum of the United Nations Office of Legal Affairs explains that a declaration is a formal and solemn instrument, reserved for special occasions when principles of great and lasting importance are being enunciated. As such a declaration cannot be binding on member nation-states, in the sense that a treaty is binding upon the parties to it. However, in view of the greater significance of the declaration, it may be considered the basis for a strong expectation that members of the international community will abide by it.

41. Richard A. Falk makes this argument in his "On the Quasi-Legislative Competence of the General Assembly," op. cit. Among the examples of this trend which he cites are: *Shimoda and Others v. Japan,* reported in the *Japanese Annual of International Law,* 1964, pp. 212-52; *Banco Nacional de Cuba v. Sabbatino,* 367 U.S. 398; and *Certain Expenses,* (I.C.J., *Reports,* 1962, pp. 151-308).

Falk maintains that:

> in a social system without effective central institutions of government, it is almost always difficult, in the absence of formal agreement, to determine when a rule of law exists. It is a matter of degree and reflects the expectations of states toward what is permissible and impermissible. Certainly norm-declaring resolutions are legal data that will be taken into account in legal argument among and within states. A main function of international law is to establish an agreed system for communication of claims and counterclaims between international actors and thereby to structure argument in diplomatic settings. In the search for basis of *justification or objection* it is clear that the resolutions of the Assembly play a crucial role — one independent of whether their status is to generate binding legal rules or to embody mere recommendations (p. 786).

See also: Higgens, *The Development of International Law Through the Political Organs of the United Nations,* op. cit.,; "Panel: Development of International Law by the United Nations," *Proceedings of the American Society of International Law at its Fifty-Ninth Annual Meeting Held at Washington, D.C., April 22-24, 1965* (Washington: American Society of International Law, 1965), pp. 108-24; and Sir Kenneth Bailey, "Making International Law in the United Nations," an address presented at the annual meeting of the American Society of International Law, *Proceedings of the American Society of International Law at its Sixty-First Annual Meeting Held at Washington, D.C., April 27-29, 1967* (Washington: American Society of International Law, 1967), pp. 233-39.

42. Since, aside from the functional legal problem areas, international law is essentially political in character, governments tend to interpret or reinterpret international law as an instrument of statecraft on a situational or circumstantial basis. While if the domestic legal model is used, this might seem to rob international law of any *legal* character, to insist on maintaining legal character is to deny international law any meaningful role in international relations outside the functional problem areas.

43. I hopefully but without delusion used a mail questionnaire in seeking unofficial statements from ministries of foreign affairs on several legal rules in air and sea law and several developing legal rules in outer space. Negative results were the rule, a result which possibly might be changed if the questionnaire could have been administered in personal interview situations. However, it is implicit in many responses that governments are reluctant even to permit officials to take unofficial positions, preferring, it seems, to preserve the greatest possible flexibility for those instances when the situation demands an official position or interpretation. It also seems very probable that most foreign ministries do not deal with abstract legal interpretations and do not even have contingency plans, but deal only with those problems which actually arise.

44. Of course, care must be exercised in using size of merchant fleet because of so-called "flags of convenience." See Bolslaw A. Boczek, *Flags of Convenience: An International Legal Study* (Cambridge: Harvard University Press, 1962) and the records of the 1958 Geneva Conference on the Law of the Sea.

2: THE LEGAL PROBLEMS
OF OUTER SPACE

INTRODUCTION

For many centuries imaginative men have been fascinated by outer space and by the notion of space travel. While many fantasies have been written about space and trips to the moon and other planets,[1] the possibility that men would ever actually be able to explore or travel in outer space seemed so unlikely that few legal scholars dealt seriously with outer space legal problems before the 1950s.[2] By then, the possibility of men venturing into outer space seemed much more likely than it had earlier.

The Germans developed the V-2 rocket during World War II. After the war, both the Soviet Union and the United States undertook rocket development programs which were initially based very largely on the V-2 and on the knowledge and skills of the German scientists who had developed it. Some legal scholars, primarily those interested in international air law,[3] became interested in legal problems which arose as a consequence of the rocket launchings made as a part of these programs. For example, as rockets were fired to higher and higher altitudes above the earth, the question of how high upward a state's sovereignty extends became a question of interest for these scholars.

However, 1955 is the first real benchmark date in space law literature. On July 29, 1955, the White House announced that the United States intended to launch an artificial satellite into earth orbit as a part of its program for the International Geophysical Year. Some two years later, on October 4, 1957, the space age actually arrived, but it was the Soviet Union and not the United States which successfully orbited the first artificial earth satellite, Sputnik I. The United States' announcement had attracted the attention of international legal scholars; Sputnik I made the space age a reality. Since 1957 the legal problems of outer space have been recognized as a very legitimate and practical subject matter which concerns governments and legal scholars alike.[4]

WHAT ARE THE LEGAL PROBLEMS OF OUTER SPACE?

It seems essential to begin this analysis with a determination and a useful categorization of the legal and political problems of outer space. In fact, without this determination there can be no certainty that this study will be at all relevant to problem-solving in that environment.

The analysis in this chapter is based on what other persons, organizations, and governments have said, written, resolved, and declared about the legal problems of outer space. The substantive aspects of these legal problems will not be discussed in this chapter;[5] the purpose of this chapter is to determine, on the basis of selected source materials, the answers to four basic questions which logically precede an analysis of the applicability of international air and sea law analogies to outer space legal problems. The four questions are:

1.   What outer space legal problems are identified in the selected source materials?

2.   Do the sources agree on these identifications of the legal problems of outer space?

3.   Do the sources agree that certain outer space legal problems should be treated as priority problems?

4.   What legal analogies have been discussed, recommended, or rejected in connection with outer space legal problems?

To obtain an answer to the first question, a large body of space law literature was canvassed. The purpose of the canvass was to develop a list which would include each distinct outer space legal problem or problem area identified in the source materials.[6] Included in this list are:[7]

Communications Satellites

Contamination or Pollution

Claims to Celestial Bodies

Definitions

Delimitation (setting boundaries)

Destructive Weapons

Electro-Magnetic (frequency interference, for example)

Exploration and Exploitation

Flight Rules

Freedom of Access and Passage

General Interference (between aircraft and spacecraft or between space experiments, for example)

General Military Problems (military operations, general references to disarmament or to rights of self defense, for example)

Inspection

Jurisdiction/Sovereignty

Legal Regime (*res nullius* or *res communis*)

Liabilty

Metalaw (prescriptions governing interactions with non-earthling sentient beings)

Peaceful/Non-peaceful Uses
Reconnaissance

Registration (including questions of nationality and identification)

Rescue and Return (downed astronauts or spacecraft, for example)

Weather Satellites.

This list gives a very general indication of agreement on the identification of legal problems of outer space. At the same time, however, this list is simply an indication that each of these problems or problem areas is identified by at least one of the sources. To determine the extent of agreement among the sources, one must know how frequently and by what sources these problems are identified. In addition, the immediate relative importance of these problems can be indicated by determining whether the sources agree that solutions to certain problems should be sought on a priority basis. This explains, then, why it is necessary to ask questions two and three concerning consensus and priority. Question four, legal analogies, is asked because the focus of this study is on the applicability of air and sea law analogies to legal and political problems in outer space.

METHOD

The analysis would be unnecessarily cumbersome if all the canvassed source materials were included. Therefore, a representative sample of these materials was selected.[8] Sample materials include the declarations, resolutions, and draft codes of associations and organizations, the proposals of various governments, official and unofficial viewpoints expressed by government officials, the work of legal scholars, and the discussions of legal problems by engineers, scientists and other persons who are neither qualified legal scholars nor government officials.[9]

These sample materials, then, are the source for data with which to answer the questions concerning consensus, priority, and analogies. The method used is a rudimentary content analysis;[10] the framework for organizing the results of this analysis consists of a categorization of problems and sources.

FRAMEWORK FOR ANALYSIS

Outer space legal problems can be categorized on the basis of their character as well as on the basis of how they are treated in the sample materials. Some are best characterized as General Problems. For example, Peaceful/Non-peaceful Uses, General Military Problems, and Definitions are really problem areas or clusters of problems rather than particular problems. On the other hand, Jurisdiction/Sovereignty, Legal Regime, and Metalaw are General Problems primarily because of their general, theoretical and philosophical character.[11]

Other outer space legal problems are best characterized as Functional Problems. These are similar to problems which have been successfully dealt with on earth and are problems which will have to be resolved if states are to interact routinely in outer space. Registration, Inspection, General Interference, Electro-Magnetic, Flight Rules, Rescue and Return, Liability, and Contamination or Pollution are Functional Problems.

A third group of problems raise political issues which are difficult to resolve. Delimitation, Claims to Celestial Bodies, Exploration and Exploitation, Communications Satellites, Destructive Weapons, Reconnaissance, Weather Satellites, and Freedom of Access and Passage are classified as Primarily Political Problems. Most of these are general problems in the sense that they are not a single problem but rather a cluster of related problems. Some raise very sensitive security issues, such as the legality of gathering military intelligence information from outer space. Others raise ideological questions; for example, should only states be permitted to establish and operate satellite communications networks?

There are, then, three categories of outer space legal problems in this analysis framework:

Category I, General Problems

Definitions
General Military Problems
Jurisdiction/Sovereignty
Legal Regime
Metalaw
Peaceful/Non-peaceful Uses

Category II, Functional Problems

Contamination or Pollution
Electro-Magnetic
Flight Rules
General Interference
Inspection
Liability
Registration
Rescue and Return

Category III, Primarily Political Problems

Claims to Celestial Bodies
Communications Satellites
Delimitation
Destructive Weapons
Exploration and Exploitation
Freedom of Access and Passage
Reconnaissance
Weather Satellites.

Four categories of sources are used in this analysis framework:

Legal Scholars — academicians and practicing attorneys;

Government Personnel — all persons officially associated with a government;

All Other Persons — all persons not classified as Legal Scholars or Government Personnel;

Organizations — governments, associations, and organizations.

The analysis framework consists, then, of three categories of outer space legal problems and four categories of source materials. The contents of the sample materials were analyzed and an enumeration was made of the identifications of outer space legal problems by source category and by year.[12] This enumeration is the basis for answering the questions concerning consensus, priority, and analogies. Furthermore, several general hypotheses can be tested when the data obtained from the content analysis are fitted into this particular analysis framework.

GENERAL HYPOTHESES

In general, it is anticipated that categories of problems or even particular outer space legal problems will be identified at different rates from year to year, and that the rates for some categories and problems will vary more than will others. Category II problems, Functional Problems, are expected to be the most variable. Levels of interest in these problems, as indicated by how frequently they are identified, are very likely to be affected by: (1) current space activities and experiments; (2) changes in space activities and experiments; and/or (3) developments in space science and technology. For example, as the number of space vehicles being launched increases, interest in liability for damages by rocket launchers, boosters, and vehicles is expected to increase. Similarly, it is expected that when manned orbital flights begin, interest in the Rescue and Return of astronauts will increase.

Levels of interest in Functional Problems may also vary because some of the problems are resolved or partially resolved. Functional Problems are the kinds of problems which most likely can be resolved. The problem of frequency interference on the earth, for example, has been dealt with some success through international agreements allocating frequencies for specific uses.

The largest variations in how frequently problems are identified are expected among Primarily Political Problems, Category III. Which particular Primarily Political Problem is most frequently identified is likely to change over time: (1) as relations between the states which are active in outer space change; and/or (2) as space activities and experiments change or intensify. For example, interest in Reconnaissance is likely to decrease when it ceases to be discussed publicly as an issue between states. Similarly, the level of interest in Weather Satellites is likely to decrease when the states active in space exploration agree to cooperate in a meteorological program.

The least variation in how frequently particular problems are identified is expected in Category I, General Problems. The very character of these problems militates against their final resolution, and, therefore, levels of interest may be expected to be relatively constant. Furthermore, levels of interest in these problems are less likely to be affected by space activities and experiments and developments in space science and technology than are problems in the other two categories.

It is also anticipated that a relationship between categories of sources and categories of problems will be established. That is, certain categories of sources are more likely to identify certain categories of problems more frequently than do other sources; moreover, certain categories of sources are more likely to identify certain categories of problems more frequently than other categories of problems.

Government Personnel are expected to identify: (1) more Functional Problems than do either of the other source categories; (2) more Functional than General or Primarily Political Problems; and (3) Primarily Political Problems more frequently than do either of the other source categories. The reason for expecting this finding is that government officials are responsible for dealing with these kinds of functional and political problems regardless of where such problems occur. It seems reasonable, therefore, to expect that government officials will frequently identify and discuss these problems.

On the other hand, Legal Scholars are expected to identify all categories of outer space legal problems at a more consistent rate than do either of the other source categories — simply because they are scholars and as such are trained to take a comprehensive perspective. Legal Scholars are also expected to identify more Category I, General Problems, than do either of the other categories of sources — because of their interest in theoretical and philosophical questions.[13]

On the question of priorities, it is anticipated that Category II problems, Functional Problems, are most likely to be identified as requiring priority treatment. This expectation is based on the character of these problems. As for analogies, when any analogy is suggested by a source, air and sea are expected to be suggested most frequently.

THE FINDINGS

THE IDENTIFIERS OF OUTER SPACE LEGAL PROBLEMS

As has already been stated, the sample materials which are the basis for this analysis were produced during the seven years, 1958 through 1964. Within these materials, 318 sources made 1,503 explicit identifications of outer space legal problems. One hundred-fifty-five of the sources are Legal Scholars, 96 are Government Personnel, 26 are All Other Persons, and 41 are Organizations (see Table 1). Almost one-half of the sources, therefore, are Legal Scholars; and together Legal Scholars and Government Personnel comprise approximately 80 percent of the 318 separate sources.

The 318 sources are predominately European and North American. South American states are more frequently represented among the sources than are either African or Asian states.[14]

TABLE I

IDENTIFIERS OF OUTER SPACE
LEGAL PROBLEMS, 1958-64

Source Category	1958	1959	1960	1961	1962	1963	1964	Total
Legal Scholars	18	20	11	21	26	27	32	155
Government Personnel	28	12	14	15	19	6	2	96
All Other Persons	5	1	0	7	5	6	2	26
Organizations	1	3	6	7	17	5	2	41
Total	52	36	31	50	67	44	38	318

THE IDENTIFICATION OF
OUTER SPACE LEGAL PROBLEMS

MOST FREQUENTLY IDENTIFIED PROBLEMS

The outer space legal problems or problem areas identified most frequently by all sources are listed in Table 2. Less than half of the 318 sources identify any one of the 22 problems or problem areas. In fact, only four problems are identified by more than one third of all sources. Three of these are General Problems — General Military, Peaceful/Non-peaceful Uses, and Jurisdiction/Sovereignty; only one, Liability, is a Functional Problem. And Liability is the sole Functional Problem included among the ten problems identified most frequently by all sources.

TABLE 2

OUTER SPACE LEGAL PROBLEMS IDENTIFIED
MOST FREQUENTLY BY ALL SOURCES, 1958-64

Problem or Problem Area	Number of Identifications	Percentage of All[a] Identifications	Percentage of[b] All Sources
General Military[c]	134	8.9	42.1
Peaceful/Non-peaceful Uses	126	8.4	39.5
Jurisdiction/ Sovereignty	124	8.1	38.9
Liability	107	7.1	33.6
Claims to Celestial Bodies	105	7.0	33.0
Delimitation	98	6.5	30.8
Legal Regime[d]	88	5.4	27.6
Communications Satellites	78	5.2	24.2
Exploration and Exploitation	67	4.5	21.1
Freedom of Access and Passage	67	4.5	21.1

[a] Based on N of 1,503.
[b] Based on N of 318.
[c] E.g., military operations, general references to disarmament or to rights of self-defense.
[d] E.g., *res nullius* or *res communis*.

Legal Scholars follow a similar pattern; that is, nine of the ten problems identified most frequently by Legal Scholars are the same as those identified by all sources (see Table 3). Jurisdiction/Sovereignty, the problem most frequently identified by Legal Scholars, is identified by more than half of all the Legal Scholar sources. Six other problems are identified by more than one third of these sources (see Table 3). There is, then, greater agreement among Legal Scholars than among all sources. And again, Liability is the only Functional Problem included among the ten problems identified most frequently.[15]

TABLE 3

OUTER SPACE PROBLEMS IDENTIFIED MOST FREQUENTLY BY LEGAL SCHOLARS, 1958-64

Problem or Problem Area	Number of Identifications by Legal Scholars	Percentage of All[a] Identifications by Legal Scholars	Percentage of All[b] Legal Scholars
Jurisdiction/ Sovereignty	87	10.0	56.1
Liability	65	7.5	41.9
General Military[c]	64	7.4	41.3
Claims to Celestial Bodies	63	7.2	40.6
Delimitation	63	7.2	40.6
Legal Regime[d]	62	7.1	40.0
Peaceful/Nonpeaceful Uses	55	6.3	35.5
Reconnaissance	41	4.7	26.5
Communications Satellites	40	4.6	25.8
Exploration and Exploitation	38	4.4	24.5

[a] Based on N of 869, the number of identifications made of all problems by Legal Scholars.
[b] Based on N of 155.
[c] E.g., military operations, general references to disarmament or to rights of self-defense.
[d] E.g., res nullius or res communis.

The ten problems identified most frequently by Government Personnel include nine of the same ten problems identified most frequently by Legal Scholars and by all sources (see Table 4). Two General Problems, General Military and Peaceful/Non-peaceful Uses, are identified by approximately one-half the 96 Government Personnel sources. Liability is again the only Functional Problem included among the ten most frequently identified problems.

TABLE 4

OUTER SPACE LEGAL PROBLEMS IDENTIFIED MOST FREQUENTLY BY GOVERNMENT PERSONNEL, 1958-64

Problem or Problem Area	Number of Identifications by Government Personnel	Percentage of All[a] Identifications by Government Personnel	Percentage of All Government[b] Personnel
General Military[c]	46	13.0	47.9
Peaceful/Non-peaceful Uses	46	13.0	47.9
Claims to Celestial Bodies	24	6.8	25.0
Communications Satellites	24	6.8	25.0
Jurisdiction/Sovereignty	21	5.9	21.9
Delimitation	20	5.6	20.8
Exploration and Exploitation	18	5.1	18.8
Freedom of Access and Passage	17	4.8	17.7
Liability	16	4.5	16.7
Destructive Weapons	16	4.5	16.7

[a] Based on N of 355, the number of identifications made of all problems by Government Personnel.
[b] Based on N of 96.
[c] E.g., military operation, general references to disarmament or to right of self-defense.

TABLE 5

OUTER SPACE LEGAL PROBLEMS IDENTIFIED BY ALL SOURCES, 1958-64

Problem Category		Frequency and Percentage of Total Identifications							
		1958	1959	1960	1961	1962	1963	1964	Total
I General Problems		89	75	57	59	128	71	73	552
	%	47.1	37.9	36.3	36.2	34.2	30.6	38.4	36.7
II Functional Problems		40	51	38	35	91	83	50	388
	%	21.2	25.8	24.2	21.5	24.3	36.1	26.3	25.9
III Primarily Political Problems		60	72	62	69	155	78	67	563
	%	31.7	36.4	39.5	42.3	41.4	33.6	35.3	37.5
Total	N	189	198	157	163	374	232	190	1503
	%	100.0	100.1	100.0	100.0	99.9	100.3	100.0	100.1

Mean Deviation:
Overall: 5.9
Category I: 3.3
Category II: 3.2
Category III: 3.3

Chi-Square: 27.93 (12 degrees of freedom); significant at .01.

NOTE: Where column total is not equal to 100 percent, the deviation is a consequence of error induced by rounding.

TABLE 6

OUTER SPACE LEGAL PROBLEMS IDENTIFIED BY
LEGAL SCHOLARS BY PROBLEM CATEGORY, 1958-64

Problem Category		Frequency and Percentage of Total Identifications							
		1958	1959	1960	1961	1962	1963	1964	Total
I General Problems		32	46	33	33	73	46	64	327
	%	38.6	40.7	36.3	39.8	37.8	31.1	40.5	37.6
II Functional Problems		20	26	22	20	43	49	40.	220
	%	24.1	23.0	24.2	24.1	22.3	33.1	25.3	25.3
III Primarily Political Problems		31	41	36	30	77	53	54	322
	%	37.3	36.3	39.6	36.1	39.9	35.8	34.2	37.1
Total	N	83	113	91	83	193	148	158	869
	%	100.0	100.0	100.1	100.0	100.0	100.0	100.0	100.0

Mean Deviation:
Overall: 5.7
Category I: 2.4
Category II: 2.3
Category III: 1.7

Chi-Square: 6.13 (12 degrees of freedom); significant at .95.

NOTE: The deviation from 100 percent in the column total is a consequence of error induced by rounding.

OVERALL

ALL SOURCES

The 1,503 separate identifications of outer space legal problems are summarized by problem category and by year in Table 5. There are significant differences in the rates of identification of categories of outer space legal problems by year. For example, the rate at which Category I problems, General Problems, are identified ranges from 47.1 percent of all outer space legal problems identified in 1958 to 30.6 percent in 1963. Similarly, the range for Category II, Functional Problems, is 21.2 (1958) to 36.1 percent (1963) and for Category III, Primarily Political Problems, 31.7 (1958) to 42.3 percent (1961).[16] This finding, of course, is contrary to what has been expected; it was expected that General Problems would be identified at a more consistent rate than either of the other categories.[17]

On the basis of the percentages reported in Table 5, it is evident that more sources have identified General and Primarily Political Problems than have identified Functional Problems. Only in 1963 were Functional Problems the most frequently identified category of outer space legal problems.

LEGAL SCHOLARS

Eight hundred sixty-nine of the total of 1,503 separate identifications of outer space legal problems were made by persons categorized as Legal Scholars. The differences in how frequently catgeories of outer space legal problems are identified by year are smaller when only Legal Scholars are considered (see Table 5, 6, and 7). The largest percentage difference in how frequently problems are identified is within Category II, Functional Problems — 22.3 percent in 1962 and 33.1 percent in 1963 (see Table 6). This finding was anticipated since it was assumed that developments in space science and technology together with changes in the activities and experiments being conducted in outer space would affect the level of interest in particular functional problems.

Legal Scholars consistently identify more General and Primarily Political Problems than Functional Problems. Of course, this was also found to be the case when all sources were considered.

TABLE 7

OUTER SPACE LEGAL PROBLEMS IDENTIFIED BY GOVERNMENT PERSONNEL BY PROBLEM CATEGORY, 1958-64

Problem Category		Frequency and Percentage of Total Identifications							
		1958	1959	1960	1961	1962	1963	1964	Total
I General Problems		41	22	16.	16	29	10	4.	138
	%	53.2	40.7	35.6	32.7	34.1	33.3	26.7	38.9
II Functional Problems		14	11	11	8	18	9	3	74
	%	18.2	20.4	24.4	16.3	21.2	30.0	20.0	20.8
III Primarily Political Problems		22	21	18	25	38	11	8	143
	%	28.6	38.9	40.0	51.0	44.7	36.7	53.3	40.3
Total	N	77	54	45	49	85	30	15	355
	%	100.0	100.0	100.0	100.0	100.0	100.0	100.0	100.0

Mean Deviation:
Overall: 9.3
Category I: 5.9
Category II: 3.3
Category III: 6.7

Chi-Square: 11.89 (12 degrees of freedom); significant at .50.

GOVERNMENT PERSONNEL

Sources categorized as Government Personnel made 355 of the 1,503 identifications of outer space legal problems. As indicated in Table 7, the rates of identification of categories of problems differ more among Government Personnel than among all sources or Legal Scholars. Government Personnel identify Functional Problems at a more consistent rate than either of the other two problems categories. However, Government Personnel consistently identify General and Primarily Political Problems at a higher rate than Functional Problems. Moreover, Government Personnel identify Functional Problems at a lesser rate than do either All Sources or Legal Scholars. These results were not anticipated since it was assumed that the responsibilities which Government Personnel have for seeking solutions to functional problems would result in their frequently identifying this category of outer space legal problems.

As was anticipated, Government Personnel do identify Primarily Political Problems more frequently than do either of the other source categories.

CATEGORY I, GENERAL PROBLEMS

Approximately one third of the 1,503 identifications of outer space legal problems are of Category I, General Problems. As was determined above, three of these problems — Peaceful/Non-peaceful Uses, General Military, and Jurisdiction/Sovereignty — are consistently the most frequently identified General Problems. Together, these three problems comprise approximately 70 percent of all the identifications of this category of outer space legal problems (see Table 8).

As was anticipated, the rates at which particular problems or problem areas are identified vary from year to year. Although these variations are not particularly large for any one Category I problem, some General Problems do vary more than do others. The order of variability, from least to greatest variability, is as follows:

Problem or Problem Area	Mean Deviation
Jurisdiction/Sovereignty	0.9
Metalaw	1.0
Legal Regime	1.5
Delimitation	1.5
Peaceful/Non-peaceful Uses	1.8
General Military	1.9.

TABLE 8

CATEGORY I, GENERAL PROBLEMS IDENTIFIED BY ALL SOURCES, 1958-64

Problem or Problem Area		Frequency and Percentage[a] of Total Identifications								
	N =	1958 (189)	1959 (190)	1960 (157)	1961 (163)	1962 (374)	1963 (232)	1964 (190)	Total (552)	Total (1503)
Peaceful/Non		27	15	11	12	33	12	16	126	126
peaceful Uses	%	14.3	7.6	7.0	7.4	8.8	5.2	8.4	22.8	8.4
General Military		24	17	17	12	37	15	12	134	134
Problems[b]	%	12.7	8.6	10.8	7.4	9.9	6.5	6.3	24.3	8.9
Jurisdiction/		15	19	13	17	25	19	16	124	124
Sovereignty	%	7.9	9.6	8.3	10.4	6.7	8.2	8.4	22.5	8.1
Legal Regime[c]		7	12	9	9	19	14	18	88	88
	%	3.7	6.1	5.7	5.5	5.1	6.0	9.5	15.9	5.4
Definitions		13	10	6	3	9	5	5	51	51
	%	6.9	5.1	3.8	1.8	2.4	2.2	2.6	9.2	3.4
Metalaw		3	2	1	6	5	6	6	29	29
	%	1.6	1.0	.6	3.7	1.3	2.6	3.2	5.3	1.9
Total	N	89	75	57	59	128	71	73	552	552
	%	47.1	37.9	36.3	36.2	34.2	30.6	38.4	100.0	36.7

NOTE: Mean Deviations within problems (by problem in the order listed): 1.8, 1.9, .9, 1.5, 1.5, 1.0.

 a Percentages are based on the N listed in parentheses. The N in each of the year columns is the total number of problems identified in that year.
 b Includes military operations, disarmament, rights of self-defense, etc.
 c I.e., res nullius, res communis, etc.
 d In order to minimize rounding errors, percentage totals are calculated independently; therefore, row and column percentages may deviate slightly from the sum of individual row and column percentages.

CATEGORY II, FUNCTIONAL PROBLEMS

Only 388 or approximately one fourth of all identifications of outer space legal problems are of Functional Problems, Category II. One problem, Liability, accounts for approximately 30 percent of all identifications of Functional Problems (see Table 9).

One of the general hypotheses stated at the beginning of this analysis was that interest in particular Functional Problems is related to current space activities, changes in space experiments and activities, and the development of new capabilities. The level of interest in Liability is generally consistent except for 1963 (see Table 9). The relatively large increase in interest in this problem in 1963 seems, at least circumstantially, to be related to instances of fragments from spacecraft or rocket boosters falling back to earth in 1962; in March, a three-pound fragment from the Atlas booster which orbited John Glenn's Mercury spacecraft fell onto a farm in South Africa;[18] and what is believed to be a piece of Sputnik IV fell on a Manitowoc, Wisconsin, street on September 4.[19]

TABLE 9

CATEGORY II FUNCTIONAL PROBLEMS IDENTIFIED BY ALL SOURCES, 1958-64

Problem	N =	Frequency and Percentage[a] of Total Identifications								
		1958 (189)	1959 (198)	1960 (157)	1961 (163)	1962 (374)	1963 (232)	1964 (190)	Total (388)	Total (1503)
Registration[b]		4	10	7	9	9	11	10	60	60
	%	2.1	5.1	4.5	5.5	2.4	4.8	5.3	15.5	4.0
Inspection		8	2	5	0	2	3	1	21	21
	%	4.2	1.0	3.2		.5	1.3	.5	5.4	1.4
Flight Rules		9	7	4	1	5	3	1	30	30
	%	4.8	3.5	2.5	.5	1.3	1.3	.5	7.7	2.0
Safety		1	2	1	2	2	2	0	10	10
	%	.5	1.0	.6	1.2	.5	.9		2.6	.7
General Interference[c]		2	3	3	1	10	5	5	29	29
	%	1.0	1.5	1.9	.5	2.7	2.2	2.6	7.5	1.9
Electro-Magnetic[d]		6	9	7	10	7	9	6	54	54
	%	3.2	4.5	4.5	6.1	1.9	3.9	3.2	13.9	3.6
Rescue and Return[e]		1	3	1	2	20	14	9	50	50
	%	.5	1.5	.6	1.2	5.3	6.1	4.7	12.4	3.3
Liability		8	11	9	9	28	27	15	107	107
	%	4.2	5.6	5.7	5.5	7.5	11.7	7.9	27.6	7.1
Contamination and/ or Pollution		1	4	1	1	8	9	3	27	27
	%	.5	2.0	.6	.5	2.1	3.9	1.6	6.9	1.8
Total[f]	N	40	51	38	35	91	83	50	388	388
	%	21.2	25.8	24.2	21.5	24.3	36.1	26.3	100.0	36.7

NOTE: Mean deviations within problems (by problems in the order listed): 1.2, 1.0, 1.3, 0.2, 0.7, 1.0, 2.2, 1.8, 0.9.

a Percentages are based on the N listed in parentheses.
b Includes questions of nationality and identification.
c E.g., interference between aircraft or interference between space experiments.
d E.g., frequency interference.
e E.g., downed astronauts and spacecraft.
f In order to minimize rounding errors, percentage totals are calculated independently; therefore, the row or column percentages may deviate slightly from the sum of individual row and column percentages.

Observe also the increase in how frequently Rescue and Return was identified beginning in 1962 (see Table 9). It may be recalled that man first entered space in 1961,[20] and that by early 1962 both the Soviet Union and the United States had orbited manned space vehicles. In fact, there were a total of five manned orbital flights in 1962;[21] the rescue and return of downed astronauts and cosmonauts had become a practical concern.[22]

Similarly, mention of General Interference indicates an overall increase in interest as the intensity of space exploration increased. By 1962 more than 50 spacecraft a year were being launched into space; the intereference problem was emphasized by spacecraft continuing to clutter up space and frequencies long after their basic missions had been completed.[23]

The controversy aroused by Project "West Ford" was perhaps another factor in the increased interest in General Interference in 1962. "West Ford" was a 1961 United States project to encircle the earth with 350 million hair-sized copper reflectors. If a military communications system could be established using this girdle of copper reflectors, it would be immune to jamming and to other kinds of interference. Many scientists opposed the project as detrimental to other space exploration projects and to studies of the earth being conducted from outer space. The United States denied the opposition claims and launched the vehicle.[24]

Problems of frequency interference — Electro-Magnetic — are apparently an example of a decrease in interest in a problem when some solution is being negotiated or has been agreed to. However, the Extraordinary Radio Administrative Conference was not successful in arriving at a compromise on the frequency allocation problem until November 8, 1963, whereas interest in the broader Electro-Magnetic problem peaked in 1961.[25]

CATEGORY III, PRIMARILY POLITICAL PROBLEMS

Approximately 33 percent of all outer space legal problems identified by all sources are Category III problems, Primarily Political Problems. It has been determined that at least five of the ten outer space legal problems identified most frequently by All Sources, Government Personnel, and Legal Scholars are Primarily Political Problems. No particular Primarily Political Problem is identified much more frequently than are all the others (see Table 10). This, it may be recalled, is in contrast to what was found when General and Functional Problems were examined.

Delimitation was the third most frequently identified outer space legal problem in 1958 and the most frequently identified in 1959 (see Table 8, 9, and 10). However, since 1959, interest in this problem has steadily decreased. This may be explained, at least in part, by the realization that the lack of a clearly defined boundary between airspace and outer space apparently does not impede space exploration.[26]

TABLE 10

CATEGORY III PRIMARILY POLITICAL PROBLEMS
IDENTIFIED BY ALL SOURCES, 1958-64

Problem	N =	Frequency and Percentage[a] of Total Identifications								
		1958 (189)	1959 (198)	1960 (157)	1961 (163)	1962 (374)	1963 (232)	1964 (190)	Total (563)	Total (1503)
Delimitation		22	23	11	8	18	11	5	98	98
	%	11.6	11.6	7.0	4.9	4.8	4.7	2.6	17.4	6.5
Claims to Celestial Bodies		11	11	12	11	24	16	20	105	105
	%	5.8	5.6	7.6	6.7	6.7	6.9	10.5	18.7	7.0
Exploration, Settlement and/or Exploration		4	7	10	8	17	10	11	67	67
	%	2.1	3.5	6.4	4.9	4.5	4.3	5.8	11.9	4.5
Weather Satellites		4	4	5	11	16	2	4	46	46
	%	2.1	2.0	3.2	6.7	4.3	.9	2.1	8.2	3.1
Communications Satellites		5	4	7	16	27	10	9	78	78
	%	2.6	2.0	4.5	9.8	7.2	4.3	4.7	13.9	5.2
Destructive Weapons		3	8	8	5	14	5	2	45	45
	%	1.6	4.0	5.1	3.1	3.7	2.2	1.1	7.9	3.0
Reconnaissance		7	7	5	3	20	13	2	57	57
	%	3.7	3.5	3.2	2.8	5.3	5.6	1.1	10.1	3.8
Freedom of Access, Passage, etc.		4	8	4	7	19	11	14	67	67
	%	2.1	4.0	2.5	4.3	5.1	4.7	7.4	11.9	4.5
Total[b]	N	60	72	62	69	155	78	67	563	563
	%	31.7	36.4	39.5	42.3	41.4	33.6	35.3	100.0	37.5

NOTE: Mean deviations within problems (by problems in the order noted): 2.7, 1.0, 1.0, 1.4, 2.0, 1.1, 1.2, 1.3.

  a   Percentages are based on the N listed in parentheses.
  b   In order to minimize rounding errors, percentage totals are calculated independently; therefore, the row and column percentages may deviate slightly from the sum of individual row and column percentages.

In 1963, Claims to Celestial Bodies was the problem most frequently identified by all sources. The increase in interest in this problem, as indicated by how frequently it was identified, is probably one consequence of the much-publicized efforts of the United States and the Soviet Union to be first in the race to put a man on the moon. The publicity, together with spectacular developments made by both the United States and the Soviet

Union in their man-on-the-moon projects, combine to make this seem a very real and immediate problem.[27]

As for Weather Satellites, the Soviet Union and the United States implemented the Bilateral Space Agreement of June 8, 1962, by a memorandum of understanding between the Academy of Sciences of the Soviet Union and the United States National Aeronautics and Space Administration in March and May, 1963.[28] These bilateral arrangements provide for cooperation in a satellite meterological program, primarily through the exchange of data collected by satellite. Note that the highest level of interest in Weather Satellites occurs in 1961, prior to the bilateral agreement, and in 1962. Note also that despite this limited agreement, Weather Satellites continues to be largely an unresolved political problem area, primarily because it overlaps with the problem of reconnaissance — the capability to observe weather phenomena includes certain reconnaissance or espionage capabilities — and the profoundly political implications of a capability to control weather.

An ideological issue which has concerned governments and space law commentators alike has been whether non-governmental organizations, corporations, or individuals should be permitted to participate in space programs, and in particular programs in space communications. The United States Congress gave its answer when it passed the Communications Satellite Act on August 31, 1962; the COMSAT Corporation was incorporated in the following February.[29] The highest level of interest in the Communications Satellites problem occurs in 1961 and 1962, and the level of interest in this problem does decrease following the enactment of the COMSAT legislation.

Interest in Reconnaissance decreased sharply in 1964. Prior to 1964, Eastern European and Soviet sources had maintained a particular interest in this problem, generally discussing the illegality of reconnaissance conducted from outer space.[30] It is usually assumed that reconnaissance is one of the unpublicized missions of the Soviet Union's multipurpose Cosmos satellite series. The first Cosmos was launched in 1962; by 1965 the Soviet Union ". . . launched dozens of Cosmos satellites that passed over the U.S."[31] After it developed its own space reconnaissance capability, the Soviet Union ceased to complain and Reconnaissance became a much less frequently discussed outer space legal problem.

An important aspect of Destructive Weapons in space was dealt with by international agreement when the Treaty Banning Nuclear Weapons in the Atmosphere, in Outer Space and Under Water was signed at Moscow on August 5, 1963. The treaty was signed by plenipotentiaries of the United Kingdom, the Soviet Union, the United States and subsequently by more than 100 other states — not including France and Red China. Note that the level of interest in Destructive Weapons decreases in 1963 and 1964.

CONCLUSIONS

The fact that 318 sources make 1,503 identifications from among only 22 outer space legal problems is an indication of a general agreement on what the legal problems of outer space are. There is evidentally no consensus that any of these 22 problems are more relevant or more important to problem-solving in outer space than are others, at least not on the basis of how frequently problems are identified. Of course, it has been determined that some outer space legal problems are identified more frequently and by more separate sources than are others. And it is evident, from the preceding analysis, that General and Primarily Political Problems are discussed by more sources than are Functional Problems. It is also evident that there is more agreement among Legal Scholars than among any of the other source categories; however, even in this case only one problem, Jurisdiction/Sovereignty, is identified by more than one-half of the 155 Legal Scholar sources.

To this point in the analysis, then, there is only implicit agreement among all sources that all 22 outer space legal problems are relevant and important to the eventual establishment of a legal order in outer space. This finding may be modified when the question concerning priorities is examined in the next section.

As was anticipated, there are variations in how frequently problems are identified both between and within categories of outer space legal problems. The variation between problem categories is very slight.

Variations in the rates of identification of particular Functional Problems within Category II, as hypothesized, do seem to be related to the activities and experiments being conducted in outer space and to the development of new capabilities. Likewise, interest in at least some Category III, Primarily Political Problems, apparently varies with changes in the relations between states, as for example when issues are resolved or otherwise cease to be issues.

Government Personnel do not identify Functional Problems as frequently as was anticipated. Government Personnel do identify General and Primarily Political Problems more frequently than do either of the other source categories. And, as expected, Legal Scholars do identify all categories of outer space legal problems at a more consistent rate than do either of the other source categories.

PRIORITIES

Only 25 of the 318 sources argue either for or against priority treatment for particular outer space legal problems. As anticipated, priority is mentioned most frequently in discussions of Functional Problems, 22 as compared to 11 for General and 12 for Primarily Political Problems.

Priorities are mentioned most frequently (ten times) by Government Personnel; Legal Scholars mention priorities nine times and Organizations, six. The following are the problems which are mentioned:

Problem or Problem Area	Frequency Mentioned[32]
Electro-Magnetic—e.g., frequency interference	10
Jurisdiction/Sovereignty	5
Legal Regime	3
Registration	3
Delimitation	3
General Military	2
Contamination or Pollution	2
Inspection	2
Claims to Celestial Bodies	2
Exploration and Exploitation	2
Metalaw	1
General Interference	1
Rescue and Return	1
Safety	1
Communications Satellites	1
Destructive Weapons	1
Freedom of Access and Passage	1
Reconnaissance	1
Weather Satellites	1

At least one source mentions priority treatment in connection with 20 of the 22 outer space legal problems. There is clearly no consensus, then, among even the 25 sources which explicitly argue either for or against priorities.

ANALOGIES

Within the sample materials, there are 172 separate identifications of analogies (see Table 11). In some instances the analogies are mentioned in relation to a particular outer space legal problem. More often, however, a reference is made to the potential applicability of an analogy to outer space legal problems in general.

TABLE 11

IDENTIFICATION OF ANALOGIES

Analogy	1958	1959	1960	1961	1962	1963	1964	Total
Air	5	7	4	6	6	7	10	45
Sea	6	17	5	7	13	7	8	63
Exploration and Discovery	1	3	2	3	3	0	2	14
Other[a]	2	9	8	8	11	6	6	50
Total	14	36	19	24	33	20	26	172
Number of Identifiers								
Legal Scholars	10	25	14	20	25	13	25	132
Government Personnel	4	8	5	2	2	3	0	24
All Other Persons	0	3	0	2	6	4	1	16
Documents	0	0	0	0	0	0	0	0
Total	14	36	19	24	33	20	26	172

[a] Includes the Antarctic analogy and general references to analogies.

International sea law is cited by slightly more than one-third of the 172 persons identifying an analogy (see Table 11). Together air and sea law comprise slightly more than 60 percent of all the analogies mentioned. Of course, this finding was anticipated and is one justification for a study of the applicability of air and sea law analogies to outer space legal problems.

SUMMARY

The focus of this study is one the applicability or relevance of international air and sea law to legal problems in outer space. But before an analysis of analogies can begin it is necessary to ascertain the legal problems of outer space. Moreover, it is desirable to know if certain problems or categories of problems are more relevant or important than are others to the eventual establishment of an outer space legal order. The purpose of this chapter, then, has been to make these determinations.

There is general agreement on 22 outer space legal problems. In fact, 318 separate sources identify these problems 1,503 times. It also has been found that interest in particular problems and categories of problems varies from year to year. These variations seem to be related either to the activities and experiments being conducted in outer space, the development of capabilities affecting future activities and experiments in outer space, or to the resolution of issues between the states which are active in outer space. When sources are categorized, it was determined that certain catgories of sources — specifically legal scholars and persons officially associated with governments — identify certain kinds of problems more frequently than they do others. These variations seem to be explained, at least in part, by the vocational interests of the source categories.

The most important finding for this study, then, is that an analysis of the applicability of international air and sea law analogies to any one of 22 outer space legal problems is regarded as relevant to problem-solving in outer space.

NOTES

1. C. Wilfred Jenks indicates that even Plato, Cicero, and Plutarch are among the "imaginative writers" who have been fascinated by the possibility of space travel (*Space Law*, op. cit., p. 10). However, most of the literature on this subject dates from the seventeenth century. Jenks lists Cyrano de Bergerac, Daniel Defoe, Francois Voltaire, Edgar Allan Poe, Jules Verne, H. G. Wells, C. S. Lewis, and Konstantin Zonkowsky as ". . . being only the most famous of the many writers on cosmic voyages . . ." (idem.). See further Jenks' brief discussion of this literature, op. cit., pp. 10-11.

2. See Jenks, op. cit., pp. 97-179, for a general review and evaluation of space law literature. One of the early works cited by Jenks is Emile Laude's *Revue international de Locomotion Aerienne* which was written in 1910. Another frequently cited early work on space law is Valdimir Mandl's *Das Weltaumrecht-Ein problem der Raumfahrt* (*Space Law — A Problem of Space Flight*). (Mannheim and Berlin-Liepsiz: Bensheimer, 1932), cited by Alex Meyer in "Legal Problems of Flight into the Outer Space," an address delivered before the Third International Astronautical Congress in Stuttgart on September 5, 1952, reprinted in United States Congress, Senate, Committee on Aeronautical and Space Sciences, *Legal Problems of Space Exploration: A Symposium*, 87th Cong., 1st sess., 1961, pp. 8-19).

3. John Cobb Cooper, Eugene Pepin, and Alex Meyer were prominent among the contributors during this period. For a more extended list, see Jenks, op. cit., pp. 102-118.

Welf Heinrich, Prince of Hanover, wrote the first doctoral thesis on space law in 1953. His thesis is reprinted in *Legal Problems of Outer Space*, op. cit., pp. 271-329. The prince was a student of Alex Meyer.

4. For some indication of when space law materials have been written, see one or more of the following bibliographies: *Bibliography of Materials in the Yale Library Pertaining to the Law of Outer Space* (New Haven: Yale University, School of Law, April, 1959); *Bibliography of the Space Law Collection* (Norman: University of Oklahoma Law Library, August 20, 1959); *Catalogue of Air and Space Law Materials* (Montreal: McGill University, Institute of Air and Space Law, July 1, 1965); Kenneth Anderson Finch, "Selected References on the Legal Problems of Space Exploration," United States Congress, Senate, Committee on Aeronautical and Space Sciences, *Legal Problems of Space Exploration: A Symposium*, 87th Cong., 1st sess., 1961, pp. 1329-92; H. Peter Kehrberger, *Legal and Political Implications of Space Research: Bibliography* (Hamburg: Verlag Weltarchiv GMBH, 1965); and Irvin L. White, Clifton E. Wilson, and John A. Vosburgh, *Law and Politics in Outer Space: A Bibliography* (Tucson: Institute of Government Research, University of Arizona, forthcoming).

5. However, substantive aspects of certain outer space legal problems will be discussed in Chapter 6.

6. A source was considered to have identified a problem if the problem was simply mentioned. That is, it was not considered necessary for the source to discuss the problem or problem area.

The problems listed by R. Cargill Hall were helpful in establishing the distinctiveness of particular problems or problem areas. Cf. his *The International Legal Problems in Space Exploration, An Analytical Review* (Sunnyvale: Lockheed Missiles and Space Co., 1964).

7. This list of problems was included in the questionnaire which was submitted to the Foreign Ministries of 123 states. Officials were asked to add any problem which in their opinion had been omitted and to indicate priorities among problems. Only the Minister of External Relations of Ecuador was willing to give an unofficial response to this part of the questionnaire. (He did not add to the list and ranked only two problems in order of priority — Peaceful/Non-peaceful Uses and General Military, in that order.) Consequently, this analysis of the extent of agreement on what the legal problems of outer space are has had to be based on available published materials.

8. The basis for selecting the sample was a knowledge of the source materials, that is, no probability model was used in selecting what are believed to be representative materials.

9. The sample includes the following materials: the *Proceedings* of the first seven colloquia on the law of outer space sponsored annually since 1958 either by the International Astronautical Federation or the International Institute of Space Law; the reports and recommendations of the United Nations *Ad Hoc* and Permanent Committees on the Peaceful Uses of Outer Space; the general debates in the First Committee of the General Assembly which are relevant to legal problems in outer space; germane General Assembly resolutions; United States Congress, Senate, Staff Report of the Committee on Aeronautical and Space Sciences, *Documents on International Aspects of the Exploration and Use of Outer Space, 1954-1962,* 88th Cong., 1st sess., 1963; resolutions and draft codes of certain international legal institutes or associations; and a number of major space law studies, including Robert D. Crane's guide to the study of Communist viewpoints in United States Congress, Senate, *Legal Problems of Space Exploration,* op. cit.; Andrew G. Haley, *Space Law and Government* (New York: Appleton-Century-Crofts, 1963); Philip C. Jessup and Howard J. Taubenfeld, *Controls for Outer Space and the Antarctic Analogy,* (New York: Columbia University Press, 1959); Leon Lipson and Nicholas deB. Katzenbach, *Report to the National Aeronautics and Space Administration on the Law of Outer Space,* op. cit.; and Myres S. McDougal, Harold D. Lasswell, and Ivan A. Vlasic, *Law and Public Order in Space,* op. cit.

10. An attempt is made to use printed materials systematically as a basis for a simple quantitative analysis. However, the analysis is rudimentary as compared, for example, to the content analysis methods described by Robert C. North, et al., *Content Analysis: A Handbook with Applications for the Study of International Crisis* (Evanston: Northwestern University Press, 1963).

Subject matter and *origin categories* and *intracontent comparisons* are used as the basis for inferences concerning the relative levels of interest in outer space legal problems. Cf. Bernard Berelson, "Content Analysis," *Handbook of Social Psychology,* 1 (Cambridge: Addison-Wesley Publishing Co., Inc., 1954), ed. Gardner Lindzey, pp. 48-522. Use of these categories in this study is described in the text.

11.   Several United Nations resolutions, including the Declaration of Legal Principles, General Assembly Resolution 1962, do indicate a general acceptance of celestial bodies as *res communis.*

Metalaw is somewhat ambiguous, for while it is now treated primarily as a question of general theoretical and philosphical interest, it may well become a practical question in the future. See, for example, Andrew G. Haley, *Space Law and Government,* Chapter 12 "Metalaw", op. cit., pp. 394-423; and Harold D. Lasswell, "Anticipating Remote Contingencies: Encounters with Living Forms," *Proceedings of the Fourth Colloquium on the Law of Outer Space* (Norman: University of Oklahoma, Research Institute, 1963) eds. Andrew G. Haley and Mortimer D. Swartz, pp. 94-104.

There are no absolutely clear distinctions between the problems or the categories. An overlap is acknowledged; however, these designations of problems and categories are meaningful and are useful for this analysis.

12.   The years 1958 through 1964 are used as data points in recording and analyzing the data, primarily because the *Proceedings* of the space law colloquia — a major source material — are available for these seven years. One of the sources, United States Congress, Senate, Staff Report of the Committee on Aeronautical and Space Sciences, *Documents on International Aspects of the Exploration and Use of Outer Space,* op. cit., includes materials for the years 1954-1962; however, only the documents issued in 1958 and subsequently are used.

13.   However, as noted above, Government Personnel may also be expectd to identify these problems frequently. For example, a propaganda advantage may be gained by advocating the peaceful uses of outer space for the benefit of all mankind.

14.   Within the United Nations, representatives of Afro-Asian states have been concerned generally with questions relating to disarmament, peaceful uses, reserving their rights to access, etc. Cf., for example, the remarks of the representatives of the United Arab Republic and of India in the United Nations, *Official Records, United Nations General Assembly, Sixteenth Session, First Committee,* 1961 (United Nations: United Nations, 1961), p. 254 and pp. 264-265. See also, United Nations, *Official Records, Seventeenth Session, First Committee,* 1962 (United Nations: United Nations, 1962); and United Nations, *Official Records, Eighteenth Session, First Committee,* 1963 (United Nations: United Nations, 1963). Even in these instances, however, only a small number of Afro-Asians address themselves to the legal problems of outer space. Perhaps one reason is that they are primarily concerned about problems associated with *emerging* as independent states.

15. See Appendix D for a summary of the States, Associations, and Organizations Represented by Identifiers of Outer Space Legal Problems, 1958-64, and for a comparison of the identification of problems by problem and source categories.

16. See also the mean deviations listed in Table 5.

17. The basis for this expectation is that these kinds of problems are neither likely to be resolved nor are they likely to be much affected by changes in activities and experiments in outer space. The frequency of identification of particular General Problems will be examined in one of the following sections.

18. New York Times, 2 March 1962, p. 20, cited by McDougal, Lasswell, and Vlasic, op. cit., p. 519.

19. Modesto Seara Vazquez, Cosmic International Law (Detroit: Wayne State University Press, 1965), Translated by Elaine Malley, p. 86. It should also be recalled that by 1963 liability had become a very practical concern as increasingly large numbers of vehicles were being launched each year.

20. The Soviet Cosmonaut Gagarin was the first man to orbit the earth. He made his one orbit flight in Vostok I on April 12, 1961. His fellow Cosmonaut Titov made 17-1/2 orbits on August 6, 1961. Two United States Astronauts made suborbital flights in 1961: Shepard on May 5, and Grissom on July 21, 1961.

21.

Astronaut or Cosmonaut	Orbits	State	Date Launched
Glenn	3	U.S.	February 20
Carpenter	3	U.S.	May 24
Nikloyev	64	U.S.S.R.	August 11
Popovich	48	U.S.S.R.	August 12
Schirra	6	U.S.	October 3

22. Interest in this problem prior to 1961 had been centered on the return of unmanned spacecraft or equipment. Much of the early discussion of this problem focused on the nature of the missions being performed. For example, the Soviet Union claimed that the United States was conducting espionage from outer space. This was alleged to be an illegal activity, and the Soviet Union took the position that it had no obligation to return "spy" satellites. See the discussion of Reconnaissance below.

23. By the end of 1966, close to 1,200 man-made objects were in orbit. Most of these are simply junk including such items as an astronaut's lost glove, space walk tethers, etc. However, some 275 of these objects are satellites, many of which continue to send a flood of data back to earth. See Newsweek for 17 October 1966, pp. 73-75.

24. Some scientists had also opposed Project "Argus" — the United States high-altitude nuclear tests between August 27 and September 7, 1958. The interest in General Interference from 1958 to 1962 is probably a carry-over from

these tests. The overall effects of these tests have not been made public, however, it is known that radio communications and radar were affected.

25. See further Horace P. Moulton, "Commercial Space Communications," *Space and Society,* ed. Howard J. Taubenfeld (Dobbs Ferry: Oceana Publications, Inc., 1964), pp. 73-90.

26. Many discussions of delimitation as a practical legal problem increasingly recommend limits based upon the functions of particular types of spacecraft. Cf., for example, McDougal, Lasswell, and Vlasic, op. cit., pp. 349-355; Sir William Hildred and Sir Frederick Tymms, "The Case Against National Sovereignty in Space," United States Congress, Senate, Committee on Aeronautical and Space Sciences, *Legal Problems of Space Exploration,* op. cit., pp. 264-270; and Spencer M. Beresford, "The Future of National Sovereignty," *Proceedings of the Second Colloquium on the Law of Outer Space,* ed. Andrew G. Haley and Welf Heinrich, Prince of Hanover (Wein: Springer-Verlag, 1960), pp. 5-10. Otherwise discussions tend to treat delimitation as a political problem; one discussed in terms of national interests (in security, for example) versus community interest (in the benefits of peaceful uses, for example).

27. Several United Nations General Assembly resolutions, including the Declaration of Legal Principles, Resolution 1962, have included a provision that celestial bodies including the moon are not subject to national appropriation. A similar provision is included in the 1966 Space Law Treaty, Article II. See Appendix A for the text of the treaty.

28. The text of these agreements is reprinted in American Society of International Law, *International Legal Materials,* 2 (January, 1963), pp. 195-198 and (September, 1963), pp. 902-926.

29. Public Law Number 87-624, 76 Stat. 419, 47 U.S.C.A. Sect. 701. Cf. Moulton, op. cit., pp. 76-77.

30. See Crane, loc. cit., and the *Proceedings* of the first six space law colloquia.

31. *Time,* 30 September 1966, p. 27.

32. Some of the 25 sources mentioned priorities for more than one problem.

PART II: A DETERMINATION OF THE
LAW-IN-ACTION WITHIN
SELECTED PROBLEM AREAS OF
INTERNATIONAL AIR AND
SEA LAW

INTRODUCTION

In the first chapter of this study, the argument is developed that international legal rules are but one decisional output of the international political system. International legal rules are those decisional outputs which order the pursuit and the realization of values through a process of interstate interaction. The focus of this study is on governmental interactions: that is, the interactions between and among the legitimate authoritative decision makers and enforcers of states.

In the analysis which follows, international legal prescriptions are examined on two dimensions, horizontal and vertical. The horizontal dimension is a measurement of the *extent* of applicability of particular legal prescriptions; that is, the question is whether a particular rule or principle is universally applicable or applicable only to some lesser *extent*. On the other hand, the vertical dimension is a measurement of the *degree* of acceptance, and the question is one of specificity, asking if what is accepted is a detailed or a general rule or principle. Presumably acceptance of a carefully specified rule or principle indicates a higher degree of acceptance than does acceptance of one formulated very generally or imprecisely.[1]

One determines what international law is at any spatial reference point by first examining claims, counterclaims, and state practice; the appropriate algorithm then is used to determine the law-in-action. The number of states which must agree to a rule or principle is not always specified in descriptions of international legal rule-making processes. In the two most informal processes, custom and general principles, legal publicists usually argue that a majority, typically an abnormal majority, must agree for a rule to be universally binding. On the other hand, the assent of each party is required to establish as binding an international legal rule between parties to a treaty or international convention.[2] However, by using the modified majority rule previously formulated, the international convention rule-making process may be used as an indicator of the status of particular rules or principles among all the states comprising the international political system.

The same basic procedures will be used to determine the law-in-action in the selected problem areas regardless of which decision-making process is being examined. The primary source materials for this determination are the records of international conferences. Where necessary, these records are supplemented with other evidence including evidence of customary practice and general principles; however, the best available evidence of explicit acceptance or rejection of particular international legal rules and principles is international conference records together with the records of signatures and ratifications or adherence to international conventions.

When the best available evidence is other than the records of an international convention, there is no attempt to establish detailed legal rules. By conducting a rigorous content analysis one might determine detailed rules on the basis of national legislation or policy statements made by authoritative and legitimate decision-makers and enforcers. Such an undertaking is beyond the scope and purpose of this study. In the present study, such sources as national legislation will be analyzed only to the degree necessary to determine whether and to what extent basic rules and general principles are accepted.[3]

Rules and principles will be determined using the modified majority rule procedure previously stated. The position on the vertical dimension — the *degree* of acceptance — will be determined on the basis of the type of evidence which is available. Only explicit acceptance will be considered acceptable for determining a binding legal *rule*. However, in the case of international conventions, signing but not subsequently ratifying will be treated as tacit consent — barring evidence of a contrary policy position. In determining a generally recognized *principle,* a vote in plenary session of an international conference for a specific conventional article will be considered acceptable — again assuming that there is no evidence to the contrary. Evidence of unilateral claims asserted in national legislation, etc., will be evaluated and in some instances may be the basis for rules or principles of varying extents of applicability.

The *extent* of acceptance — the horizontal dimension — will be determined by simply counting the number of states supporting the rule or principle. Legal rules will be considered universally binding when the three requirements stated in the modified majority rule are satisfied. Similarly, general principles will be considered universally recognized when these same three requirements are met. Of course, rules may be less than universally applicable and still be international law-in-action between some subsystems within the international political system. Obviously, an international convention ratified or adhered to by the required number of parties and regularly observed in practice is international law-in-action between the parties. That this is the case is of interest here and will be important in the analysis in Part III; however, the primary purpose of the analyses in the following two chapters is to determine if rules or principles are more broadly applicable; that is, applicable to the entire population of states included within the 1964 international political system.

The determination of legal rules in the following two chapters is less than comprehensive. However, the applicability and utility of the approach, methods, and techniques are believed to be demonstrated. Furthermore, areas of air and sea law have been selected for analysis which seem particularly relevant to certain of the twenty-two outer space legal problems determined in Chapter 2.

NOTES

1.   Richard A. Falk, in his *The Role of Domestic Courts in the International Legal Order* (Syracuse: Syracuse University Press, 1964), uses the terms horizontal and vertical ". . . to describe the two basic distributions of power in a legal order" (p. 22). He contends that "there are two primary dimensions of order. There is vertical or hierarchical order among many formally unequal centers of legal authority; there is horizontal or nonhierarchical order among equal centers of legal authority" (pp. 21-22).

A similar conception of the horizontal dimension is used here. To determine the extent of applicability of a particular legal prescription, one determines how many states — the equal centers of legal authority in the nonhierarchical international legal order — accept the particular legal prescription. The range is from universal acceptance to universal rejection.

A somewhat different vertical or hierarchical dimension is used in this study. Degrees of acceptance of legal prescriptions may range from the very specific to the very general. Positions on this continuum, as will be discussed in the text which follows, are established on a number of bases including the kind of decision-making process used in formulating the prescription and the explicitness of the best available evidence; however, only the two poles of the continuum will be used in this study.

2. Some agreements do purport to bind third parties. For example, see the United Nations Charter, Articles 6 and 50.

The point was made in Chapter I that this is a "best evidence" procedure, that is, satisfying the requirements of the modified majority rule provides the best available evidence of what the universally applicable international law is at any given point in time.

3. Legal publicists will be cited; however, publicists' claims which appear to be primarily normative or unsubstantiated will not be accepted. There is no assurance that to accept such claims is not to become an agent in either myth perpetuation or in the advancement of some other writer's value preferences. An example of this risk would be to accept the claim of an universally cited sea law specialist that there is a rule establishing the right of innocent passage for merchant vessels. It is very likely that this is a universally binding rule. (See the discussion of the conventional rule later in this chapter.) However, this particular scholar's evidence consists of the opinions of several of his illustrious predecessors together with a resolution accepted by an international legal association and a draft produced by the 1930 Hague conference. The question must be raised as to the relevance to contemporary international legal rules and rule-making of a determination on the basis of such evidence.

Other legal writers are, of course, important to this study. Not only do other writers provide instruction and guidance, but in some instances, such writers are a source of acceptable evidence and/or offer conclusions based on acceptable evidence. In general, however, it seems that one of the most important consequences of normative legal writings is the effect of these writings on decision-makers either as one of the ingredients shaping the decision-maker's conception of what particular international legal rules or principles are or as a basis for justifying certain of his actions.

3: A DETERMINATION OF THE LAW-IN-ACTION WITHIN SELECTED PROBLEM AREAS OF INTERNATIONAL SEA LAW

INTRODUCTION

C. John Colombos contends that international law, ". . . as it is understood today, is little more than three hundred years old."[1] Legal publicists and government officials have maintained a substantive interest in the law of the sea throughout these approximately 300 years. In fact, the law of the sea constitutes a substantial portion of international law.

The law of the sea frequently has been identified as a body of law comprised for the most part of customary rules. However, since World War II, United Nations-sponsored efforts to codify and progressively develop international law have resulted in widespread acceptance of several important international conventions dealing with many facets of the law of the sea. Consequently, although customary rules are still important, international sea law seemingly is becoming a law embodied in international conventions formally agreed to by a majority of the governments of the states comprising the international political system.

In certain problem areas of international sea law, governments make what are essentially claims to a right to exercise exclusive authority. The degree of *exclusive* authority claimed varies from area to area. For example, governments regularly claim a more comprehensive authority over their territorial sea than over special purpose contiguous zones.[2]

Certain other areas of international sea law are analytically distinctive as areas within which the *inclusive* interests seems to be paramount. Freedom of the high seas and the conservation of living resources are examples.

A third area which may be distinguished is comprised of deviations or exceptions to claims within either the exclusive or the inclusive categories. The right of innocent passage and the questionable right of a government to establish temporary testing zones of various kinds on the high seas are examples which might be included in this category.[3]

The terms inclusive and exclusive have been used by Myres S. McDougal.[4] As McDougal uses the terms, the differentiation seems to be between two poles of a continuum ranging from ". . . relatively unique demands and expectations of a high degree of particular impact upon a single claimant . . .",[5] to ". . . shared demands and expectations of high degrees of impact upon collective processes . . . ."[6] A somewhat different distinction is intended here. As noted above, a distinction is made between demands and expectations on the basis of the primary purpose and function of the demand rather than on the impact made upon the decisional process by the demand and the expectations which the demand arouses. Demands which are made primarily in support of an exclusive interest might well have a high degree of impact upon collective decision-making processes. Conversely, so might demands made primarily in the inclusive interest have "a high degree of particular impact upon a single claimant."

As an example, the primary purpose and function of claims to varying degrees of authority in the various sea zones and over the continental shelf appear to be the protection of primarily exclusive interests. These include national security and the economic development and exploitation of living and mineral resources either in or underlying the sea zones or continental shelf claimed. On the other hand, the primary purpose and function of free-primarily exclusive interests of some states, particularly those with large dom of the high seas is to maximize and facilitate joint use — although maintaining this freedom also may be functional to the attainment of the merchant fleets, for example.

This three-fold division — Claims Primarily in Support of an Exclusive Interest, Claims Primarily in Support of an Inclusive Interest, and Deviations or Exceptions to Exclusive or Inclusive Authority — will be used to categorize claims in this analysis to determine the law-in-action of selected problem areas of international sea law. At least one rule or principle in each of these categories will be analyzed in this chapter.

CLAIMS PRIMARILY IN SUPPORT
OF AN EXCLUSIVE INTEREST

DELIMITATION

States generally recognize four separate and distinct legal regimes of the sea: internal waters; territorial sea; special purpose contiguous zones; and the high seas.[7] Both internal waters and the territorial sea are usually considered to be subject to the sovereignty or the comprehensive jurisdiction of the adjacent state. Contiguous zones are considered to be subject to the jurisdiction of the adjacent state only for specified special purposes. The high seas, on the other hand, generally are considered to be free. However, there are exceptions in all four legal regimes — for example, the right of innocent passage and numerous claims to jurisdiction, in some instances sovereignty, over, on, and under the high seas.

The most comprehensive claims to authority are made over internal waters (ports or waters within some coastal indentations), and adjacent waters located between the coast and certain islands or rocks located offshore.[8] States generally agree to the extent of state authority within internal waters; however, not all states seem to agree on the extent of the internal waters themselves.[9]

States generally claim territorial sovereignty in both internal waters and the territorial sea;[10] the basic distinction between the two legal regimes is the extent or comprehensiveness of the authority claimed. It may be assumed that claims to authority in internal waters will differ, if at all, by being more rather than less comprehensive than those examined in determining the law-in-action of delimitation of the territorial sea. Therefore, internal waters will not be discussed separately in this analysis.

TERRITORIAL SEA

States seem generally to agree that there is a limit to the extent of the territorial sea.[11] There are several bases for claims to particular breadths. Some national decision-makers claim that a particular breadth of territorial sea is either required or sanctioned by customary international law;[12] others claim a right to a different breadth based on the right of states to protect one or more exclusive interest: security, economic — such as development and exploitation of resources — or conservation of sea resources. Of course, the claim that there is a sanction in customary law for a particular breadth of territorial sea is challenged by the counterclaims of states which claim other breadths on other bases.

CONVENTIONAL RULES

There have been two major post-World War II attempts to codify the international law of the sea, the 1958 and 1960 Geneva Conferences on the Law of the Sea.[13] At both of these conferences, efforts to codify a rule establishing a specific breadth for the territorial sea failed. In fact, the major reason for convening the Second United Nations Conference on the Law of the Sea in 1960 was to try once again to draft an acceptable compromise rule delimiting the territorial sea.

In this examination of the voting records of states represented at the 1958 and 1960 conferences, states will be characterized as either possessing or not possessing a special interest in the international law of the sea. This characterization is based on an objective definition of what constitutes a special interest. Size of merchant fleet, extent of port and fishing activity, and the size of naval security forces are the quantitative indicators used as the bases for this objective definition. Data on each of these indicators have been collected for the 121 independent states comprising, at least for this study, the population of the 1964 international political system.

As objectively defined here, a state is considered to have a special interest in the legal rules of the sea if it is either Very Large or Very Active, Large or Active, or Medium or Moderately Active, as indicated by the selected interest indicators named above.[14]

Eighty-six states have a special interest in the law of the sea. A summary of the extent of these states' maritime activity is presented in Table 12.

When it became evident at the 1958 conference that the three-mile limit would not be adopted, delegates of the United Kingdom and the United States, seeking a compromise solution, sponsored and actively supported proposals providing for a territorial sea of up to six miles, together with an extension of a contiguous zone to twelve miles for certain limited exclusive fishing rights.[15]

Three major proposals were offered for consideration by the First Committee (Territorial Sea and Contiguous Zone). These were sponsored by Canada, the United States, and jointly by India and Mexico.

Canada's proposal provided for a territorial sea of up to six miles. In an additional six mile zone ". . . the coastal state was to have the same rights in respect of fishing and the exploitation of the living resources of the sea as it has in its territorial sea."[16]

TABLE 12

STATES WITH A SPECIAL INTEREST IN THE SEA REPRESENTED AT THE 1958 AND 1960 GENEVA CONFERENCES ON THE LAW OF THE SEA

State	Merchant[a] Marine Fleet	Port[b] Activity	Fishing[e] Activity	Naval Forces:[d] Large and Small Combatants
Argentina		3		
Australia		3		
Belgium		2		
Brazil		1		
Canada		2	2	3
Chile			2	
China (Nat.)		3		
Colombia		3		
Denmark		2	3	
Ecuador		3		
Finland		3		
France	3	1	2	2
Germany (W.)	3	1	3	3
Greece	2	3		
Iceland			3	
India		3	2	
Indonesia			3	3
Iran		2		
Italy	3	1	2	3
Japan	2	1	1	3
Korea (S.)		3	3	
Liberia	1			
Malaysia[e]		2		
Mexico				3
Netherlands	3	1		3
Norway	2	3	2	
Pakistan		3		
Panama	3			
Peru		2	1	
Philippines		2	3	
Poland		3		
Portugal		3	3	

TABLE 12 (Continued)

State	Basis of Special Interest			
	Merchant[a] Marine Fleet	Port[b] Activity	Fishing[c] Activity	Naval Forces:[d] Large and Small Combatants
South Africa			3	
Spain		2	2	3
Sweden	3	3	2	3
Thailand			3	
Turkey				3
USSR	2	1	2	2
UAR		1		
UK	1	1	3	2
US	1	1	2	1
Venezuela		1		
Total	13	33	22	14

[a] Based on data furnished by the American Bureau of Shipping for seagoing steam and motor vessels of 1,000 gross tons and over as of December 31, 1964, and supplemented where necessary by data obtained from the United Nations, *Statistical Yearbook, 1965* (United Nations: United Nations, 1966). Codes: (1) Very Large (more than 10% of the world total); (2) Large 4-10% of the world total); and (3) Medium (2-3.9% of the world total).

[b] Based on data contained in the United Nations, *Statistical Yearbook, 1965*, ibid., for thousand gross registered tons vessels entering and clearing ports, excluding vessels in ballast. Codes: (1) Very Active (more than 55,000); (2) Active (20-55,000); and (3) Moderately Active (6-19,999).

[c] Based on data reported in Food and Agricultural Organization, *Yearbook of Fishery Statistics, 1964* (Rome: Food and Agriculture Organization, 1965). Codes: (1) Very active (more than 10% of world total fishing catch); (2) Active (2-10% of world fishing catch); and (3) Moderately Active (1-1.9% of world total fishing catch).

[d] Based on data reported by Raymond V. B. Blackman, ed., *Jane's Fighting Ships 1965-66* (Great Missenden Bucks: Jane's Fighting Ships, 1966), and supplemented with data obtained in S. H. Steinberg, ed., *The Statesman's Yearbook 1965-66* (New York: St. Martin's Press, 1965). Codes: (1) Very Large (more than 1,000 large and/or small combatants); (2) Large (70-1,000 large and/or small combatants); and (3) Medium (25-69 large or small combatants).

[e] Data reported here are on Malaysia; however, at the time of the 1958 and 1960 conferences, this state was still the Federation of Malaya.

The joint Indian and Mexican proposal permitted states to claim a territorial sea of up to twelve miles. No reference was made to any additional state authority beyond the twelve-mile maximum limit.[17]

The United States proposed a territorial sea of six miles and the same fishing rights as in the territorial sea out to a distance of twelve miles. In this proposal, the United States also attempted to protect the fishing rights of states whose fishermen had fished regularly in these waters for the preceding five years.[18]

Arguments in support of the Canadian proposal stressed that the twelve-mile limit recognized economic interests and needs. The proponents of the Indian-Mexican proposal based their arguments on the security needs and interests of coastal states.[19]

The Canadian proposal, the first proposal to be voted on in the First Committee, was treated as two separate proposals. The six-mile limit for the territorial sea was soundly defeated, 11 in favor, 48 against, with 23 abstaining.[20] Nine of the 11 votes for a six-mile territorial sea were cast by delegates of states identified in Table 12 as having a special interest in the law of the sea. Twenty-four of the 48 negative votes were the votes of states with a special interest.[21]

The proposal for a contiguous six-mile fishing zone was adopted by 37 votes to 35, with nine abstentions. Nineteen of the 37 votes in favor and 19 of the 35 votes against were cast by the delegations of states with a special interest in the law of the sea. Nineteen of those voting against include such major maritime states as France, Italy, Japan, the Soviet Union, the United Kingdom, and the United States.[22]

The proposal submitted jointly by India and Mexico for a territorial sea of up to twelve miles was rejected by a tie vote of 35 to 35, with 12 abstentions. A request by the Ecuadorian delegate that his abstention be registered as a vote in favor was denied by the committee chairman. On appeal, the full committee upheld the chairman's decision. Only 12 states with a special interest favored, whereas 23 opposed the Indian-Mexican proposal for a twelve-mile territorial sea.[23]

The First Committee also rejected the United States proposal for a six-mile territorial sea with fishing rights as in the territorial sea out to twelve miles. Fifteen states with a special interest were included among the 38 opposed; twenty of the 36 states favoring the United States proposal possess a special interest in the law of the sea.[24]

In plenary session, the United States proposal received 45 affirmative votes. This was greater support than any other proposal had received; however, an affirmative two-thirds vote was required for conference approval and the 45 affirmative votes were still short of this requirement. The vote by states with a special interest was 24 in favor, 15 against, with 3 abstaining.[25]

The 1958 voting records of the states with a special interest in the law of the sea are summarized in Table 13. Under the rules of the conference, no conventional rule on the maximum extent of the territorial sea was agreed upon. A six-mile extent for the territorial sea without some provision for a contiguous zone was defeated by a large margin. Similarly, a proposal for a twelve-mile territorial sea was rejected two to one by states with a special interest. Although the United States proposal for a six-and-six rule was rejected in the First Committee by a majority of the delegates voting, this proposal won majority support in plenary — but failed to obtain the necessary two-thirds vote. With the failure of the attempted compromise, a number of governments reaffirmed their claims to other breadths of territorial sea.[26] There was, then, no conventional rule establishing a particular maximum breadth of the territorial sea at the conclusion of the 1958 Geneva Conference on the Law of the Sea.

In March 1960, the Second United Nations Conference on the Law of the Sea convened in Geneva; 88 states were represented. And seven proposals relating to the breadth of the territorial sea were submitted.[27]

The Soviet Union proposal authorized states to claim a territorial sea of up to a maximum limit of twelve miles. States claiming a lesser territorial sea were authorized to claim a contiguous fishing zone up to the twelve-mile extent. Mexico offered a similar proposal, as did a sixteen-power group of Asian, African, and Arab states. The distinguishing feature of the latter proposal was the inclusion of the principle of reciprocity. A state would be entitled to exercise sovereignty and/or exclusive fishing rights up to the limits fixed by the other state in its adjacent waters. For example, if state A claimed exclusive fishing rights to a twelve-mile limit and states B and C claimed similar rights to only six miles, the six-mile limit would apply between B and C. However, state A would be required to observe a twelve-mile limit off the coasts of B and C unless it granted them the right to fish within six miles of its own coast.

A composite plan which included features of both the Mexican and the sixteen-power plan was proposed by a group of eighteen powers. This group consisted of the sixteen powers together with Mexico and Venezuela.

The separate United States and Canadian plans were essentially the same as their plans of 1958. However, these two states also offered a joint proposal which provided for a territorial sea of up to six miles in breadth and an additional exclusive fishing zone extending to a twelve-mile maximum.

This joint proposal also protected the rights of those states whose vessels had fished regularly in the outer six-mile zone for a period of five years immediately preceding January 1, 1958. A third article in this joint proposal provided that the 1958 Convention on Fishing and Conservation of the Living Resources of the High Seas would apply *mutatis mutandis* to the settlement of disputes arising out of the application of the other provisions.[28]

TABLE 13

VOTING SUMMARY OF STATES WITH A
SPECIAL INTEREST IN THE LAW OF THE SEA
REPRESENTED AT THE 1958 GENEVA CONFERENCE
ON THE LAW OF THE SEA

State	Canadian[a]		Indian-[b] Mexican	United[c] States	Plenary United[c] States
Argentina	Y	Y	Y	N	N
Australia	N	N	N	Y	N
Belgium	N	N	N	Y	Y
Brazil	N	N	N	Y	Y
Canada	Y	Y	N	N	Y
Chile	N	Y	A	A	N
China (Nat.)	A	A	N	Y	N
Colombia	N	N	A	N	Y
Denmark	A	A	N	Y	N
Ecuador	N	Y	A	N	Y
France	N	N	N	Y	N
Finland	A	A	A	A	Y
Germany (W.)	N	N	N	Y	A
Greece	Y	N	N	Y	Y
Iceland	N	Y	A	N	Y
India	N	Y	Y	N	N
Indonesia	N	Y	Y	N	N
Iran	A	Y	Y	A	N
Italy	A	N	N	Y	Y
Japan	Y	N	N	A	Y
Korea (S.)	A	Y	A	N	A
Liberia	Y	Y	N	Y	N
Malaysia[d]	N	Y	Y	N	Y
Mexico	N	Y	Y	N	Y

TABLE 13 — Continued

| | First Committee | | | | Plenary |
State	Canadian[a]		Indian-[b] Mexican	United[c] States	United[c] States
Netherlands	N	N	N	Y	N
Norway	Y	Y	N	Y	Y
Pakistan	A	N	N	Y	Y
Panama	N	Y	Y	N	N
Peru	N	Y	A	N	Y
Philippines	N	Y	Y	A	Y
Poland	N	N	Y	N	Y
Portugal	A	N	N	Y	N
South Africa	N	N	N	Y	N
Spain	A	N	N	Y	A
Sweden	Y	N	N	A	N
Thailand	Y	Y	N	Y	Y
Turkey	Y	Y	N	Y	Y
USSR	N	N	Y	N	Y
UAR	N	Y	Y	N	Y
UK	N	N	N	Y	Y
US	N	N	N	Y	Y
Venezuela	N	A	Y	N	N
Total	Y=9 N=24 A=9	Y=19 N=19 A=4	Y=12 N=23 A=7	Y=20 N=16 A=6	Y=24 N=15 A=3
Total Conference Vote	Y=11 N=48 A=23	Y=37 N=35 A=9	Y=35 N=35 A=12	Y=36 N=38 A=9	Y=45 N=33 A=7

[a] First vote is on six mile territorial sea; second vote is on an additional six mile fishing zone. (Y = in favor; N = against; and A = abstention).

[b] Proposal for a territorial sea of up to 12 miles.

[c] Proposal for a territorial sea of six miles and a fishing zone of up to 12 miles together with protection for fishing rights of present users.

[d] Data is on what was then the Federation of Malaya.

Only two of the seven proposals advanced to the voting stage in the Committee of the Whole: the eighteen-power proposal and the joint United

States-Canadian proposal. The difference between the two plans centered on the extent of state authority in the seas between the six- and twelve-mile limits.[29]

The eighteen-power proposal was rejected in the Committee of the Whole by a vote of 39 to 36 with 13 abstentions.[30] Only thirteen of the votes in favor were cast by delegates of states with a special interest in the law of the sea. Twenty-three votes against were cast by delegates of states with a special interest.

The committee adopted the joint United States-Canadian proposal together with a proposal by Iceland for dealing with its special dependence on the sea.[31] Representatives of states with a special interest cast 23 of the 43 votes in favor whereas only 12 of the 33 negative votes were votes of delegates of these states.

In plenary session, the joint United States-Canadian proposal failed by one vote to obtain the necessary two-thirds majority.[32] The vote was 54-28-5 with 39 of the votes cast for or against being the votes of representatives of states with a special interest. Twenty-seven of these 39 were votes in favor.

The 1960 voting records of the states with a special interest in the law of the sea are summarized in Table 14. Again, as in 1958, no conventional rule on the maximum extent of the territorial sea was agreed upon. The proposal most favorably received, the joint United States-Canadian proposal, provided for a six-mile territorial sea and a six-mile contiguous zone. This proposal was favored by 27 of the states with a special interest in the law of the sea as well as by 27 of the other states represented at the conference. However, as in 1958, when the compromise solution was defeated, the United Kingdom and the United States reaffirmed their position that customary international law sanctioned three miles as the maximum permissible breadth of territorial sea.

CUSTOMARY RULES

If there is a rule in international law on the maximum breadth of the territorial sea, it apparently is rooted in custom.[33] When does a practice or usage become a customary rule in international law? It may be recalled from the discussion that the answer usually given by publicists is that when a practice or usage comes to command general assent, it becomes a rule of conduct; a customary rule is based not merely on a habit of action, but also on general approval.[34]

TABLE 14

VOTING SUMMARY OF STATES WITH A
SPECIAL INTEREST IN THE LAW OF THE SEA
REPRESENTED AT THE 1960 GENEVA CONFERENCE
ON THE LAW OF THE SEA

| | Committee of the Whole | | Plenary |
State	18-Power[a]	US-Canadian[b]	US-Canadian[b]
Argentina	A	A	Y
Australia	N	Y	Y
Belgium	N	A	Y
Brazil	N	Y	Y
Canada	N	Y	Y
Chile	A	N	N
China (Nat.)	N	Y	Y
Colombia	A	Y	Y
Denmark	N	Y	Y
Ecuador	Y	N	N
Finland	A	A	Y
France	N	A	Y
Germany (W.)	N	Y	Y
Greece	N	Y	Y
Iceland	Y	N	N
India	Y	A	N
Indonesia	Y	N	N
Iran	Y	N	A
Italy	N	Y	Y
Japan	N	Y	A
Korea (S.)	N	Y	Y
Liberia	N	Y	Y
Malaysia[c]	Y	Y	Y
Mexico	Y	N	N
Netherlands	N	Y	Y
Norway	N	Y	Y
Pakistan	A	Y	Y
Panama	Y	N	N
Peru	N	N	N
Philippines	Y	A	A
Poland	Y	N	N

TABLE 14 — Continued

| State | Committee of the Whole | | Plenary |
	18-Power[a]	US-Canadian[b]	US-Canadian[b]
Portugal	N	Y	Y
South Africa	N	Y	Y
Spain	N	Y	Y
Sweden	N	A	Y
Thailand	N	Y	Y
Turkey	A	Y	Y
USSR	Y	N	N
UAR	Y	N	N
UK	N	Y	Y
US	N	Y	Y
Venezuela	Y	N	N
Total	Y=13	Y=23	Y=27
	N=23	N=12	N=12
	A=6	A=7	A=3
Total	Y=36	Y=43	Y=54
Conference	N=39	N=33	N=28
Vote	A=13	A=12	A=5

[a] Up to twelve mile territorial sea or a combination territorial sea and contiguous zone of up to twelve miles in extent (Y = in favor; N = against; and A = abstention).

[b] A six mile territorial sea and a six mile contiguous zone.

[c] Data is on what was then the Federation of Malaya.

The basic questions to be raised, then, are: (1) what breadth of territorial sea does a majority of states claim? and (2) does this majority include a majority of the major users of states which otherwise have a special interest in a legal rule establishing a particular maximum breadth for the territorial sea? In Table 15, the claims made by the 121 states comprising the 1964 international political system are summarized.

Although a simple majority of all states represented at the 1958 and 1960 Conference on the Law of the Sea indicated a willingness to accept a territorial sea of six miles when combined with a six-mile contiguous zone, less than a simple majority of all states claim a territorial sea of six miles or less in practice. In order to obtain a simple majority, the category of claims of more than six but equal to or less than twelve miles must be included (see Table 15).

TABLE 15

CLAIMS TO PARTICULAR BREADTHS OF TERRITORIAL SEA

Claim[a]	Total	Number of States Claiming With Special Interest in:[b]				
		Merchant Fleet	Port Activity	Fishing Activity	Security Forces	One or More Interest
3	36	7	22	8	7	22
>3 but ≦6	23	4	9	7	4	14
>6 but ≦ 12	33	2	9	5	4	13
12 +	7	0	2	2	0	3
Landlocked	21					
Ambiguous	1	0	1	1	0	1
Total	121	13	43	23	15	53

[a] Claims in miles. Data obtained from the "Synoptical Table Concerning the Breadth and Juridical Status of the Territorial Sea and Adjacent Zones," (U.N. Doc. A/Conf. 19/4) (1960), in Second United Nations Conference on the Law of the Sea, *Official Records, Summary of Plenary Meetings and Meetings of the Committee of the Whole* (U.N. Doc. No. A/Conf. 19/8) (1960), pp. 157-164; and *Sovereignty of the Sea, Geographic Bulletin* No. 3 (April, 1965), (Washington: Department of State, 1965), pp. 26-27. In case of conflict, the Department of State data are accepted, although the claims listed there are not necessarily official. See Appendix B for a listing of states and their claims.

[b] Algeria, Red China, Gabon, Ivory Coast, Jamaica, Kenya, Nigeria, Senegal, Syria, Tanzania, and Trinidad and Tobago, in addition to the forty-two states listed in Table 12 are the states with a special interest in the law of the sea in the 1964 international political system. See Appendix E for an indication of the bases for these states' special interest. Note that a state may have a special interest on the basis of more than one of these indicators. The One or More Interest column indicates that 53 of the 100 states which claim a particular number breadth of territorial sea have a special interest.

A simple majority of all states may be obtained by extending the limit to ten miles;[35] however, this still does not include a number of states with a special interest in the law of the sea. The conclusion must be, then, that there is no customary rule which establishes a specific breadth for the territorial sea. No single breadth commands the generality of assent needed to establish a rule by means of the customary international law decision-making process. The United Kingdom and the United States, for example, have indicated an unwillingness to accept an extent in excess of three miles unless such a limit is established by international convention. Moreover, the twelve-mile proposal has been voted down by two international conferences on the law of the sea. It seems that the only legal rule established concerning the breadth of the territorial sea is the three-mile minimum extent.

CONTIGUOUS ZONE

Delegates to the 1958 Geneva Conference on the Law of the Sea were successful in codifying certain rules applicable to special purpose contiguous zones. Article 24 of the Convention on the Territorial Sea and the Contiguous Zone provides:

1. In a zone of the high seas contiguous to its territorial sea, the coastal state may exercise the control necessary to:

a) Prevent infringement of its customs, fiscal, immigration, or sanitary regulations within its territory or territorial sea;

b) Punish infringement of the above regulations committed within its territory or territorial sea.

2. The contiguous zone may not extend beyond twelve miles from the baseline from which the breadth of the territorial sea is measured.[36]

Only 15 of the 53 states with a special interest in the law of the sea included within the 1964 international political system have ratified this convention. As indicated in Table 16, an additional 11 such states signed but have not subsequently ratified. Only 26 states with a special interest and only 53 states altogether have indicated any degree of approval of the legal rules concerning the contiguous zone set forth in Article 24 of the Convention on the Territorial Sea and the Contiguous Zone.

In the First Committee, the article on the contiguous zone was adopted 50-18-8.[37] This same article was rejected in plenary session 40-27-9. However, a United States-sponsored substitute, the present Article 24, was adopted 60-0-13.[38]

In practice, 52 states have established at least one special purpose contiguous zone.[39] Thirty-four of these are states with a special interest in the law of the sea. Thirty-nine states with a special interest have ratified the convention and/or unilaterally have claimed at least one special purpose contiguous zone (see Table 17 for unilateral claims). Both the United States and the Soviet Union are included among the 39. Furthermore, a total of 70 of the 121 states included within the 1964 international political system have ratified the convention and/or unilaterally have claimed at least one purpose zone.

TABLE 16

ACCEPTANCE OF CONVENTIONS ON THE TERRITORIAL SEA, THE CONTINENTAL SHELF, AND THE HIGH SEAS BY STATES WHICH HAVE A SPECIAL INTEREST IN THE LAW OF THE SEA

State	Convention		
	Territorial Sea and Contiguous Zone	Continental Shelf	High Seas
Argentina	S	S	S
Australia	R	R	R
Belgium			
Brazil			
Canada	S	S	S
Chile		S	
China (Nat.)	S	S	S
China (Red)			
Colombia	S	R	S
Denmark	S	R	S
Ecuador		S	
Finland	R	R	R
France		R	S
Gabon			
Germany (W.)		S	S
Greece			
Iceland	S	S	S
India			
Indonesia		S	R
Iran	S	S	S
Italy	R		R
Ivory Coast			
Jamacia	R	R	
Japan			
Kenya			
Korea (S.)			
Liberia	S	S	S
Malaysia	R	R	R
Mexico	R	R	R

TABLE 16 — Continued

State	Convention		
	Territorial Sea and Contiguous Zone	Continental Shelf	High Seas
Algeria			
Netherlands	R	R	R
Nigeria	R		
Norway			
Pakistan	S	S	S
Panama	S	S	S
Peru		S	
Philippines			
Poland		R	R
Portugal	R	R	R
Senegal	R	R	R
South Africa	R	R	R
Spain			
Sweden		R	
Syria			
Tanzania			
Thailand	S	S	S
Trinidad and Tobago			
Turkey			
USSR	R	R	R
UAR			
UK	R	R	R
US	R	R	R
Venezuela	R	R	R
Total	S=11 R=15	S=14 R=18	S=13 R=15
Total Ratifications By All States	S=24 R=29	S=25 R=33	S=25 R=36

NOTE: Based on data obtained from the Treaty section, The Legal Division, United Nations Secretariat in June, 1966, this table excludes Byelorussian and Ukrainian S.S.R., the Holy See, Monaco, and San Marino. If these political entities are included, totals are: Territorial Sea 29 ratified, High Seas 25 signed and 38 ratified. Otherwise, no changes. (S = Signed; R = Ratified or otherwise adhered).

TABLE 17

UNILATERAL CLAIMS TO SPECIAL PURPOSE
CONTIGUOUS SEA ZONES
AND TO THE ADJACENT CONTINENTAL SHELF
MADE BY STATES WITH A SPECIAL INTEREST
IN THE LAW OF THE SEA

| State | Claim | |
	At Least One Contiguous Sea Zone[a]	Continental Shelf[b]
Algeria		
Argentina	X	X
Australia	X	X
Belgium	X	
Brazil	X	X
Canada	X	
Chile	X	X
China (Nat.)	X	
China (Red)		
Colombia	X	
Denmark	X	
Ecuador	X	X
Finland	X	
France	X	
Gabon		
Germany (W.)	X	
Greece	X	
Iceland	X	X
India	X	X
Indonesia		
Iran		X
Italy	X	
Ivory Coast		
Jamaica		X
Japan	X	X
Kenya		
Korea (S.)	X	X
Liberia		
Malaysia		

TABLE 17 — Continued

State	Claim At Least One Contiguous Sea Zone[a]	Continental Shelf[b]
Mexico	X	
Netherlands	X	
Nigeria		
Norway	X	
Pakistan	X	X
Panama	X	X
Peru	X	X
Philippines		X
Poland	X	
Portugal	X	X
Senegal	X	
South Africa	X	
Spain	X	
Sweden	X	
Syria		
Tanzania		
Thailand	X	
Trinidad and Tobago		X
Turkey		
USSR		
UAR		X
UK[c]	X	X
US	X	X
Venezuela	X	X
Total	34	21
Total All States	52	32

[a] Based on data obtained from "Synoptical Table Concerning the Breadth and Juridicial Status of the Territorial Sea and Adjacent Zones," (U.N. Doc. A Conf. 19/4) (1960), in Second United Nations Conference on the Law of the Sea, *Official Records, Summary of Plenary Meetings and Meetings of the Committee of the Whole* (U.N. Doc. No. A/Conf. 19/8) (1960), pp. 157-164.

[b] Based on data obtained from "Synoptical Table . . . ," Ibid., and Shigeru Oda, *International Control of Sea Resources* (Leyden: A. W. Sythoff, 1963), pp. 148-150.

[c] The United Kingdom claims are for territorial possessions.

There is, then, a universally-applicable rule with regard to the contiguous zone. The rule establishes the right of states to claim contiguous sea zones for certain special purposes. Although the votes in the Committee of the Whole and in plenary session indicate wide-spread support for the special purposes listed in the convention, these purposes cannot be considered definitive. Some of the unilateral claims to authority in contiguous zones are for purposes other than those specified in paragraph 1, Article 25 of the convention. There is no practical way to determine what other purposes might be approved by the parties to the convention. Moreover, it is not possible to determine whether states making unilateral claims to contiguous zones but not ratifying the convention would agree to paragraphs 2 and 3 of Article 24. The universally-applicable rule seems to be, then, that states are authorized to establish special purpose contiguous sea zones for certain purposes; purposes perhaps not limited to but at least including enforcement of customs, fiscal, immigration, and sanitary regulations.[40]

CONTINENTAL SHELF[41]

Delegates to the 1958 Convention on the Law of the Sea also were able to agree on a draft convention on the continental shelf. This convention was signed by the representatives of 46 states, and has been in force since June 10, 1964, more than the required 22 ratifications and/or accessions having been deposited by that date.[42]

Under the provisions of this convention, states may exercise sovereign rights over the adjacent continental shelf. This sovereign right is limited, however, to the right of exploration and exploitation of natural resources of the continental shelf.[43]

Eighteen of the states which have ratified this convention have a special interest in the law of the sea (see Table 16). Altogether 33 states have ratified or otherwise adhered. Thirty-one states, 20 of which have a special interest, make unilateral claims to exclusive rights over adjacent continental shelves (see Table 17). In combination, a total of 32 states with a special interest have ratified or otherwise adhered to the convention and/or make unilateral claims to certain exclusive rights.[44] A total of 53 states have ratified and/or made unilateral claims. Fourteen other states, including six with a special interest, have indicated a tacit consent by signing but not subsequently ratifying the convention. None of these 14 have asserted unilateral claims to exclusive rights in the continental shelf. In summary, then, 64 states, including 35 with a special interest, have accepted the principle that coastal states have certain exclusive rights over the adjacent continental shelf, although 14 and 6 have accepted the principle only tacitly.

It seems reasonable to contend that there is a universally-applicable rule with regard to the continental shelf. This rule provides that the adjacent coastal states may exercise sovereign rights in the exploration and exploitation of the natural resources of the continental shelf. Although not universally binding as conventional rules, the definitions included in the Convention on the Continental Shelf are universally recognized — this convention was adopted 57-3-8 in plenary session of the 1958 convention.[45] It is evident, therefore, that a majority of all states, including a majority of the states with a special interest, recognize these definitions.

CLAIMS PRIMARILY IN SUPPORT OF AN INCLUSIVE INTEREST

HIGH SEAS

To maintain that the high seas are free in the inclusive interest borders on stating a truism. So widely accepted is this principle that the 1958 Geneva Conference on the Law of the Sea adopted unanimously the two articles articulating it.[46] The Convention on the High Seas as a whole was accepted in plenary session by a vote of 65-0-1.[47]

In Article 1, the high seas are defined as all waters beyond the territorial sea, and in Article 2, the high seas are declared ". . . open to all nations . . . ."[48] This freedom is said to comprise, for all states, coastal and non-coastal, freedom of navigation, fishing, freedom to lay submarine cables and pipelines, and freedom to fly over the high seas.[49]

Article 3 provides that landlocked states should have free access to the sea. States located between landlocked states and the sea shall agree to accord:

> (a) To the state having no sea-coast, on a basis of reciprocity, free transit through their territory; and
>
> (b) To ships flying the flag of that state treatment equal to that accorded to their own ships, or to ships of any other states, as regards access to seaports and the use of ports.[50]

Furthermore, states located between landlocked states and the sea

> . . . shall settle, by mutual agreement with the latter, and taking into account the rights of the coastal State or State of transit and the special conditions of the State having no sea-coast, all matters relating to freedom of transit and equal treatment in ports, in case such States are not already parties to existing international conventions.[51]

Thirty-six states, including fifteen with a special interest in the law of the sea, have ratified or otherwise adhered to the Convention on the High Seas (see Table 16). An additional 24 states, including thirteen with a special interest, signed the convention, but have not subsequently ratified.[52]

There clearly is an established and universally recognized general principle of the freedom of the high seas. However, because of the lack of widespread support for the Convention on the High Seas, the special provisions of the convention are not universally applicable.[53]

NATIONALITY, REGISTRATION, AND SAFETY AT SEA

There is a degree of ambiguity as to whether the claim to authority to endow a vessel with the nationality of a state is primarily an exclusive or inclusive claim. Significantly, the question is dealt with in an international convention dealing with a primarily inclusive interest, the Convention on the High Seas. The claim is treated here as an inclusive claim since apparently one of the primary reasons for insisting that a ship have a nationality is to give some state the responsibility for ensuring that international safety standards are enforced, that crews be licensed in accordance with some basic minimum international standards, and so forth.

The question of nationality is dealt with in Article 5 of the Convention of the High Seas. This article provides that "each state shall fix the conditions for the grant of its nationality to ships, for the registration of ships in its territory, and for the right to fly its flag."[54]

The protection of an inclusive interest is emphasized by the provision, also in Article 5, that "there must exist a genuine link between the State and the ship; in particular, the State must effectively exercise its jurisdiction and control in administrative, technical and social matters over ships flying its flag."[55]

The controversy stimulated by introduction of the genuine link requirement will not be discussed here. However, it does seem that the inclusion of this requirement is in the nature of an assurance that some state is assigned effective responsibility for every ship.

The Convention on the High Seas is not universally applicable; however, 64 states within the 1964 international political system, including 39 with a special interest in the law of the sea, have statutes which establish rules and regulations concerning the acquisition of nationality by ships. Furthermore, this same legislation details the procedures for registration.[56]

It is beyond the scope of this study to determine what the detailed rules concerning nationality and registration are; however, at a minimum states seem to agree to rules that: (1) a ship possesses the nationality of the state whose flag it flies;[57] (2) each state establishes its own conditions for granting its nationality; and (3) each state establishes its own conditions and procedures for registering ships.[58]

The Convention on the High Seas also assigns responsibilities to the flag state for ensuring safety at sea

. . . with regard *inter alia* to:

(a)   The use of signals, the maintenance of communications and the prevention of collisions;

(b)   The manning of ships and labor conditions for crews, taking into account the applicable international labor instruments.

(c)   The construction, equipment and seaworthiness of ships.[59]

Article 12 of the Convention on the High Sea deals with rescue and assistance to distressed persons at sea. States are to ". . . require the master of a ship sailing under its flag, in so far as he can do so without serious danger to the ship, the crew or passengers . . ." to render assistance and to attempt to rescue persons in danger of being lost or who are otherwise distressed and in need of assistance.[60]

The extent of applicability of this convention has been discussed previously and it has been concluded that the detailed provisions of the convention are applicable only between parties. However, a number of other international conventions treat with safety at sea, including the International Load Line as modified in 1938 and 1957, and the 1948 and 1960 Safety of Life at Sea Conventions. The preamble of the International Load Line Convention indicates that the contracting governments ". . . desiring to promote safety of life and property at sea by establishing in common agreement uniform principles and rules with regard to the limits to which ships on international voyages may be loaded, have resolved to conclude a Convention for that purpose . . . ."[61] Furthermore, the principle of registration previously discussed is referred to in Article 3.[62]

The 1948 and 1960 Safety of Life at Sea Conventions specify regulations on survey and certificates, casualties, construction, subdivisions, and stability, electrical installations, fire protection, life saving appliances, radio-telegraphy, radiotelephony, and some other areas.[63]

The International Load Line Convention, as modified, has been ratified or otherwise adhered to by 73 states, including 44 with a special interest in the law of the sea (see Table 18). The 1948 Convention on the Safety of Life at Sea has been ratified or otherwise adhered to by 69 states, including 36 with a special interest (see Table 18). Thirty-two states, of which 23 have a special interest, have ratified the 1960 version of this convention (see Table 18). The provisions of the 1948 and 1960 conventions are very similar and in combination 75 states including 40 with a special interest in the law of the sea have ratified or otherwise adhered.

TABLE 18

ACCEPTANCE OF SAFETY AT SEA CONVENTIONS BY STATES WHICH HAVE A SPECIAL INTEREST IN THE LAW OF THE SEA

State	Convention		
	Load Line	1948	1960
Algeria	X	X	X
Argentina	X	X	
Australia	X	X	X
Belgium	X	X	X
Brazil	X	X	
Canada	X	X	X
Chile	X	X	
China (Nat.)	X	X	
China (Red)	X		
Colombia			
Denmark	X		X
Ecuador	X		
Finland	X	X	X
France	X		X
Gabon			
Germany (W.)	X	X	X
Greece	X	X	
Iceland	X	X	X
India	X	X	
Indonesia	X		
Iran	X	X	X
Italy	X	X	X
Ivory Coast	X	X	
Jamaica			
Japan	X	X	
Kenya			
Korea (S.)	X	X	
Liberia	X	X	X

TABLE 18 — Continued

| | Convention | | |
State	Load Line	1948	1960
Malaysia	X	X	
Mexico	X	X	X
Netherlands	X	X	X
Nigeria	X	X	
Norway	X	X	X
Pakistan	X	X	
Panama	X	X	X
Peru	X		
Philippines	X	X	X
Poland	X	X	X
Portugal	X	X	
Senegal		X	
South Africa	X	X	
Spain	X	X	X
Sweden	X		X
Syria			
Tanzania			
Thailand	X		
Trinidad and Tobago			
Turkey	X	X	
USSR	X	X	
UAR	X	X	X
UK	X		X
US	X	X	X
Venezuela	X	X	X
Total	44	36	23
Total All States	73	69	32

NOTE: Data on parties to these three conventions obtained from Department of State, *Treaties in Force: A List of Treaties and Other International Agreements in Force on January 1, 1966* (Washington: Government Printing Office, 1966), pp. 264-266.

It is beyond the scope of this study to attempt to determine the specific safety rules which are established by these three conventions. However, it seems that a general rule may be asserted based on the findings here. This universally-applicable general rule establishes the authority of the collective community to formulate rules and to exercise and establish international control over several aspects of safety on the seas.[64]

DEVIATIONS OR EXCEPTIONS
TO EXCLUSIVE OR INCLUSIVE AUTHORITY

INNOCENT PASSAGE

The right of innocent passage is provided for in Part I, Section III of the Convention on the Territorial Sea and the Contiguous Zone. Ships of all states are said to ". . . enjoy the right of innocent passage through the territorial sea."[65] The ships of all states are authorized to navigate through the territorial sea without entering the internal waters of the coastal state. Such vessels also may navigate through the territorial seas in proceeding to the international waters of the coast state and in proceeding from the internal waters to the high seas.[66] Ships may stop and anchor if this is incidental to ordinary navigation or if distress or a *force majeoure* makes stopping or anchoring necessary.[67]

Passage is innocent so long as it is not prejudicial to the peace, good order, or security of the coastal state.[68] Fishing in the territorial sea during passage apparently is prejudicial to peace and good order, for fishing vessels are admonished to observe the laws and regulations of the coastal states establishing rules for fishing in the territorial sea.[69] Warships generally and submarines specifically are treated as a potential threat to peace, good order, and security. A warship may be required to leave the territorial sea if it fails to comply with regulations or if it disregards requests by the host state that it comply with such regulations.[70] "Submarines are required to navigate on the surface and to show their flag."[71]

It is the duty of the coastal state not to hamper innocent passage, and to publicize dangers to navigation.[72] It is the right of the coastal state to prevent non-innocent passage, to establish conditions for entry into internal waters, and to ". . . suspend temporarily in specified areas of its territorial sea the innocent passage of foreign ships if such suspension is essential for the protection of its security."[73]

The criminal jurisdiction of the coastal state over merchant ships and government ships operated for commercial purposes are detailed in Articles 19 and 20.[74] In general, these provisions are statements of what states are not authorized to do in exercising jurisdiction on board foreign vessels passing through the territorial sea. These rules regarding criminal jurisdiction do not apply to government ships which are operated for non-commercial purposes.[75]

Support of the Convention on the Territorial Sea and the Contiguous Zone has been examined in the subsection treating with the contiguous zone. As noted there, the convention is not universally applicable for it fails to meet the requirements of the modified majority rule. The articles dealing with the right of innocent passage do have widespread support, however. In plenary session at Geneva, each of these 10 articles was adopted by large majorities. The article receiving least support was adopted by a vote of 62-9-4.[76]

This widespread support is indicative of the positive acceptance of the general principle of a right of innocent passage. In some cases, the detailed provisions of Section III of the convention are supported by national legislation, but not to the extent required here to establish universally-applicable rules.[77]

SUMMARY

The claims which states make in various problem areas in international law may be characterized as: Claims Primarily in support of an Exclusive Interest; Claims Primarily in Support of an Inclusive Interest; and Deviations or Exceptions to Exclusive or Inclusive Authority. Claims are categorized on the basis of what the primary purpose or function of the claim appears to be. At least one problem in each of these categories has been examined in this chapter.

The analysis here has not been comprehensive; rather, only selected legal problem areas in international sea law have been analyzed. Moreover, there has been no attempt to be comprehensive in the determination of legal rules and principles within the selected problem areas. The purposes have been: (1) to determine the *extent* of applicability and the *degree* of acceptance of certain legal prescriptions; (2) to demonstrate the applicability of an approach and certain techniques or a method in the analysis of international law; and (3) to examine certain legal problems in the sea environment which seem particularly relevant to certain outer space legal problems determined in Chapter 2.

It has been determined that:

1. There is neither a customary rule nor a general principle establishing a specific maximum breadth for the territorial sea. However, there is general agreement on a minimum breadth of three miles.

2. States have the legal right to establish contiguous sea zones for special purposes including enforcement of customs, fiscal, immigration, and/or sanitary regulations.

3. Coastal states may exercise sovereign rights in the exploration and exploitation of the natural resources of the adjacent continental shelf.

4. The principle of the freedom of the high seas is universally recognized. Conventional legal rules concerning the high seas are not universally applicable.

5. At a minimum, states seem to agree to international legal rules that: (a) a ship possesses the nationality of the state whose flag it flies; (b) each state establishes its own conditions for granting its nationality to vessels; (c) each state establishes its own conditions and procedures for registration of vessels; and (d) there is a universally applicable general rule that a state should register and exercise control over ships flying its flag.

6. There are a number of detailed international safety at sea legal rules; however, for purposes of this study, only the general rule has been determined: a universally-applicable general rule that the collective community may establish and exercise international controls over certain aspects of safety on the seas.

7. States accept a general principle of a right of innocent passage through territorial seas. The detailed procedures regarding innocent passage in the Convention on the Territorial Sea and the Contiguous Zone are widely supported; however, the degree of acceptance is inadequate to establish binding rules other than between parties to the convention.

The question of why legitimate and authoritative decision-makers accept these rules and principles as the law-in-action in the selected legal problem areas in the sea environment will be analyzed in Part III.

NOTES

1. *The International Law of the Sea,* 5th rev. ed. (London: Longmans, Green and Co., Ltd., 1962), p. 8. For Colombos, international law ". . . is a body of rules which states consider they are bound to observe in their mutual relations" (p. 7). He dates the beginning of international law from Hugo Grotius' *De Jure Bellis ac Pacis* which was published in 1625.

2. Although the net effect of claims and counterclaims in a particular problem area may be in the inclusive interest of the international political system, the claims referred to here are analytically distinctive as claims made primarily in the exclusive interest of the particular state.

3. There are possible ambiguities within this categorization scheme. For example, one might argue that innocent passage is an inclusive interest rather than a deviation or an exception to an exclusive claim to authority over the territorial sea. The emphasis, however, as noted above, is on what the *primary* purpose or function of the claim appears to be.

It should be noted, as was pointed out to me by Myres S. McDougal, that the fundamental question here concerns accommodation. This is not only the case between exclusive and inclusive interests; often there also must be an accommodation between competing exclusive interests.

4. See his *Public Order* series generally, and specifically see McDougal and Burke, *Public Order of the Oceans,* op. cit.

5. Ibid., p. viii.

6. Idem.

7. The continental shelf can be considered an additional regime. This regime will be discussed separately.

8. See, for example, United Nations Legislative Series, *Laws and Regulations on the Regime of the Territorial Sea* (United Nations: United Nations, 1957) (St/Leg/Ser. B16) (1956). States claim the authority to: control access; apply authority to vessels in such matters as pollution, pilotage, etc.; control resources; prescribe policy both externally, and to certain events aboard vessels within internal waters. State legislative enactments relating to vessels other than warships, on navigation, security, fiscal, custom, and sanitation matters are collected in Chapter II, pp. 59-360. Legislation regarding warships is collected in Chapter III, pp. 361-420.

9. See generally: *Anglo-Norwegian Fisheries* (1951), International Court of Justice *Reports,* 1951, p. 116; on adjacent islands see *United States v. California* (1947), 332 U. S. 19; and on rugged and complex coastal configurations see the *Anglo-Norwegian Fisheries,* idem., and International Law Commission, *Reports,*

United Nations General Assembly, *Official Records,* 9th Session, Supplement No. 9 (A2693) (1954), 10th Session, Supplement No. 9 (A/2934) (1955), and 11th Session, Supplement No. 9 (A/3159) (1956).

10. See United Nations Legislative Series, *Laws and Regulations on the Regime of the Territorial Sea,* op. cit., and the Convention on the Territorial Sea and the Contiguous Zone, Articles 1 and 2, in United Nations Conference on the Law of the Sea, *Official Records,* 2, (United Nations: United Nations, 1958) (U.N. Doc. A/Conf. 13/38) (1958), pp. 132-135.

11. On the territorial sea, in addition to McDougal and Burke, op. cit., and Colombos, op. cit., see: Henry Reiff, *The United States and the Treaty Law of the Sea* (Minneapolis: University of Minnesota Press, 1959); Research in International Law of the Harvard Law School, *The Law of Territorial Waters, American Journal of International Law, Supplement,* 23 (April, 1929); S. Whittemore Boggs, "Delimitation of Seward Areas Under National Jurisdiction," *American Journal of International Law,* 45 (April, 1951), pp. 240-266; Edward W. Allen, "Territorial Waters and Extraterritorial Rights," *American Journal of International Law,* 47 (July, 1953), pp. 478-480; H.S.K. Kent, "The Historical Origins of the Three-Mile Limit," *American Journal of International Law,* 48 (October, 1954), pp. 537-553; and Philip C. Jessup, "The Law of the Sea Around Us," *American Journal of International Law,* 55 (January, 1961), pp. 104-109.

12. McDougal and Burke, op. cit., p. 487. McDougal and Burke review "Claims to Determine the Width of the Territorial Sea," pp. 446-564.

13. The 1930 Hague Codification Convention was an earlier attempt to codify the law of the sea. Although delegates to the Hague convention were unable to agree on a sea law convention, a draft on "The Legal Status of the Territorial Sea" was prepared. For a summary of the accomplishments and voting records of the 1930 convention, see Colombos, op. cit., pp. 94-97.

For discussion and evaluation of the 1958 and 1960 conferences, see: Arthur H. Dean, "The Geneva Conference on the Law of the Sea: What was Accomplished," *American Journal of International Law,* 52 (October, 1958), pp. 607-628; Arthur H. Dean, "The Second Geneva Conference on the Law of the Sea," *American Journal of International Law,* 54 (October, 1960), pp. 750-789; and Philip C. Jessup, "The Geneva Conference on the Law of the Sea," *American Journal of International Law,* 52 (October, 1958) pp. 730-733.

14. Following the Banks and Textor example, code cutting points have been established at what appear to be natural breaking points within the raw data distributions rather than on the basis of some equal interval measurement [Arthur S. Banks and Robert B. Textor, *A Cross-Polity Survey* (Cambridge: The M.I.T. Press, 1963), pp. 56-57].

Note that the relationship between the concept "special interest" and the variables selected to define "special interest" is based on active utilization of the sea by nation-states or their nationals. It is not practical to attempt to deal directly with the possibility that certain official decision-makers perceive a special national interest in problems within which their state is not objectively defined as having a special interest. However, in some instances, the apparent perceptions of national decision-makers will be treated in Part III. In any case, the effort here has been to be liberal in defining special interest in an attempt to avoid omitting relevant actors.

There is also the question of intensity. Perhaps some measure of intensity might be obtained by relating the degree of activity or size within categories and the number of categories within which a state qualifies as the possessor of a special interest to the rule preferences of a state's decision-makers; however, no attempt is made in this study to deal with this interesting question.

15. See United Nations Conference on the Law of the Sea, *Official Records*, 3 (United Nations: United Nations, 1958), (U.N. Doc. No. A/Conf. 13) (1958). These were separate proposals, not a joint UK-US proposal. In fact, when the representatives of the United Kingdom originally proposed a six-mile maximum, not to affect existing rights of passage outside three miles, the United States delegation did not support the proposal. However, it was only two weeks later that the United States Delegation itself proposed a six-mile territorial sea with a six-mile contiguous zone. See ibid., pp. 105, 153, and 163, and McDougal and Burke, op. cit., pp. 529-530.

16. United Nations Conference on the Law of the Sea, *Official Records,* op. cit., p. 232.

17. Ibid., p. 233.

18. Ibid., p. 253.

19. Why states accept or reject particular rules or principles will be analyzed in Part III.

20. Although represented at the conference, the Byelorussian S.S.R., the Ukrainian S.S.R., the Holy See, Monaco, and San Marino are not included in the 1964 international political system for this study.

21. In favor: Argentina, Cambodia, Canada, Greece, Haiti, Japan, Liberia, Norway, Sweden, Thailand, and Turkey. Against: Afghanistan, Albania, Australia, Belgium, Bazil, Bulgaria, Burma, Byelorrussian S.S.R., Ceylon, Chile, Colombia, Cuba, Czechoslovakia, Dominican Republic, Ecuador, El Salvador, France, West Germany, Guatemala, Hungary, Iceland, India, Indonesia, Iraq, Lebanon, Libya, Luxembourg, Federation of Malaya, Mexico, Monaco, Morocco, Netherlands, New Zealand, Panama, Peru, Philippines, Poland, Romania, Saudi Arabia, South Africa, the Soviet Union, Tunisia, Ukrainian S.S.R., UAR, UK, US, Uruguay, and Venezuela. Abstaining: Austria, Bolivia, China (Nat.), Costa Rica, Denmark, Finland, Ghana, the Holy See, Honduras, Iran, Ireland, Israel, Italy, South Korea, Nepal, Nicaragua, Pakistan, Paraguay, Portugal, Spain, Switzerland, Vietnam, and Yugoslavia. United Nations Conference on the Law of the Sea, *Official Records,* 3, op. cit., p. 176.

22. In favor: Afghanistan, Argentina, Burma, Cambodia, Canada, Ceylon, Chile, Costa Rica, Ecuador, El Salvador, Ghana, Guatemala, Iceland, India, In-

donesia, Iran, Iraq, Ireland, South Korea, Liberia, Libya, Federation of Malaya, Mexico, Morocco, Nepal, Norway, Panama, Peru, Philippines, Saudi Arabia, Thailand, Tunisia, Turkey, UAR, Uruguay, Vietnam, and Yugoslavia. Against: Albania, Australia, Belgium, Brazil, Bulgaria, Byelorussian S.S.R., Colombia, Cuba, Czechoslavakia, Dominican Republic, France, West Germany, Greece, Haiti, Hungary, Israel, Italy, Japan, Luxembourg, Monaco, Netherlands, New Zealand, Nicaragua, Pakistan, Poland, Portugal, Romania, South Africa, the Soviet Union, Spain, Sweden, Switzerland, Ukrainian S.S.R., UK, and US. Abstaining: Austria, Bolivia, China (Nat.), Denmark, Finland, the Holy See, Honduras, Lebanon, and Venezuela. Ibid., pp. 176-177.

23. In favor: Afghanistan, Albania, Argentina, Bolivia, Bulgaria, Burma, Byelorussian S.S.R., Cambodia, Ceylon, Czechoslovakia, Ghana, Guatemala, Hungary, India, Indonesia, Iran, Iraq, Lebanon, Libya, Federation of Malaya, Mexico, Morocco, Nepal, Panama, Philippines, Poland, Romania, Saudi Arabia, Tunisia, Ukrainian S.S.R., the Soviet Union, UAR, Uruguay, Venezuela, and Yugoslavia. Against: Australia, Austria, Belgium, Brazil, Canada, China (Nat.), Cuba, Denmark, Dominican Republic, El Salvador, France, West Germany, Greece, Haiti, Ireland, Israel, Italy, Japan, Liberia, Luxembourg, Monaco, Netherlands, New Zealand, Nicaragua, Norway, Pakistan, Portugal, South Africa, Spain, Sweden, Switzerland, Thailand, Turkey, UK, and US. Abstaining: Chile, Colombia, Costa Rica, Ecuador, Finland, the Holy See, Honduras, Iceland, South Korea, Paraguay, Peru, and Vietnam. Ibid., p. 177.

24. In favor: Australia, Austria, Belgium, Bolivia, Brazil, Cambodia, China (Nat.), Cuba, Denmark, Dominican Republic, France, West Germany, Greece, Haiti, Honduras, Ireland, Israel, Italy, Liberia, Luxembourg, Monaco, Netherlands, New Zealand, Nicaragua, Norway, Pakistan, Paraguay, Portugal, South Africa, Spain, Switzerland, Thailand, Turkey, UK, US, and Vietnam. Against: Afghanistan, Albania, Argentina, Bulgaria, Burma, Byelorussian S.S.R., Canada, Ceylon, Colombia, Czechslovakia, Ecuador, El Salvador, Ghana, Guatemala, Hungry, Iceland, India, Indonesia, Iraq, Jordan, South Korea, Lebanon, Libya, Federation of Malaya, Mexico, Morocco, Panama, Peru, Poland, Romania, Saudi Arabia, the Soviet Union, UAR, Uruguay, Venezuela, and Yugoslavia. Abstaining: Chile, Costa Rica, Finland, the Holy See, Iran, Japan, Nepal, Philippines, and Sweden. Ibid., p. 180.

25. In favor: Australia, Austria, Belgium, Bolivia, Brazil, Cambodia, Ceylon, China (Nat.), Denmark, Dominican Republic, France, West Germany, Ghana, Greece, Haiti, the Holy See, Honduras, India, Iran, Ireland, Israel, Italy, Laos, Liberia, Luxembourg, Federation of Malaya, Monaco, Netherlands, New Zealand, Nicaragua, Norway, Pakistan, Paraguay, Portugal, San Marino, South Africa, Spain, Sweden, Switzerland, Thailand, Turkey, UK, US, and Vietnam. Against: Albania, Argentina, Bulgaria, Burma, Byelorussian S.S.R., Canada, Chile, Colombia, Czechoslovakia, Ecuador, El Salvador, Guatemala, Hungary, Iceland, Indonesia, Jordan, South Korea, Lebanon, Libya, Mexico, Morocco, Panama, Peru, Poland, Romania, Saudi Arabia, the Soviet Union, Tunisia, Ukrainian S.S.R., UAR, Uruguay, Venezuela, and Yugoslavia. Abstaining: Afghanistan, Costa Rica, Finland, Iraq, Japan, Nepal, and Philippines. United Nations Conference on the Law of the Sea, *Official Records,* 2, op. cit., p. 39.

26. The United States and the United Kingdom, for example, reaffirmed their claim that customary international law provided for a maximum breadth of three miles.

27. All proposals are reprinted in Second United Nations Conference on the Law of the Sea, *Official Records, Summary Records of Plenary Meetings and of Meetings of the Committee of the Whole* (U.N. Doc. No. A/Conf. 19/8), pp. 164-169.

28. Ibid., p. 173.

29. Arguments for the eighteen-power proposal were based primarily on exclusive economic and security interests. See ibid., pp. 70-71, 98, 102, 104-106, and 146. These arguments will be discussed in Part III.

30. In favor: Albania, Bulgaria, Burma, Byelorussian S.S.R., Cambodia, Czechoslovakia, Ecuador, Ethiopia, Ghana, Guinea, Hungary, Iceland, India, Indonesia, Iran, Iraq, Jordan, Lebanon, Libya, Federation of Malaya, Mexico, Morocco, Panama, Philippines, Poland, Romania, Saudi Arabia, the Soviet Union, Sudan, Tunisia, Ukrainian S.S.R., UAR, Uruguay, Venezuela, Yemen, and Yugoslavia. Against: Australia, Belgium, Brazil, Cameroons, Canada, China (Nat.), Costa Rica, Denmark, Dominican Republic, El Salvador, France, West Germany, Greece, Haiti, Honduras, Ireland, Israel, Italy, Japan, South Korea, Laos, Liberia, Luxembourg, Monaco, Netherlands, New Zealand, Nicaragua, Norway, Peru, Portugal, San Marino, South Africa, Spain, Sweden, Switzerland, Thailand, UK, US, and Vietnam. Abstentions: Argentina, Austria, Bolivia, Ceylon, Chile, Colombia, Cuba, Finland, Guatemala, the Holy See, Pakistan, Paraguay, and Turkey. Ibid., p. 151.

31. In favor: Australia, Austria, Bolivia, Brazil, Cameroons, Canada, Ceylon, China (Nat.), Colombia, Costa Rica, Denmark, Dominican Republic, West Germany, Greece, Haiti, Honduras, Ireland, Israel, Italy, Japan, South Korea, Laos, Liberia, Luxembourg, Federation of Malaya, Monaco, Netherlands, New Zealand, Nicaragua, Norway, Pakistan, Paraguay, Portugal, San Marino, South Africa, Spain, Switzerland, Thailand, Turkey, UK, US, Uruguay, and Vietnam. Against: Albania, Bulgaria, Burma, Byelorussian S.S.R., Chile, Czechoslovakia, Ecuador, El Salvador, Ethiopia, Guinea, Hungary, Iceland, Indonesia, Iran, Iraq, Jordan, Lebanon, Libya, Mexico, Morocco, Panama, Peru, Poland, Romania, Saudi Arabia, the Soviet Union, Sudan, Tunisia, Ukrainian S.S.R., UAR, and Venezuela. Abstaining: Argentina, Belgium, Cambodia, Cuba, Finland, France, Ghana, Guatemala, the Holy See, India, Philippines, and Sweden. Ibid., p. 152.

32. In favor: Argentina, Australia, Austria, Belgium, Bolivia, Brazil, Cameroons, Canada, Ceylon, China (Nat.), Colombia, Costa Rica, Cuba, Denmark, Dominican Republic, Ethiopia, Finland, France, West Germany, Ghana, Greece, Guatemala, Haiti, the Holy See, Honduras, Ireland, Israel, Italy, Jordan, South Korea, Laos, Liberia, Luxembourg, Federation of Malaya, Monaco, Netherlands, New Zealand, Nicaragua, Norway, Pakistan, Paraguay, Portugal, San Marino,

South Africa, Spain, Sweden, Switzerland, Thailand, Tunisia, Turkey, UK, US, Uruguay, and Vietnam. Against: Albania, Bulgaria, Burma, Byelorussian S.S.R., Chile, Czechoslovakia, Ecuador, Guinea, Hungary, Iceland, India, Indonesia, Iraq, Libya, Mexico, Morocco, Panama, Peru, Poland, Romania, Saudi Arabia, the Soviet Union, Sudan, Ukrainian S.S.R., UAR, Venezuela, Yemen, and Yugoslavia. Abstaining: Cambodia, El Salvador, Iran, Japan, and Philippines. Ibid., p. 30.

33.   For a discussion of claims to unilateral competence to establish the breadth of the territorial sea, see McDougal and Burke, op. cit., pp. 490-498. On the international aspects of such claims, see the *Anglo-Norwegian Fisheries,* op. cit. In Colombus' opinion, there is a customary rule establishing a maximum extent of three miles (op. cit., p. 100).

34.   See, for example: Pitt Cobbett, *Cases on International Law* (6th. ed.: London: Sweet and Maxwell, Ltd., 1947), cited in William W. Bishop, Jr., *International Law: Cases and Materials,* op. cit., p. 23; and Sir Humphrey Waldock, ed. *J. L. Brierly, The Law of Nations: An Introduction to the International Law of Peace,* op cit., p. 61.

35.   See Appendix C for a listing of the claims of all the states.

36.   United Nations Conference on the Law of the Sea, *Official Records,* 2, op. cit., p. 135. Paragraph 3, which is omitted here, deals with the measurement of contiguous zones between states which are opposite or adjacent to each other.

37.   See "Report of First Committee," ibid., p. 117. This was not a roll call vote.

38.   Ibid., p. 40. This was not a roll call vote.

39.   See "Synoptical Table Concerning Breadth and Jurisdicial Status of the Territorial Sea and Adjacent Zones," (U.N. Doc. A/Conf. 19/4) (1960) in Second United Nations Conference on the Law of the Sea, *Official Records, Summary of Plenary Meetings and Meetings of the Committee of the Whole* (U.N. Doc. No. A/Conf. 19/8) (1960), pp. 157-164. See also the decision in *Church v. Hubbart,* 2 Cranch 187 (U.S. 1804), for an early statement on contiguous zones. On claims for military exercises, etc., for temporary periods, see McDougal and Schlei, "The Hydrogen Bomb Tests in Perspective: Lawful Measures for Security," *Yale Law Journal,* 64 (April, 1955), pp. 648-710; and Emanuel Margolis, "The Hydrogen Bomb Experiments and International Law," *Yale Law Journal,* 64 (April, 1955), pp. 624-647. On contiguous zones in general, see McDougal and Burke, op. cit., pp. 565-729.

In October, 1966, the United States Congress enacted a bill extending exclusive fishing rights to twelve miles. And a bill was introduced which would extend these rights to the limits of the continental shelf. Cf. Geoffrey E. Carlisle, "Three Mile Limit: Obsolete Concept?" *United States Naval Institute Proceedings,* 93 (February, 1967), pp. 25-33.

40. McDougal and Burke assert that "the proposed limitation of permissible purposes for contiguous zones in the reference to 'customs, fiscal, sanitary and immigration' is certainly no accurate summary of the purposes for which states have in the past demanded and been accorded, an occasional exclusive competence in contiguous waters" (op. cit., pp. 606-607). This is a correct assertion; however, there is general agreement on at least these specified permissible purposes. On the other hand, McDougal and Burke are able to cite only eight cases in which zones have been established to protect security and power as an example of a type of claim to authority in contiguous sea areas which are omitted from Article 24 of the 1958 convention. See McDougal and Burke, op. cit., pp. 613-619 for a review of legal publicists' views on this point.

41. On the continental shelf in general see: Herbert W. Briggs, "Jurisdiction over the Sea Bed and Subsoil Beyond Territorial Waters," *American Journal of International Law,* 45 (April, 1951), pp. 338-342; Andres A. Aramburuy Menchaca, "Character and Scope of the Rights Declared and Practiced Over the Continental Sea and Shelf," *American Journal of International Law,* 47, (January, 1953), pp. 120-123; J.A.C. Gutteridge, "The Regime of the Continental Shelf," *Transactions of the Grotius Society,* 44 (1957), pp. 77-89; D. P. O'Connell, "Sedentary Fisheries and the Australian Continental Shelf," *American Journal of International Law,* 49 (April, 1955), pp. 185-209; C. H. M. Waldock, "The Legal Basis of Claims to the Continental Shelf," *Transactions of the Grotius Society,* 36 (1950), pp. 115-148; Josef L. Kunz, "Continental Shelf and International Law: Confusion and Abuse," *American Journal of International Law,* 50 (October 1956), pp. 828-853; Richard Young, "The Geneva Convention on the Continental Shelf: A First Impression," *American Journal of International Law,* 52 (October, 1958), pp. 733-738; and Richard Young, "Sedentary Fisheries and the Convention on the Continental Shelf," *American Journal of International Law,* 55 (April, 1961), pp. 359-373.

42. These data were furnished by the Treaty Section, Legal Division of the United Nations Secretariat in June, 1966.

The term "continental shelf" is defined in the convention

> . . . as referring (a) to the sea bed and subsoil of the submarine areas adjacent to the coast but outside the area of the territorial sea, to a depth of 200 meters or, beyond that limit, to where the depth of the superjacent waters admits of the exploitation of the natural resources of the said areas; (b) to the sea bed and subsoil of similar submarine areas adjacent to the coasts of islands (United Nations Conference on the Law of the Sea, *Official Records,* 2, op. cit., p. 142).

43. The natural resources referred to in these articles consist of the mineral and other non-living resources of the sea bed and subsoil together with living organisms belonging to the sedentary species, that is to say, organisms which, at the harvestable stage, either are immobile on or under the sea bed or are unable to move except in physical contact with the sea bed or the subsoil (idem.).

44. As noted in Table 17, the data on these claims were obtained from the "Synoptical Table . . . ," op. cit., and Shigeru Oda, *International Control of Sea Resources* (Leyden: A. W. Sythoff, 1963).

Oda discusses claims to the continental shelf in Part II, Chapter I, pp. 147-159, of his study. He summarizes scholarly viewpoints and proceeds to rationalize an argument which seems divorced from state practice.

45. United Nations Conference on the Law of the Sea, *Official Records*, 2, op. cit., p. 61.

It should be noted that the definition incorporated in the 1958 convention is a compromise political definition, the delegates being unable to agree on a strictly geological definition. This definition is open-ended, the maximum extent of shelf which may be claimed ultimately being determined by the development of a technology for exploiting resources at depths exceeding 200 meters. The problems which arise as a consequence of this definition are becoming ever more apparent both at the United Nations and at Geneva.

46. McDougal and Burke, op. cit. pp. 526-528, as cited by Marjorie M. Whiteman, ed. *Digest of International,* 4 (Washington: U.S. Government Printing Office, 1965), p. 79.

47. United Nations Conference on the Law of the Sea, *Official Records,* II, op. cit., p. 61.

48. Ibid., p. 136. Article 2 was included in Part I of the Fifth Committee's Report; Part I was adopted in plenary session by a vote of 67-0-3. (Ibid., p. 29).

49. Idem. For a more extensive list of claims, see McDougal and Burke, op. cit., p. 744, and Chapter 7 in general (pp. 730-1007).

50. United Nations Conference on the Law of the Sea, *Official Records,* 2, op. cit., p. 136.

51. Idem. Article 3 was included in Part II of the Fifth Committee's Report; Part II was adopted in plenary session by a roll call vote of 67-0-6. In favor: Afghanistan, Albania, Argentina, Australia, Austria, Belgium, Bolivia, Brazil, Bulgaria, Burma, Byelorussian S.S.R., Cambodia, Canada, Ceylon, Chile, China (Nat.), Colombia, Costa Rica, Czechoslovakia, Denmark, Dominican Republic, Ecuador, Finland, France, Germany (W.), Ghana, Guatemala, Haiti, the Holy See, Hungary, Iceland, India, Indonesia, Ireland, Israel, Italy, Japan, Liberia, Libya, Luxembourg, Mexico, Monaco, Morocco, Nepal, Netherlands, New Zealand, Norway, Peru, Philippines, Poland, Romania, San Marino, Saudi Arabia, Spain, South Africa, the Soviet Union, Sweden, Switzerland, Thailand, Tunisia, Ukrainian S.S.R., United Arab Republic, United Kingdom, United States, Uruguay, Vietnam, and Yugoslavia. Abstaining: Iran, Pakistan, Paraguay, Portugal, Turkey, and Venezuela (ibid., p. 29).

52. These data were furnished by the Treaty Section, Legal Division of the United Nations Secretariat in June, 1966. The convention has been in force since September 30, 1962.

53. Rules regarding claims to jurisdiction on the high seas, as onboard vessels, for example, will not be examined. Rules dealing with this concern and with others might be determined by analyzing policy statements, national legislation, etc. However, for the purpose of this study, the primary interest in the high seas is in the freedom of access and use. A determination of more detailed rules must be left for a later time — or for others.

54. United Nations Conference on the Law of the Sea, *Official Records,* 2, op. cit., p. 136. See further Max Sorensen, "The International Law of the Sea," *International Conciliation,* No. 520 (1958); McDougal and Burke, op. cit., pp. 1011-1012; *Lauritzen v. Larsen,* (1953), 345 U.S. 571; *The Schooner Exchange v. McFadden,* 7 Cranch 187 (U. S. 1871); and Myres S. McDougal, William T. Burke, and Ivan A. Vlasic, "Maintenance of Public Order at Sea and the Nationality of Ships," *American Journal of International Law,* 54 (January, 1960), pp. 25-116.

55. Idem. On the genuine link, see Boleslaw Adam Boczek, *Flags of Convenience: An International Legal Study* (Cambridge: Harvard University Press, 1962). See also McDougal and Burke, op. cit., Chapter 8, pp. 1008-1140.

56. United Nations Legislative Series, *Laws Concerning the Nationality of Ships* (United Nations: United Nations, 1955) (St/Leg/Ser B/5) (1955); and United States Legislative Series, *Supplement to Laws and Regulations on the Regime of the High Seas (Volumes I and II) and Laws Concerning the Nationality of Ships* (United Nations: United Nations, 1959) (St/Leg/Ser/B/8) (1959).

57. This basic rule is not challenged by the flag of convenience or genuine link controversy. That controversy centers on what the requirements are for granting nationality. Both Liberia and Panama, for example, grant their nationality to ships owned by corporations headquartered in their states. See United Nations Legislative Series, *Laws Concerning the Nationality of Ships,* op. cit., pp. 98 and 129. See Boczek, op. cit., for an analysis of the arguments.

58. See Boczek, op. cit., for a discussion of these rules.

59. United Nations Conference on the Law of the Sea, *Official Records,* 2, op. cit., p. 136.

60. Idem.

61. League of Nations, *Treaty Series,* 135 (1932-1933), p. 302. An International Conference on Load Lines met in London in March and April, 1966. The delegates of 60 states drafted an International Load Line Convention of 1966. It is too early to assess the extent of acceptance of this new convention.

62. The length of this convention is a rough indicator of the detail of its provisions. Together with annexes, this convention is 61 pages in length.

63. The earlier 1929 Safety of Life at Sea Convention was replaced by the 1948 convention. The 1960 convention, in turn, replaces the 1948 convention as between parties, and in addition, a number of parties to the 1960 convention have given notice of withdrawal from the 1948 convention, in most instances effective May, 1966. For the text of the 1948 convention, see United Nations, *Treaty Series,* 164, p. 113, and for the 1960 convention, see *United States Treaties and Other International Agreements,* 16, Part 1, page 198.

See Article II of the 1948 convention as it refers to registration. The 1960 provision is comparable.

64. The determination of the general rule is adequate for the purposes of this study. However, it seems evident on the basis of the data presented that one could determine detailed rules by making a thorough and rigorous content analysis of conventions and national legislation on safety on the seas.

The International Maritime Consultative Organization has not been mentioned in this discussion. It should be noted that the IMCO is responsible for administering several international conventions, including the 1948 and 1960 Safety of Life at Sea and International Regulations for the Preventing Collisions at Sea Conventions. On the IMCO and its role in safety at sea see L. W. Goddu, Jr., "IMCO: An Assistance to the American Merchant Marines," *United States Naval Institute Proceedings,* 92 (December, 1966), pp. 70-83.

65. Article 14, paragraph 1, United Nations Conference on the Law of the Sea, *Official Records,* 2, op. cit., p. 133. At the Hague conference in 1930, the Second Commission drafted an article which stated that under international law coastal states could not legally raise obstacles against the innocent passage of foreign vessels other than warships through their territorial sea (Haley, op. cit., p. 69). See also Leo Gross, "Geneva Conference on the Law of the Sea and the Right of Innocent Passage Through the Gulf of Aqaba," *American Journal of International Law,* 53 (July, 1959), pp. 564-594, for a discussion of the right of innocent passage.

66. Article 14, paragraph 2, idem.

67. Article 14, paragraph 3, idem.

68. Article 14, paragraph 4, idem.

69. Article 14, paragraph 5, ibid., p. 134.

70. Article 23, idem.

71. Article 14, paragraph 6, idem.

72. Article 15, idem. An additional duty is not to levy charges on vessels solely by reason of their innocent passage (idem.).

73. Article 16, paragraph 3, idem. Innocent passage through straits used for international navigation may not be suspended.

74. Idem.

75. See Article 22, idem. This provision places the general question of the immunities enjoyed by these vessels outside the scope of this convention.

76. Ibid., p. 64. In plenary session articles were voted on using the numbers as assigned in the First Committee Report. The numbers used here are as articles appear in the convention. The vote on the 10 articles, in plenary session, was 14, 68-0-2; 15, 65-1-1; 16, 62-1-9; 17, 72-0-2; 18, 72-0; 19, 80-0; 20, 76-0; 21, 62-9-4; 22, 74-0-2; and 23, 76-0-1 (ibid., pp. 65-68). Only one roll call was taken on the section dealing with innocent passage. This was on an article concerning warships; the article was rejected.

77. On this point, see, for example: United Nations *Legislative Series, Laws and Regulations on the Regime of the Territorial Sea,* op. cit.; Whiteman, *Digest,* op. cit., pp. 343-480; and McDougal and Burke, op. cit., pp. 179-180.

4: A DETERMINATION OF THE LAW-IN-ACTION WITHIN SELECTED PROBLEM AREAS OF INTERNATIONAL AIR LAW

INTRODUCTION

International air law originates in classical Roman law; however, for the most part, international air law has been formulated and agreed upon in the twentieth century.[1] In contrast to the law of the sea, international air law generally is identified as a body of law which has been developed through treaties and multilateral conventions. Technological change has proceeded at an exponential rate during the twentieth century. In both military and civil aviation, the almost simultaneous application of these technological developments has militated against an evolutionary, leisurely formulation of legal rules and principles regulating the international effects of airspace flight.

We live in an age in which commercial passenger airliners regularly fly at speeds in excess of 600 miles per hour; velocities of up to twice the speed of sound are commonplace for military aircraft. In fact, speeds of more than 1,800 miles per hour are planned for the supersonic transports now being developed as the next generation of commercial airliners.

Living in a world in which such developments in aviation are accepted very casually, it is sometimes difficult to remember that Orville and Wilbur Wright made the first controlled powered flight in an airplane as recently as 1903. In fewer than 70 years, national decision-makers have been required to deal with the myriad of legal problems literally forced upon them by spectacular developments in civil and military aviation.

As in international sea law, claims in international air law may be characterized as being made either primarily in the exclusive interest of the particular state, in the inclusive interest of the collective community, or as deviations or exceptions to the exclusive or inclusive categories. The claim to sovereign rights in the superjacent airspace, for example, is a claim made primarily in the exclusive interest of the particular state. Likewise, claims relating to the joint use of airspace over the high seas clearly are made in the inclusive interest, although the net effect of these claims may be functional to certain exclusive interests as well. In air law, as in sea law, claims to certain rights of innocent passage are examples of claims made primarily as deviations or exceptions to exclusive or inclusive authority. This trichotomy — Claims Primarily in Support of an Exclusive Interest, Claims Primarily in Support of an Inclusive Interest, and Deviations or Exceptions to Exclusive or Inclusive Authority — will be used again to categorize claims and counterclaims made by national decision-makers. At least one air law problem in each of these three categories will be analyzed.

The modified majority rule is used here, as in Chapter 3, in determining the law-in-action. States are divided into two groups on the basis of an objective definition of a special interest in air law. This objective definition is based on a determination of the degree of a state's activity in international civil aviaton; the degree of activity being measured in terms of passenger kilometers and/or kilometers flown in international civil aviation. Those states which are Very Active, Active, or Moderately Active on this basis are considered to have special interest in international air law (see Table 19).

CLAIMS PRIMARILY IN SUPPORT OF AN EXCLUSIVE INTEREST

TERRITORIAL AIRSPACE

Since the days of the Roman Empire, the problems associated with claims to sovereignty and/or jurisdiction over superjacent airspace have attracted the interest of legal scholars and government officials alike.[2] The question of national sovereignty over superjacent airspace has been dealt with in international conventions and in national legislation. Article I of the Paris convention of 1919 provided that every state had complete and exclusive authority over its superjacent airspace.[3] The more recent 1944 Chicago Convention on International Civil Aviation contains an almost identical provision.[4]

The Chicago convention has been ratified or otherwise adhered to by 109 of the 121 states which are included within the 1964 international political system.[5] Thirty-one of the 33 states with a special interest in international air law have ratified or otherwise adhered to this convention (see Table 20). Furthermore, some 100 states have asserted claims in their national legislation either to comprehensive jurisdiction or to sovereignty over airspace superjacent to their national territory.[6] Neither Red China nor the Soviet Union have ratified the Chicago convention; however, both are among the 100 asserting claims either to comprehensive jurisdiction or to sovereignty over superjacent airspace.[7]

TABLE 19

STATES WITH A SPECIAL INTEREST IN INTERNATIONAL AIR LAW

State[a]	Degree[b] of Activity
Argentina	3
Australia	2
Belgium	2
Brazil	3
Canada	2
China (Red)	9
Colombia	3
Denmark	3
France	2
Germany (West)	2
Greece	3
Iceland	3
India	2
Ireland	3
Israel	2
Italy	2
Japan	2
Mexico	3

TABLE 19 — Continued

State[a]	Degree[b] of Activity
Netherlands	2
New Zealand	3
Norway	3
Pakistan	3
Peru	3
Portugal	3
South Africa	3
Spain	2
Sweden	2
Switzerland	2
Trinidad and Tobago	3
USSR	9
UK	2
US	1
Venezuela	3
Total	33

[a] Data is not available on a large number of states. Except for the "Communist bloc" it seems unlikely that any of the other states for which data are not available would possess a special interest. Data are not available for: Afghanistan, Albania, Bulgaria, Burundi, Cambodia, Cameroon, Central African Republic, Chad, China (Red), Congo (Leopoldville), Congo (Brazzaville), Costa Rica, Cyprus, Dahomey, Dominican Republic, El Salvador, Gabon, Germany (East), Guinea, Haiti, Hungary, Ivory Coast, Jamaica, Kenya, Korea (North), Kuwait, Laos, Lebanon, Liberia, Libya, Luxembourg, Malawi, Malta, Mauritania, Mongolia, Nepal, Niger, Panama, Paraguay, Rumania, Rwanda, Saudi Arabia, Senegal, Sierre Leone, Somalia, Tanzania, Togo, Uganda, the Soviet Union, Upper Volta, Vietnam (North), Yemen, and Zambia. It has been assumed that the Soviet Union and Red China possess special interests.

[b] Based on data obtained from the United Nations, *Statistical Yearbook, 1965* (United Nations: United Nations, 1966). Codes: (1) Very Active (more than 200 million kilometers flown and/or more than 50 billion passenger kilometers); (2) Active (20-200 million kilometers flown and/or 1-49.9 billion passenger kilometers); (3) Moderately Active (10-19.9 million kilometers flown and/or 300-999.9 million passenger kilometers); and (9) Not Ascertained. In each instance, the degree of activity was coded in the higher category when there was conflict between kilometers flown and passenger kilometers.

TABLE 20

ACCEPTANCE OF INTERNATIONAL AIR LAW
CONVENTIONS BY STATES WHICH HAVE A
SPECIAL INTEREST IN THE LAW OF THE AIR

	Convention			
State	Warsaw[a] 1929	Chicago[a] 1944	Air[a] Services	Rome[b] (1952) Surface Damages
Argentina	X	X	X	X
Australia	X	X	X	X
Belgium	X	X	X	X
Brazil	X	X		X
Canada	X	X	X	X
China (Red)	X			
Colombia		X		
Denmark	X	X	X	S
France	X	X	X	S
Germany (West)	X	X	X	
Greece	X	X	X	S
Iceland	X	X	X	
India	X	X	X	S
Ireland	X	X	X	
Israel	X	X	X	S
Italy	X	X		X
Japan	X	X	X	
Mexico	X	X	X	S
Netherlands	X	X	X	S
New Zealand	X	X	X	
Norway	X	X	X	S
Pakistan	X	X	X	X
Peru		X		
Portugal	X	X	X	S
South Africa	X	X	X	
Spain	X	X	X	X
Sweden	X	X	X	S
Switzerland	X	X	X	
Trinidad and Tobago	X	X	X	

TABLE 20 — Continued

State	Warsaw[a] 1929	Chicago[a] 1944	Air[a] Services	Rome[b] (1952) Surface Damages
USSR	X	X	X	
UK	X	X	X	S
US[c]	X	X	X	
Venezuela	X	X	X	
Total	31	31	27	S=12 X=7
Total All States	86[d]	109	72	S=18 X=20

[a] Based on data obtained from Department of State, *Treaties in Force: A List of Treaties and Other International Agreements in Force in January 1, 1966* (Washington: Government Printing Office, 1966), pp. 227-228. (X = party).

[b] Data on signatures and ratifications or adherence furnished by the International Civil Aviation Organization in September, 1966. (S = signed; X = party).

[c] The United States denounced the Warsaw convention in 1965 (Department of State Press Release No. 268, 15 November 1965), but withdrew the denouncement in May, 1966 (Department of State Press Release No. 110, 13 May 1966).

[d] There now have been a total of 87 ratifications and/or adherences to this convention; however, one ratifying state, Gambia, is not included in the 1964 international political system for this study.

The right of a state to exercise sovereign rights in the airspace above its national territory is clearly an established universally-binding international legal rule. Claims which define, at least in part, the specific content of this general rule are included in both the Chicago convention and in the various national rules and regulations which have been referred to previously.[8] The widespread acceptance of the Chicago convention gives to the specific provisions included therein the status of universally-binding international legal rules. Among these are the following which are based on claims made primarily in the exclusive interest.

1. States must give special permission for scheduled international air services to be operated over or into their territory.[9]

2. States have the right to control all cabotage within their territory.[10]

3. Flights by pilotless aircraft over the territory of another state are prohibited unless made with the special authorization of that state.[11]

4. States may establish prohibited areas ". . . for reasons of military necessity or public safety. . . ."[12] Furthermore, ". . . in exceptional circumstances or during a period of emergency, or in the interest of public safety. . . ," a government may temporarily prohibit or restrict all flight within its territorial airspace.[13]

5. States may require all aircraft entering into and departing from their territorial airspace to land at designated customs airports.[14]

6. States have the right ". . . without unreasonable delay. . . ," to search aircraft landing or departing and to ". . . inspect the certificates and other documents. . ." which such aircraft are required to possess.[15]

7. States may prohibit ". . . for reasons of public order and safety. . ." the carriage of any article over its territory.[16]

8. States ". . . may prohibit or regulate the use of photographic apparatus in aircraft above its territory."[17]

The general rule which establishes the sovereign right of states in the airspace above their territory is given more specific meaning by the rules which have been listed here. No doubt, additional rules can be determined; however, these particular rules illustrate two basic aspects of the claims which states make in regard to their superjacent airspace. That is, states claim comprehensive competence to control all: (1) activities taking place within their territorial airspace; and (2) access into their territorial airspace.[18]

CLAIMS PRIMARILY IN SUPPORT OF AN INCLUSIVE INTEREST

NATIONALITY AND REGISTRATION[19]

In Chapter III, Article 17 of the Chicago convention it is asserted that "aircraft have the nationality of the state in which they are registered."[20] The primarily inclusive character of this basic claim is clarifed by related claims also asserted in this convention.

Dual registration is invalidated by the provisions of Article 19;[21] Article 20 provides that ". . . aircraft engaged in international air navigation shall bear . . . appropriate nationality and registration marks."[22] In Article 21, provisions are made for exchange of data on registration and ownership of particular aircraft when such data are demanded; such information on registration and control is also to be furnished when requested by or required in reports to the International Civil Aviation Organization.[23] It is Article 12, however, which best emphasizes the inclusive character of claims made regarding the registration and nationality of aircraft. This article assigns to the state registering and/or granting nationality to aircraft the responsibility for insuring that: (1) all aircraft comply with the rules governing flight and maneuvering in its own airspace; (2) *all aircraft of its nationality or registration* comply with the rules established under the convention controlling flight over the high seas.[24]

As has been stated in the preceding section, 109 states, including 31 with a special interest in international air law, either have ratified or adhered to the Chicago convention. Ninety-nine states, including nine which have not accepted the Chicago convention, have enacted municipal legislation providing for registration and/or granting of nationality to aircraft.[25] Both Red China and the Soviet Union are included among these 99.[26] Therefore, the general international legal rule on registration and nationality has been accepted by 118 nations including all 33 which have a special interest in international air law.

The detailed provisions of the Chicago convention are universally binding as international legal rules on the basis of the widespread acceptance of that convention. Moreover, it seems likely that the results of a thorough content analysis of national air law legislation would indicate an even more universal explicit support for these detailed rules.[27]

LIABILITY

There are two major international conventions which deal with problems of liability[28] in international civil aviation: the Convention for the Unification of Certain Rules Relating to International Transportation by Air (Warsaw, 1929, as modified by the 1955 Hague Protocol); and the Convention on Damage Caused by Foreign Aircraft to Third Parties on the Surface (Rome, 1952).[29] Chapter III of the Warsaw convention treats with the question of the liability of air carriers. Carriers are held liable for damage resulting from the death of or injury to a passenger ". . . if the accident which caused the damage so sustained took place on board the aircraft or in the course of any of the operations of embarking or disembarking."[30] Carriers also are liable for damage caused by loss, destruction, or damage to checked baggage or goods when such damage is sustained during transportation by air.[31] In addition, carriers ". . . shall be liable for damage occasioned by delay in the transportation by air of passengers, baggage or goods."[32]

Articles 20 and 21 provide that the carrier shall not be liable in certain instances, for example: (1) if he and his agents took all possible steps to avoid the damage or if it was impossible for such steps to be taken; (2) if ". . . the damage was occasioned by an error in piloting, in the handling of the aircraft, or in navigation and that in all other respects, he and his agents have taken all necessary measures to avoid the damage;"[33] and (3) if he can prove that negligence of the injured person caused or contributed to the damage.[34] This latter provision either may completely relieve the carrier of liability, or such proof may result in a lesser award for damages.[35]

The liability of the carrier under the Warsaw convention is a limited liability. As provided by the 1955 Hague Protocol, ". . . the liability of the carrier for each passenger is limited to the sum of two hundred and fifty thousand francs."[36] A limit of 250 gold francs per kilogram applies to registered baggage and cargo unless a special declaration of value is made when the baggage is registered.[37] However, if the damage to passengers, baggage, and/or cargo is caused by the willful misconduct of the carrier, the liability limitation provisions of the convention do not apply.[38] Moreover, the carrier is prevented from giving effect to contract provisions which either fix a lower limit or completely relieve the carrier of liability.

The United States announced in November 1965 that it was denouncing the Warsaw convention.[39] The position of the United States for some time had been that the limited liability sums fixed by the convention were unjust.[40] An interim agreement was concluded with a majority of the international air carriers which provided for a limit of $75,000 per passenger and no recourse by the carrier under Article 20, Paragraph 1.[41]

In May, 1966, the United States withdrew its denouncement.[42] Although dissatisfied with the liability limitations, the United States indicated that the interim agreement would protect its interest while it continued to work for more just compensation for damages within the Warsaw framework.

Eighty-six states have ratified or otherwise adhered to the Warsaw convention as modified by the 1955 Hague Protocol. Thirty-one of the ratifying or adhering states possess a special interest in international air law (see Table 20). The particular rules included within this convention are, therefore, universally-binding legal rules.

In contrast to the Warsaw convention, the Rome convention of 1952 is based on the principle of absolute liability.[43] Under the Rome convention, any person who suffers damage on the surface who can prove ". . . that the damage was caused by an aircraft or by any person or things falling there-from . . ."[44] is entitled to compensation. The sole limitation is that the da-mage must be a direct consequence of some incident other than ". . . the mere fact of passage of the aircraft through the airspace in conformity with existing air traffic regulations."[45] The operator of the offending aircraft is the person liable; the operator is presumed to be the registered owner unless that person proves that some other person was the operator at the time the damage was caused and has taken measures to make that other person a party to the proceedings.[46]

The amount of the absolute liability of the operator is limited based on the maximum authorized take-off weight of the aircraft. Amounts of com-pensation range from 500,000 gold francs for a 1,000 kilogram or less aircraft weight to 10,500,000 gold francs plus 100 francs per kilogram over 50,000 kilograms for aircraft weighing in excess of 50,000 kilo-grams.[47] Compensation for loss of life or personal injury is limited to 500,000 francs per person.[48] Again, however, as in the Warsaw conven-tion, if the damage is caused by a deliberate act or omission intended to cause damage, liability is unlimited.[49]

A separate chapter of the convention, Chapter III, deals with the problem of insuring that operators will be able to compensate for damages which they cause. States may require the aircraft operator to be insured up to the liability limits provided in the convention.[50]

Unlike the Warsaw convention, the 1952 Rome convention has not at-tracted widespread support. In fact, only 38 states have signed or ratified it, 19 of which are states with a special interest in international air law. Only 7 states with a special interest and a total of 20 states have ratified (see Table 20).[51] It is evident that the detailed provisions concerning the liability of foreign aircraft operators for damage to persons on the ground are the law-in-action only for the parties to the Rome convention.

DEVIATIONS OR EXCEPTIONS TO EXCLUSIVE OR INCLUSIVE AUTHORITY

INNOCENT PASSAGE

The right of innocent passage was explicitly provided for in both the 1919 Paris and the 1928 Habana conventions.[52] By both conventions, con-tracting states were obligated to permit the innocent passage over their terri-tory by the aircraft of other contracting states during peacetime. Aircraft undertaking such passage were obliged to observe the conditions laid down in the conventions regulating such passage.[53]

In Article 5 of the Chicago convention, provision is made for a right of innocent passage by aircraft not engaged in scheduled international air services.[54] This right is subject to the overflown state's right in certain cases to prescribe routes and to require special permission. Article 6 of the Chicago convention prohibits entry into territorial airspace by foreign aircraft engaged in scheduled international air service except with the authorization of the state whose airspace is being entered.[55]

The International Air Service Transit Agreement includes a provision which grants to other contracting states: "(1) the privilege to fly across its territory without landing; and (2) the privilege to land for non-traffic purposes."[56] As in the Chicago convention, states may designate routes and airports.[57]

It has been stated that the provisions of the Chicago convention are universally binding as international legal rules since that convention is so widely accepted. Support for the International Air Services Transit Agreement is not so widespread. However, 72 states, including 27 with a special interest in international air law, have ratified or otherwise adhered to this agreement (see Table 20). Therefore, the provisions of the International Air Service Transit Agreement would seem to be universally-binding legal rules. However, a number of representatives of the 1958 Conference on the Law of the Sea made statements which indicate that the right of innocent passage by aircraft is only a conventional right. The delegates of Canada and the United Kingdom, for example, argued that the extension of the territorial sea would restrict international air commerce since aircraft do not enjoy a right of innocent passage comparable to the right of ships.[58] Comments by the International Civil Aviation Organization on the International Law Commission's draft articles for a convention on the law of the sea support this interpretation. In fact, these comments indicate very explicitly that the right of innocent passage by aircraft is a conventional right or one granted by some special authorization.[59]

SUMMARY

States have been characterized as either possessing or not possessing a special interest in international air law on the basis of an objective definition of what constitutes such a special interest. The fundamental assumption which is made is that states which are at least moderately active in international civil aviation as determined by passenger kilometers or kilometers flown in international scheduled air services have a special interest in the legal rules which regulate the international effects of airspace flight. A majority of states which have a special interest in international air law as well as a majority of all states included within the international political system must accept a particular rule if the rule is to be universally binding. Selected provisions of international civil aviation conventions have been examined to determine the degree and extent of acceptance of particular legal rules or principles.[60] There has been no attempt to be comprehensive; rather, particular legal rules and principles have been selected which seem especially relevant to one or more of the legal problems in outer space which have been determined in Chapter 2.

It has been determind that:

1.   States claim a comprehensive competence to control all activities taking place within their territorial airspace.[61]

2.   States claim a comprehensive competence to control all access into their territorial airspace.[62]

3.   The right of innocent passage for aircraft is a conventional rule.

4.   All aircraft have the nationality of the state in which they are registered. A state assumes certain responsibilities, such as ensuring compliance with flight rules and regulations, for the aircraft to which it grants its nationality.

5.   The liability provisions of the 1929 Warsaw convention as modified by the 1955 Hague Protocol are universally binding, except that an interim agreement between the United States and certain international air carriers supplements these conventional provisions as between the United States and these carriers.

Why these rules are accepted as the law-in-action in these selected international legal problem areas of civil aviation will be analyzed in Part III.

NOTES

1. See, for example, the history of the development of air law by Peter H. Sand, et al., *An Historical Survey of the Law of Flight* (Montreal: Institute of Air and Space Law, McGill University, 1961), and Francesco Lardone, "Airspace Rights in Roman Law," *Air Law Review,* 3 (November, 1931), pp. 455-467.

2. See, for example: DeForest Billyou, *Air Law* (New York: Ad Press, Ltd., 1963); Bin Cheng, "The Right to Fly," *Transactions of the Grotius Society,* 42 (1957), pp. 99-131; John C. Cooper, *The Right to Fly* (New York: Henry Holt and Co., 1947); D. Goedhius, "Sovereignty and Freedom in the Air Space," *Transactions of the Grotius Society,* 41 (1956), pp. 137-152; D. H. N. Johnson, *Rights in Air Space* (Manchester: Manchester University Press, 1965); Andrew G. Haley, *Space Law and Government,* op. cit., Chapter 4, "The Limits of National Sovereignty," pp. 75-117; J. P. Honig, *The Legal Status of Aircraft* (The Hague: Martinus Nijhoff, 1956), particularly Chapter 1, "Sovereignty Over the Air Space;" Albert I. Moon, Jr., "A Look at Airspace Sovereignty," *Journal of Air Law and Commerce,* 29 (Autumn, 1963), pp. 328-345; Sand, et al., op. cit., pp. 1-58; H. A. Wassenbergh, *Post-War International Civil Aviation Policy and the Law of the Air* (2nd rev. ed.; The Hague: Martinus Nijhoff, 1962); and Raymond W. Young, "The Aerial Inspection Plan and Air Space Sovereignty," United States Congress, Senate, Committee on Aeronautical and Space Science, *Legal Problems of Space Exploration,* op. cit., pp. 46-64.

3. Convention Relating to the Regulation of Aerial Navigation, Article 1, League of Nations, *Treaty Series* (1922), p. 173; United States Congress, Senate, Committee on Commerce, *Air Laws and Treaties of the World,* 89th Cong., 1st sess., 1965, 3, p. 3085.

4. Convention on International Civil Aviation, Article I, 61 Stat. 1180; ibid., p. 3166. The same claim is asserted in Article I of the Convention on Commercial Aviation, signed at Habana on February 20, 1928; [League of Nations, *Treaty Series* (1932), p. 225; ibid., p. 3094]. Only five governments ratified the Habana convention — Guatemala, Mexico, Nicaragua, Panama, and the United States. Both the Paris and Habana conventions were superseded by the Chicago convention (Article 80, ibid., p. 3188).

5. The source of data on ratification or adherence is Treaty Affairs Staff, Office of the Department of State, *Treaties in Force: A List of Treaties and Other International Agreements in Force on January 1, 1966* (Washington: Government Printing Office, 1966), p. 228.

6. United States Congress, Senate, Committee on Commerce, *Air Laws and Treaties of the World,* 89th Cong., 1st sess., 1965, I and II, pp. 1-3083.

7. On China, see ibid., pp. 435-445. There appears to be no basic air law for the Chinese Peoples' Republic; however, provisions of customs laws and certain bilateral treaties do indicate the acceptance of certain principles and/or rules. On

the Soviet Union, see the Air Code of the Union of Soviet Socialists Republics of 1961, Article I, ibid., p. 2545.

8. As noted in Chapter 3, the rigorous content analysis required to determine specific rules on the basis of national legislation is beyond both the purpose and scope of this study. Therefore, only selected rules included with international conventions will be analyzed here.

9. Convention on International Civil Aviation, Article 6, United States Congress, Senate, *Air Laws and Treaties of the World*, 2, op. cit., p. 3167. But see also the determination of a rule of innocent passage below.

Article 3 limits the applicability of the convention to civil aircraft, thereby specifically excluding ". . . aircraft used in military, custom and police services" (ibid., p. 3166). There are, however, two provisions which do apply to state aircraft: (1) flight by state aircraft over the territory of another state may be made only when authorized by that state; and (2) regulations for state aircraft are to provide for ". . . the safety of navigation of civil aircraft" (Article 3, idem.).

10. Article 7, ibid., pp. 3167-3168.

11. Article 8, ibid., p. 3168.

12. Article 9, idem. The provision applies to territorial airspace, but see also McDougal and Schlei, op. cit., on temporarily prohibiting flight in areas over the high seas.

13. Idem.

14. Article 10, ibid., pp. 3168-3169.

15. Article 16, ibid., p. 3170.

16. Article 35, ibid., p. 3175. The same article prohibits the carriage of munitions or implements of war except by special permission.

17. Article 36, ibid., p. 3176. When Francis Gary Powers' U-2 was shot down over the Soviet Union on May 1, 1960, he was flying what later was admitted to be a clandestine espionage mission which included the use of sophisticated aerial photographic apparatus. The debate which followed focused on his allegedly unauthorized use of aerial photographic apparatus as well as on his allegedly unauthorized entry into Soviet airspace. See the following: Spencer M. Beresford, "Surveillance Aircraft and Satellites: A Problem of International Law," *Journal of Air Law and Commerce,* 27 (Spring, 1960), pp. 107-118; Oliver J. Lissitzyn, "The Treatment of Aerial Intruders in Recent Practice and International Law," *American Journal of International Law,* 47 (October, 1953), pp. 559-589; and Quincy Wright, "Legal Aspects of the U-2 Incident," *American Journal of International Law,* 54 (October, 1960), pp. 836-854.

18. McDougal et al., *Law and Public Order in Outer Space,* op. cit., p. 254.

The upward limit on the extent of territorial airspace is left as an open question since it arises primarily as a question of the law of outer space rather than as a question of international air law. The question will be discussed in Chapter 6.

19. See Honig, op. cit., pp. 41-57, for a concise review of claims and the history of the development of rules concerning the registration and nationality of aircraft.

20. Convention on International Civil Aviation, United States Congress, Senate, Committee on Commerce, *Air Laws and Treaties of the World,* III, op. cit., p. 3171.

21. Idem.

22. Idem.

23. Idem.

24. Ibid., p. 3169. On the interpretation of this provision concerning flight over the high seas, see Jean Carroz, "International Legislation on Air Navigation Over the High Seas," *Journal of Air Law and Commerce,* 26 (Spring, 1959), pp. 158-172. He argues that it was not intended that this provision encompass the annexes to the convention. His major argument is that the provision applies only to rules established under the convention, and that the annexes do not constitute such rules.

25. United States Congress, Senate, Committee on Commerce, *Air Laws and Treaties of the World,* 1-2, op. cit., pp. 1-3083.

26. In the case of Red China, the existence of such national legislation is implicit in certain agreements. For example, an agreement with North Vietnam which entered into force in 1956 includes a requirement for aircraft of each party to carry markings of nationality and registration certificates (Air Transport Agreement Between the Government of the People's Republic of China and the Government of the Democratic Republic of Vietnam, Article II, ibid., I. p. 443). On the other hand, Chapter II of the Air Code of the Union of Soviet Socialist Republics of 1961 includes explicit provisions concerning registration and nationlity (ibid., 2, pp. 2546-2547).

27. See the national legislation in ibid., 1 and 2, passim.

28. See, among others: Elizabeth Gaspar Brown, "The Rome Conventions of 1933 and 1952: Do They Point a Moral?" *Journal of Air Law and Commerce,* 28 (Autumn 1961-62), pp. 418-443; Jose A. Cabranes, "Limitations of Liability in International Air Law: The Warsaw and Rome Conventions Reconsidered," *International and Comparative Law Quarterly,* 15 (July 1964), pp. 660-689; Lee S. Kreindler, "The Denunciation of the Warsaw Convention," *Journal of Air Law and Commerce,* 31 (Autumn 1965), pp. 291-303; Gerd Rinck, "Damage Caused

by Foreign Aircraft to Third Parties," *Journal of Air Law and Commerce,* 28 (Autumn 1961-62), pp. 405-417; and Peter H. Sand, "Air Carriers' Limitation of Liability and Air Passengers' Accident Compensation Under the Warsaw Convention," *Journal of Air Law and Commerce,* 28 (Summer 1961-62), pp. 260-284.

29.   The earlier Convention for the Unification of Rules Relating to Damages Caused by Aircraft to Third Parties on the Surface (Rome, 1933), was ratified by only five governments: Belgium, Brazil, Guatemala, Romania, and Spain (Honig, op. cit., p. 117). For the text of all three conventions, see United States Congress, Senate, Committee on Commerce, *Air Laws and Treaties of the World,* 3, op. cit., pp. 3103-3139 (Warsaw), pp. 3147-3155 (Rome, 1933), and 3221-3237 (Rome, 1952). The text of the Warsaw convention referred to here is the text as modified by the 1955 Hague Protocol.

30.   Article 16 ibid., p. 3119. On the right of action, see: *Noel, et al. v. Linea Aeropostal Venezolana,* 24 *International Law Reports* 580 (1957); and *Komolos v. Compagnie Nationale Air France, Royal Indemnity Co. v. Compagnie Nationale Air France,* 20 *International Law Reports* 417 (1953). The viewpoint asserted in these decisions is that the Warsaw Convention does not create a right of action for wrongful death, rather a presumption of liability results from the occurence of the accident [20 *International Law Reports* 421 (1953)].

See further Julian G. Verplaetse, *International Law in Vertical Space: Air, Outer Space, Ether* (South Hackensack, New Jersey: Fred B. Rothman and Co., 1960), pp. 308-310, for a description of the case law concerning the right of the passenger to bring action. He cites Rhyne (*Aviation Accident Law*) on this point.

> It seems to be settled by the few decisions of the Courts on the point that the wrongful death statutes of the place where the accident causing the damage occurred shall be applied as the Convention creates no right of action (p. 310).

Verplaetse concurs in this conclusion and appears to base his concurrence on several decisions handed down by French, Italian, and United States courts. There is some question, then, as to the appropriateness of so broad a generalization.

The notion of a law-in-action is a notion of a living law [on the *living law,* see F. S. C. Northrup, "Contemporary Jurisprudence and International Law," *Yale Law Journal,* 61 (May, 1952), pp. 623-654], a law which may be shaped in part and perhaps decisively by decisions in municipal courts. However, it seems unwarranted to assert a rule or a modification to a conventional rule on the basis of such limited data as several judicial opinions made within a very small minority of the states which collectively comprise the international political system. Unfortunately, the judicial decisions of very few states are generally available to the legal scholar. While it may be correct to maintain the development and modification of legal rules within these select few states affect the development of international law more than do similar developments and modifications in other municipal systems, it cannot be asserted, on the basis of more than opinion and scholarly insight, that such developments and/or modifications are universally applicable. This is especially correct when a particular conventional rule exists on the question being litigated.

In the contemporary international political system, one consequence of the decentralization of authority is that a majority of all international litigation is conducted in municipal courts. These courts, then, do have a significant role in shaping the law-in-action. It is not uncommon, however, to find provisions in international conventions stipulating the forum for settling disputes which arise under the provisions of the convention. It seems, then, that in such cases, the courts of the forum state develop rules of interpretation which are applicable only in their municipal system and in accordance with their own legal order. Collectively, however, the decisions of the various municipal systems may develop and/or modify conventional rules. So long as the basic organizational unit in the international political system continues to be the state, one still determines the law-in-action by applying the modified majority rule which has been implicit in many authoritative interpretations of international law and which is made explicit in this study.

On the role of municipal courts in the development of international law, compare the following: O'Connell, *International Law,* op. cit., pp. 28-36; Bishop, *International Law,* op cit., pp. 37-38; Falk, op. cit.; Friedmann, *The Changing Structure of International Law,* op. cit.; and *The S. S. Lotus,* 2 Hudson, *World Court Reports* 71 (1935).

Of course, there are numerous international arbitrations which contribute to the development of legal rules and principles. And the interaction between foreign offices and negotiations between governments and other actors must be considered.

On the more general problem of possibly overemphasizing the contributions of civilized, Christian, Western political subsystems to the development of international law within the contemporary international political system, see, for example: B.V.A. Röling, *International Law in an Expanding World* (Amsterdam: Djambatan N.V., 1960); C. Wilfred Jenks, et al., *International Law in a Changing World* (Dobbs Ferry: Oceana Publication, Inc., 1963); and Friedmann, op. cit.

31. Article 18, United States Congress, Senate, Committee of Commerce, *Air Laws and Treaties of the World,* op. cit., 3, p. 3119.

32. Article 19, idem.

33. Article 20, idem. On the somewhat ambiguous reasonable care provision see, for example, the following: *Palleroni v. S. A. di Navigazione Aeria, Revista de diritto aeronauticao* (1938), p. 52 (diligence of an ordinary man), cited by O'Connell, op. cit., p. 591; *Csillag v. Air France,* Lemione, *Traite de droit aerien* (1947), p. 825 (reasonable and normal measures to avoid damage), cited by O'Connell, idem.; *Grien v. Imperial Airways, Ltd., King's Beach* 50 (1937) (the accident could not have been avoided by the exercise of reasonable care by the carrier); *Ritts v. American Overseas Airlines, U. S. Aviation Reports* 65 (1949) (a very high degree of care); *American Smelting and Refining Co., et al., v. Philippine Airlines, Inc.,* 21 *International Law Reports* 286 (1954) (all possible precautions to avoid damage were taken); and *Rotterdam Zoological Gardens v. Air France,* 24 *International Law Reports* 645 (1957) (all necessary measures which

in the circumstances could reasonably be expected). This latter case involved the death of animals and the reasonable care provision was interpreted in terms of what constituted proper care of animals.

34.   Articles 20 and 21, idem.

35.   It should be noted that the passenger or damaged party must offer proof of a contract with the carrier in order for the latter to be liable.

36.   Article 22, ibid., p. 3122. The francs referred to consist of 65½ milligrams of gold of millesimal (a thousandth part) fineness. On the limits of liability, see: *Ulen v. American Airlines*, U.S. *Aviation Reports* 161 (1948); *Flying Tiger Lines, Inc., v. United States*, 28 *International Law Reports* 99 (1963); and *American Smelting and Refining Co., et al., v. Philippines Airlines, Inc.*, op. cit.

37.   Idem. In the latter instance, the passenger or consignor may be required to pay a supplemental sum if required by the air carrier.

38.   Article 25, ibid., p. 3123. On willful misconduct see: *Rashap v. American Airlines, Inc.*, U.S. and C. *Aviation Reports* 593 (1955); *Garcia v. Pan American Airways*, U.S. *Aviation Reports* 496 (1946); *Pauwel v. Sabena*, U.S. *Aviation Reports* 367 (1950); *Hennessy v. Air France*, *Revue francais de droit aerien* 62 (1954), cited by O'Connell, op. cit., p. 594; *Grey et al., v. American Airlines*, 22 *International Law Reports* 527 (1951); and *Ross v. Pan American Airways*, U. S. *Aviation Reports* 541 (1948). The consensus which seems to emerge from these decisions is that the plaintiff must accept the burden of proof when the court is asked to set aside the liability limitations on the basis of willful misconduct.

In *Grey et al., v. American Airlines*, an appeal before the Court of Appeals, Second Circuit, the court stated that:

> there is no dispute as to what constitutes willful misconduct. The instructions require proof of a conscious intent to do or omit doing an act from which harm results to another, or an international omission of a manifest duty. There must be a realization of the probability of injury from the conduct, and a disregard of the probable consequences of such action (op. cit., p. 165).

American Airlines v. Ulen, op. cit., and *Goepp v. American Overseas Airlines*, op. cit., are cited as precedents in support of this view.

An extended list of cases in United States courts arising from application and interpretation of the Warsaw Convention may be found in Bishop, op. cit., p. 375. See also Billyou, op. cit., pp. 268-285; Verplaetse, op. cit., pp. 316-318; and O'Connell, op. cit., p. 594. Each of these writers cites cases from a very few states. See again footnote 30 above.

39.   Department of State Press Release No. 268, 15 November, 1965.

40.   See Cabranes, op. cit.

41.   Ibid., p. 688. See the discussion of Article 20 above.

42.   Department of State Press Release No. 111, 14 May 1966. See also No. 110, 13 May 1966, in which the interim agreement is described. Text of these releases are cited in *Journal of Air Law and Commerce*, 33 (Summer, 1966), pp. 247-248.

43.   Cf. Honig, op. cit., pp. 117-120; Haley, *Space Law and Government*, op. cit., pp. 237-240, and Chapter 8 in general; and Verplaetse, op. cit., pp. 298-338.

44.   Article 1. United States Congress, Senate Committee on Commerce, *Air Laws and Treaties of the World*, 3, op. cit., p. 3221. Recall in contrast, that under the provisions of the Warsaw Convention, there must be proof of a contract before the injured party may state the extent of damages.

45.   Idem.

46.   Article 2, ibid., pp. 3221-3222.

47.   Article 11, ibid., pp. 3223-3224. This range in U.S. dollars and in pounds is $33,162.50 for aircraft weighing 2,204.6 pounds or less to $693,000 plus $3.00 per pound over 110,230 pounds for aircraft which weigh more than 110,230 pounds (idem.).

48.   Idem. The gold franc referred to here has the same value as those mentioned in the Warsaw convention, i.e., 65½ milligrams of gold of millesimal fineness.

49.   Article 12, ibid., p. 3224.

50.   Article 15, ibid., p. 3225. See further, pp. 3225-3228.

51.   Data on signatures and ratifications and/or adherences were furnished by the International Civil Aviation Organization in September 1966.

52.   See Wassenbergh, op. cit., pp. 107-109; Goedius, op. cit., pp. 137-152; and Elmer Plische, "Transpolar Aviation Jurisdiction Over Arctic Airspace," *American Political Science Review*, 37 (December 1943), pp. 999-1013.

53.   United States Congress, Senate, Committee on Commerce, *Air Laws and Treaties of the World*, 3, op. cit., pp. 3085-3102. No rule can be determined on the basis of these two treaties, both of which were superseded by the 1944 Chicago convention.

54.   Ibid., p. 3167.

55.   Article 6, idem.

56.   Article 1, Section 1, ibid., p. 3203.

57.   Article 1, Section 4, ibid., pp. 3203-3204.

58.   United Nations Conference on the Law of the Sea, *Official Records,* 3, op. cit., pp. 8 and 104 (U.K.) and pp. 90-91 (Canada). See also statements by the Burmese delegate, pp. 122-123. This interpretation was not challenged. However, when those opposed to extending the territorial sea argued that freedom of navigation by ships would be adversely affected, they were challenged. Those favoring extending the territorial sea contended that the right of innocent passage of ships would minimize any interference with sea commerce. It seems significant, then, that a similar argument was not made concerning the right of innocent passage for aircraft.

59.   "Comments by the International Civil Aviation Organization on the Draft Articles Concerning the Law of the Sea Adopted by the International Law Commission at its Eighth Session" (U.N. Doc. A/Conf. 13/31), United Nations Conference on the Law of the Sea, *Official Records,* 1, op. cit., pp. 336-338.

Bishop agrees. In his *International Law,* op. cit., he contends that "it seems clear, especially in the light of statements made at the 1958 Geneva Conference on the Law of the Sea, that aircraft are not entitled to 'innocent passage' through the airspace above the territorial waters of a foreign state, except by treaty" (p. 371).

Briggs, in *The Law of Nations,* op. cit., contends that "the freedom of innocent passage . . . , in so far as it exists, has been recognized as a conventional right based upon international agreement between States" (p. 325). On this point, see also Stephen Latchford, "The Right of Innocent Passage in International Civil Air-Navigation Agreements," *Department of State Bulletin,* 11 (July 2, 1944), pp. 19-24.

Wassenberg, op. cit., takes exception. He expresses the opinion that, with the exception of Red China, the Soviet Union and "the satellite countries,"

> . . . the right of innocent passage has acquired the force of customary law, it being an established practice to expect or accord this right if states are satisfied as to the innocent character of the passage concerned, in the conviction that in receiving or granting such a right of passage, they are exercising a right or fulfilling a duty (p. 109).

The right of entry in distress has not been dealt with here since no conventional provision is made for such entry. Bishop indicates that this is a more likely right than the more general right of innocent passage, but still not so clearly established as a similar right for ships (op. cit., p. 371). Lissitzyn also argues that such a right exists when entry is caused by a *force majeure* (op. cit., pp. 588-589).

60.   See the Introduction to Part II of this study.

61.   McDougal et al., *Law and Public Order in Space,* op. cit., p. 254.

62.   Idem.

PART III: AN ANALYSIS OF WHY
NATIONAL DECISION-MAKERS
ACCEPT OR REJECT PARTICULAR
INTERNATIONAL LEGAL RULES
AND PRINCIPLES AND WHETHER
THESE RULES AND PRINCIPLES
ARE APPLICABLE TO
OUTER SPACE

INTRODUCTION

The two major analytic goals for Part III are: (1) to clarify or partially explain *why* national decision-makers accept or reject the selected international legal rules and principles analyzed in Part II; and (2) to determine the applicability or relevance of selected rules and principles of the law-in-action in international air and sea law to certain legal problems in outer space.

In Chapter 5, two distinct methods are used in an attempt to achieve the first goal. The first method is to analyze statements made by governmental officials concerning the air and sea law rules and principles which have been determined in Part II.[1] On the basis of these explicit statements of policy positions, a number of hypotheses are formulated. The assertion made in these hypotheses is that rule acceptance and rejection can be clarified or explained, at least in part, by determining the relationship between acceptance and rejection and certain economic, political, and social indicators. These assertions are tested by means of a computer variance reduction routine. This routine is used to determine which combination from among the selected indicators explains the greatest proportion of variance between states in rule acceptance or rejection.[2]

The results of the analysis of the relationship between certain interests such as security, conservation, and economic, for example, and rule acceptance and rejection in the air and sea environments may be used in the analysis of similar relationships in the space environment. Once the *why* of rule acceptance and rejection has been examined, a meaningful analysis of the probable applicability of selected air and sea law rules and principles to outer space legal problems can be made. This, then, is the goal in Chapter 6.

NOTES

1. Since for the most part only conventional rules have been analyzed, the source for these statements will be limited to the records of the appropriate international conference.

2. In the traditional language of the scholar, the claims made here for the degree of explanation are carefully limited. There is, of course, no assurance that even the critical variables or indicators have been isolated and included in this analysis of variance. See Chapter 5 for a more complete discussion of this point.

The computer program which is used is the Inter-University Consortium's AID (3). This program and its uses are described by John A. Sonquist and James N. Morgan in *The Detection of Interaction Effects: A Report on a Computer Program for the Selection of Optimal Combinations of Explanatory Variables* (Ann Arbor: Survey Research Center, Institute for Social Research, The University of Michigan. Monograph No. 35, 1964).

5: AN ANALYSIS OF WHY NATIONAL DECISION-MAKERS ACCEPT OR REJECT PARTICULAR INTERNATIONAL LEGAL RULES AND PRINCIPLES

INTRODUCTION

The analytic goal in this chapter is to clarify or to explain in part *why* national decision-makers accept or reject international air and sea legal rules and principles. This, then, requires an examination of the causal relationships between two sets of variables — decisions and the identifiable interests or preconditions which apparently have some causal role in shaping these decisions.

Social scientists are handicapped in dealing with the question of causation. The nature of the subject matter of social science and the nonexperimental character of most social science studies constitute rather formidable obstacles; ones which many, if not most, social scientists prefer to avoid.[1] However, the question of causation has intrigued social scientists and has been discussed by them beginning at least with Aristotle. Recently, a new system and a more rigorous approach have been introduced by two sociologists, Herbert A. Simon and Hubert M. Blalock, Jr.[2]

Given the present "state of the art" of social science methods, all efforts to deal with causation require a willingness to make simplifying assumptions. Simon, in fact, deals entirely with so-called hypothetical models, not attempting to bridge the gap between the model and the real or physical world. Blalock, building on Simon's earlier work, also works with simplified models. Simplification, of course, means that the models are so conceptualized as to include a specific set of variables, but as Blalock indicates

> the basic difficulty [in causal arguments] is a fundamental one: there seems to be no systematic way of knowing for sure whether or not one has located all of the relevant variables. Nor do we have any foolproof procedures for deciding which variables to use.[3]

One isolates what appears to be the relevant variables on the basis of knowledge of subject matter. The model is shaped, then, by one's knowledge of content since as Blalock points out ". . . there is nothing absolute about any particular model . . . ."[4]

One set of variables for the analysis in this chapter already has been selected: the decisions made by certain national decision-makers in accepting or rejecting particular international air and sea legal rules and principles. The beginning point in selecting the second set of variables is an explication of what these decision-makers *say* their reasons are for accepting or rejecting these rules and principles. The causal question, then, is what caused or motivated these decision-makers to make a particular decision.[5]

Given the two sets of variables, an analysis of variance will determine which combination from among the selected predictor variables explains the greatest proportion of variance between states in their acceptance or rejection of international rules and principles.

The question of causation or motivation is not met head-on. However interesting and important the deterministic question of causation, the primary research interest and goal here is to learn more about the relationships between interests and/or preconditions and classes of legal rules and principles. The results of the analysis of variance are suggestive and help to clarify or partially explain the *why* question upon which this chapter focuses. Certainly, the deterministic causal question is not conclusively answered. The more general research interest and goal is necessary in part as a consequence of the exploratory character of this part of the study. Moreover, the simplifying assumptions made in selecting predictor variables act as a restraint upon any tendency to overgeneralize on the basis of an analysis of variance between and among these variables. Of course, it is hoped that this study will help to provide a basis for a more direct confrontation with the causal question in the future and thereby to provide a better basis for predicting rule and principle acceptance or rejection.

AN ANALYSIS OF DECISION-MAKERS' STATEMENTS

CLAIMS PRIMARILY IN SUPPORT OF AN EXCLUSIVE INTEREST

SEA

TERRITORIAL SEA AND CONTIGUOUS ZONES

On the basis of the analysis in Chapter 3, it seems there is general agreement that the maximum extent of the territorial sea is limited. It is equally evident that a majority of states do not agree upon what that maximum limit is.

At the 1958 and 1960 Conferences on the Law of the Sea, delegates supported various particular maximum limits on a number of bases. Statements were made by a number of delegates who represented states opposed to any extension of the territorial sea and to the establishment of contiguous zones within which the adjacent coastal state would enjoy exclusive fishing rights.[6] Two basic points were generally made in these statements. First, it was maintained that any extension of the territorial sea would threaten a fundamental freedom of navigation. Second, extension of the territorial sea or the establishment of contiguous exclusive fishing zones could result in severe dislocations in some national economies.

Arthur H. Dean, chairman of the United States Delegation, argued, for example, that a number of adverse economic effects would result from either or both of these extensions. First, merchant vessels would take longer and consequently more costly routes in order to avoid traversing extended territorial seas. All states would suffer from the resulting increased cost of maritime transportation and communication. Second, national economies which depend upon marine products for domestic livelihood or for export would suffer severe economic dislocation if their fishermen were denied traditional fishing grounds. A further adverse economic effect would result from the increased cost of effectively patrolling these extended sea zones.[7]

The delegates of a number of states whose fishermen engage in distant-water fishing contended that excluding their fishing vessels from traditional high seas fisheries would adversely affect their economies. The chairman of the 1960 Japanese Delegation, Katsuzo Okumura, stated that to extend the territorial sea or a zone of exclusive fishing rights out to twelve miles or beyond would not be compatible with the principles of justice and equity if states were excluded ". . . which had for many years been fishing in the areas of the high seas affected, and whose economy and national livelihood largely depended on fishing in distant waters."[8] He pointed out that his country, one of the leading fishing states of the world with an annual catch of some five million tons, took most of its catch in distant waters. Fish were the source of almost 70 percent of the animal protein in the diet of his countrymen. Moreover, Japan's economy was heavily dependent upon foreign trade and shipping and would be affected adversely if territorial seas were extended.[9]

The delegate of the United Kingdom argued a similar case. Specifically, he predicted that a direct economic effect would be the unemployment of a large number of fishermen. There would be also a number of indirect effects, such as shore workers being denied their markets, for example. He argued that these effects surely would follow any serious curtailment of distant water fishing by British fishermen.[10]

Several other delegations — Australia, Belgium, Canada, West Germany, Greece, Liberia, Netherlands, New Zealand, Pakistan, Paraguay, Portugal, Sweden, and Switzerland — made similar arguments in favor of what they considered to be the fundamental freedom of navigation.[11] With the exception of Paraguay, Sweden, and Switzerland, all the states whose delegates made these statements claim a territorial sea of three miles. Paraguay and Switzerland are landlocked and Sweden claims a territorial sea of four miles. Thirteen of these states possess a special interest in the law of the sea.[12] Most of these states expressed a willingness to compromise in order to obtain agreement on a conventional rule fixing specific limits and rights. This explains, at least in part, why these states proposed and/or supported in 1958 and 1960 breadths in excess of three miles and, under certain conditions, exclusive fishing zones.

Statements in support of an extension of the territorial sea and/or the establishment of a contiguous exclusive fishing zone were made by the delegates of 36 states at either the 1958 and/or the 1960 conferences. Three identifiable interests are mentioned in a majority of these statements: conservation, economic, and security. For example, the chairman of the Indian Delegation, Shri A. K. Sen, stated that

> . . . it is significant to note that the dominant feature of this group [of states supporting a twelve-mile territorial sea] is the predominance of what we call the newer and younger states . . . . It is not a mere accident that these newer and younger nations should be asking for a wider territorial sea, whereas the older maritime powers should be wanting a narrow territorial sea. Their past history, their sufferings, their economic under-development and, the most important thing, their passionate craving for a better life explain their eagerness to cling to and appropriate to themselves for their exclusive use and occupation

their adjacent seas as far as possible. For one thing, they have not the men or the equipment to sail the high seas or to exploit them. For another, they feel rightly or wrongly, that a wider territorial sea would give them an insulated life, free from the interference from the Great Powers.[13]

He added that these small and younger states do not welcome foreign warships coming into their adjacent sea and remaining there for long periods. These states are ". . . anxiously worried about the possibility of such warships coming in the future and staying within the waters adjacent to their seas."[14]

Other delegates made similar but less detailed statements identifying conservation, economic and/or security interests. Bulgaria's delegate echoed the viewpoint of the Indian delegate. He, too, thought it significant that the states favoring the twelve-mile limit were ". . . newly independent countries, having no powerful warships, merchant navies or fishing fleets, some of them economically underdeveloped, and all of them concerned for their security and the protection of their economic interest."[15]

The chairman of the delegation of the United Arab Republic, Abdel Fattah Hassan, argued forcefully that coastal states need a reasonably broad territorial sea in order to ensure ". . . that foreign warships and military aircraft . . . [are] unable to pass through or over areas closely adjacent to its coast for purposes of intimidation.[16] Small states, he added, are particularly concerned about the security aspect of the breadth of the territorial sea. As a consequence, at the 1958 conference, a majority of these states ". . . had consistently opposed the adoption of any provision that did not explicitly recognize the right of the coastal State to make movements of foreign warships in its territorial sea subject to its authorization."[17] He continued by noting that although some of his fellow delegates questioned the importance of a twelve-mile territorial sea to a state's security, small states are particularly apprehensive about naval and aerial demonstrations off their coasts.[18]

An example of the arguments made to justify the extension of the territorial sea and/or the establishment of exclusive fishing zones for economic and conservation reasons is found in the statement made by Dr. Enrique Garcia Sayan of Peru. He stated that 90 percent of his country's fertilizer needs are supplied by guano. The sea birds which produce the guano depend upon certain stocks of fish for their food. Overfishing threatened these stocks of fish. If the relationship between the sea birds and their food was disturbed, the guano would not be produced and the effect on Peruvian agriculture would be disastrous. Consequently, conservation measures had to be taken by his government to protect the stocks of fish upon which the sea birds feed. Moreover, he said, in 1956, there were in Peru only 0.17 hectares of cultivated area per capita. With the population expected to double by 1980, it would be necessary to depend increasingly upon the sea as a major source of food.[19]

Dr. Alfredo Martinez Moreno, chairman of the El Salvadorian Delegation, identified the basic difference between the economic needs of the various states in their contiguous sea zones. He maintained that for some states the contiguous sea zones are simply additional areas in which to seek profits and to add to already healthy and developed national economies; however, for many of the so-called under-developed states, these sea areas represent a major part of their limited national resources.[20]

One or more of these three interests — conservation, economic, and security — also was explicit mentioned in statements made by the delegates of Albania, Argentina, Burma, Ceylon, Chile, Costa Rica, Czechoslovakia, Ecuador, Ethiopia, Ghana, Hungary, Iceland, Indonesia, Israel, Jordan, South Korea, Libya, Norway, Panama, Phillippines, Spain, Sudan, Tunisia, Turkey, Uruguay, Venezuela, Vietnam, and Yemen, in addition to the statements already cited.[21]

In some cases, there is evidently a difficulty in balancing interests. For example, Norway's delegate favored a twelve-mile fishing zone as a minimum protection for his country's economic interests. He also favored a three or four mile limit for the territorial sea. Of course, these are not antithetical positions, yet this does emphasize the potential conflict among interests for states such as Norway and Canada. Where their interests lie is much clearer for states such as Japan, France, and Italy. In these latter instances, fishing interests and an interest in maintaining freedom of navigation are more nearly congruent.

CONTINENTAL SHELF

In Chapter 2, it was determined that there is a universally binding legal rule that coastal states may exercise sovereign rights in the exploration and exploitation of the natural resources of the continental shelf. Delegates to the 1958 Conference on the Law of the Sea were not so explicit in indicating why they accept or reject this rule as they were in indicating why they accept or reject rules related to the territorial sea and contiguous zones.

An almost universal acceptance of the general rule of the coastal state's priority of rights in exploring and exploiting the continental shelf seems to underlie discussion and debate in the Fourth Committee. In fact, only two delegations, West Germany and Japan, questioned this general rule. Delegates of both expressed concern lest the inclusive interests of the international community be derogated in favor of exclusive interest of certain states.[22] The Japanese Delegation took the position that it was not necessary to vest "a monopoly of rights" in the adjacent state.[23] West Germany's position was that the freedom to explore and exploit the continental shelf should be subject to the same restrictions as other high seas freedoms. The West Germans proposed, then, a system of "regulated freedom" under international supervision.[24]

The majority view clearly was that the continental shelf is geographically an extension of the mainland and that the adjacent coastal state either should have "exclusive rights," "sovereign rights," or should exercise "jurisdiction and control."[25] Discussion and debate centered on the problem of definition and delimitation.

There was extended debate as to whether the rights of the coastal state should be considered sovereign or exclusive or whether the phrase jurisdiction and control was more appropriate.[26] Two other questions which occupied the committee concerned the problems of delimiting the extent of the continental shelf and defining what was meant by natural resources.[27] Delegates seem to have made the fundamental assumption that it was in the inclusive as well as the exclusive interest that the continental shelf be explored and its resources exploited. It should be recalled that by 1958 some thirty states had made unilateral claims to the continental shelf adjacent to their territorial sea. Furthermore, it seemed unlikely that states would permit other states to exploit resources close to their shores. It seemed, then, that it was in the interest of *progress* to assign priority exploration and exploitation rights to the adjacent coastal states. In the long run, this apparently appeared to be the best available means of ensuring that these resources were developed for the benefit of the entire community.

Two exclusive interests were mentioned which were to be protected in any conventional rule on the continental shelf — economic and security. Both interests are implicit in the statements of many delegates and several delegates explicitly mentioned one or both interests in their statements. For example, Dr. Jose Joaquin Caicedo Castilla, a Colombian delegate, recognized an "imperative economic need" for states to claim exclusive or sovereign rights over the resources on the shelf.[28] Predrog Nicolic of Yugoslavia maintained that "economic needs" made recognition of the "concept" of the continental shelf essential.[29] The Ghanian member of the Fourth Committee, R. A. Quarshie, referred to the economic and social interests of the smaller states in exploiting their adjacent continental shelves.[30]

Only two delegates made explicit reference to the security interests of the adjacent coastal states in exclusive or sovereign rights to explore and exploit. Admiral D. Carlos Carbajal of Uruguay contended that it was unlikely that even a "great Power would permit the vessels of another State to approach its shores so closely for the purpose of exploiting the resources of the continental shelf."[31] Buu-Kinh, Republic of Vietnam, argued that "both legally and politically, the presence of installations [on the continental shelf] belonging to a foreign State would constitute a constant threat to the security of the coastal State. . . ."[32]

On the basis of an examination of statements made by the delegates to the 1958 conference, it seems reasonable to assume that states make claims to sovereign rights over the adjacent continental shelf in order to protect or enhance two primarily exclusive interests — economic and security. It seems clear that the most basic interest which they seek to protect is economic.[33]

AIR

TERRITORIAL AIRSPACE

It has been determined that states possess sovereign rights in the airspace over their territory. In fact, 109 states have ratified or otherwise adherd to the Chicago convention which explicitly provides that every state has complete and exclusive authority over its superjacent airspace.

The widespread acceptance of this rule is evident in policy position statements made by several delegates at the Chicago conference in 1944. For example, Adolf B. Berle, Jr., a United States delegate and president of the conference, stated that "the United States believes in and asserts the rule that each country has a right to maintain sovereignty of the air which is over its land and its territorial waters. There can be no question of alienating or qualifying this sovereignty."[34]

Apparently acceptance of the complete and exclusive sovereignty of each state in its superjacent airspace is based primarily on exclusive economic and security interests. These two interests are evident in the Australian position as articulated by the chairman of that delegation, Arthur S. Drakeford. In advocating an international civil aviation authority, Drakeford contended that

> . . . in the interests of the future peace of the world and in order to facilitate the rational development of the world's air commerce, an international air transport authority should be appointed, which, through an appropriate organization would own the aircraft and operate prescribed international routes on behalf of all nations; and that such an international air transport authority should be an organ of the world security organization to be established.[35]

Drakeford added, "at the same time, we fully realize that it is the sovereign right of each nation to develop air services within its own territory for the benefit of its own people."[36]

This caveat to acceptance of any general international control also was made explicit by Colonel Pedro A. Chapa, chairman of the delegation of Mexico. He stated that ". . . we concur on a general plan to attain the greatest freedom of the air while maintaining full recognition of the sovereignty of nations."[37] However, he indicated that his country reserved its right to authorize, "according to its own criteria," the establishment and control of any air transportation over its territory. And he was very careful to add that cabotage within his country was at the time of the conference exclusively Mexican and that his government wished it to remain so.[38]

The United Kingdom's proposal also reaffirmed the principle of national sovereignty.[39] In stating his country's position, Lord Swinton identified an economic and security interest which extended beyond the territorial airspace. He contended that "every nation, which aspires to be in the air, will wish to have, and indeed will insist on it, in addition to its own internal traffic, a fair share of its external traffic as well."[40] He explained that "it is not just a matter of prestige. It is bound up in large measure with security."[41]

C. D. Howe, chairman of the Canadian Delegation, also recognized economic and security interests which extended beyond the limits of territorial airspace. However, he argued for recognition and protection of these primarily as inclusive rather than as exclusive interests. He favored an international authority and "four freedoms." In calling attention to the importance of air transport to the prosperity, security, and prestige of nations, he stated that "an enlightened settlement of the problem of international air transport will mean that the nations of the world have gone a long way toward establishing a lasting peace and a new order of security."[42]

It seems, then, on the basis of these policy position statements, that decision-makers accept the complete and exclusive authority of each state in its superjacent airspace primarily because of perceived national economic and security interests in this airspace. Moreover, these economic and security interests apparently extend to airspace outside territorial boundaries as well.

CLAIMS PRIMARILY IN SUPPORT OF AN INCLUSIVE INTEREST

SEA

HIGH SEAS

No attempt was made in Chapter 3 to determine detailed rules relating to the high seas, rather only a universally recognized general principle of the freedom of the high seas was determined. For the most part, delegates in the Second Committee, High Seas: General Regime seem to have accepted this freedom as a fundamental principle of the international law of the sea.[43]

Several specific interests were identified in statements made before the Second Committee. Commander Joaquin Carlos Esteves Cardoso, Portugal, stated that freedom of communications is ". . . essential to the well-being and security of all states."[44] The Tunisian delegate, Hamida Ben Salem, ". . . regarded the high seas as a common domain which all nations . . . [are] equally free to use as a means of communications and a source of wealth."[45] The importance of the freedom of the high seas to the development of shipping was referred to by Abdallah El Erian of the United Arab Republic.[46] Sir Alec Randall, United Kingdom, stressed the great importance of the principle to states possessing merchant fleets,[47] and the United States' delegate to the Second Committee, Admiral Oswald S. Colclough, identified the sea as the world's principal highway.[48]

Commander A. Hameed, Pakistan, noted that the high seas are the main means of communication between the two parts of his country. He added that his country also has ". . . high aspirations for its small but growing merchant fleet and the trade . . . [is] so vital for its economic development."[49] Freedom of the high seas is, therefore, in his opinion, essential to his country.

Even the few statements made by opponents of certain aspects of the general principle of the high seas as formulated by the Second Committee based their opposition on essentially economic grounds. Chile and Peru, for example, had a vested interest as a consequence of their claims to sovereignty over waters to a distance of 200 miles from their coastline. Both stressed that the freedom of the high seas is not an unlimited freedom.[50] And Fernando Garello Fitz-Henry, Chile, took the position that the freedom "to fish anywhere on the high seas" is not a traditional freedom as is the freedom of navigation thereon.[51]

The statements cited here make explicit what seems to be implicit in the committee's acceptance of the general principle of the freedom of the high seas. Exclusive and inclusive interests appear to be congruent in this instance. Safeguarding the inclusive interest in shared usage is functional also to the exclusive interests of states dependent upon the high seas for communications or transportation and fishing, for example. The basic interest, then, seems to be economic.[52]

NATIONALITY, REGISTRATION, AND SAFETY

As was noted in Chapter 3, there is a universally applicable rule that: a ship possesses the nationality of the state whose flag it flies; each state establishes its own conditions for granting its nationality; and each state establishes its own conditions and procedures for registering vessels. The question of primary interest in the Second Committee at the 1958 conference was the question of a genuine link between the vessel and the flag state.[53] In a very real sense, of course, "genuine link" was a challenge to the stated rules.

Evidently, the inclusive interest, as articulated by a number of delegates — including those from Australia, Nationalist China, Denmark, Japan, Liberia, Netherlands, Pakistan, Sweden, United Kingdom, and United States — is that a right of a state to permit ships to sail the high seas bearing its flag and nationality entails a concommitant duty to exercise effective jurisdiction and control over these ships.[54] For example, Admiral Colclough, United States, stated that "admittedly, the right of a State to sail vessels on the high seas . . . [carries] with it the corresponding duty to exercise control and effective jurisdiction over those vessels in the interest of order on the high seas . . . ."[55] W. Riphagen, of the Netherlands Delegation, argued that the real proof of a genuine connection between a vessel and the state which granted it its nationality is the exercise of effective jurisdiction and control.[56] The chairman of the Chinese Delegation, Liu Chieh, said that the principle of the genuine link is ". . . essential in order to enable the flag state to exercise control over the ship and to discharge its responsibility with regard to safety and other regulations."[57] In commenting on the obligations of the registering state, Toreis Valdemar Andreas Oldenburg, Denmark, asserted that "those obligations . . . [imply] complete jurisdiction and the exercise of effective control, especially with regard to internationally adopted standards of safety and social conditions of the crew."[58]

When safety of life at sea is discussed, the focus seems to be primarily on the technical aspects of safety appliances and practices. The basic inclusive needs and interests apparently are accepted without question. That this is the prevailing viewpoint is evident in a statement made by the French delegate at the closing session of the 1960 Conference on Safety of Life at Sea. He said that

> representatives at the Conference . . . [have] worked hard, their aim being to assure the greatest security possible for their vessels. The role of the merchant navy . . . [is] a historic one, and, despite the advent of the aeroplane, transport of merchandise at sea . . . [is] still essential. Members of the Conference . . . [can] return to their countries

in the knowledge of a job well done for the merchant navies of the world, which . . . [are] instruments of prosperity, of better social standards and, consequently, of peace.[59]

The Liberian delegate recognized a similar common objective when he observed that ". . . the minds of all . . . [have] been [concentrating] on one common objective — the security, preservation and safety of life at sea."[60] This underlying humanitarian interest in safeguarding lives is evident in a number of other statements as well. In the *Report of the United States Delegation* to the 1948 conference, it is pointed out that the 1929 conference had been called largely because of reaction to the loss of the *Titanic* with an attendant heavy loss of passengers. The United States Congress responded by proposing that an international conference be held to provide means for preventing any such disasters in the future.[61] Likewise, a press release of the United States Coast Guard Headquarters states that "the [1960] Conference was called primarily as a result of the collision of the liners STOCKHOLM and ANDREA DORIA on July 25, 1956, in which fifty persons lost their lives and the ANDREA DORIA sank."[62]

However, as pervasive and compelling as the underlying humanitarian interest appears to be, it seems that economic interests also must be satisfied if the rules are to be accepted. The 1948 *Report of the United States Delegation,* for example, indicates that states whose vessels were designed to meet the standards of the 1929 regulations "with little or no margin," were not willing in 1948 to agree to any changes in standards without being aware of what the impact of these changes would be on their "particular maritime conditions."[63]

The two primary interests which decision-makers say they seek to protect when formulating rules concerning the nationality and registration of ships and the safety of life at sea are economic and humanitarian. Based on the records examined here, it is evident that the two interests are interrelated and that decision-makers perceive that both interests are best served by rules providing for effective control and jurisdiction by the flag state.

AIR

NATIONALITY AND REGISTRATION

Acceptance of the international rules concerning registration and nationality of aircraft appears not to have been discussed at Chicago in 1944; at least no such discussion is evident in the published *Proceedings* of that conference. The Chicago convention, as was noted in Chapter 4, does include detailed provisions concerning nationality and registration. Apparently these inclusive interests were so widely accepted in 1944 that discussion could focus on the technical aspects of the question rather than on particular policy positions. It does seem reasonable, however, to assume that particular interests in nationality and registration are approximately the same as in the sea environment: to provide for jurisdiction and effective control with regard to regulations made in the inclusive interest, thereby protecting and enhancing economic and social interests.

LIABILITY

Discussions of liability at the Conference on Private International Air Law which met in Rome in 1952 focused on two questions: (1) should a system of absolute liability (as was embodied in the 1933 Rome convention) be adopted? and (2) what should be the limits of the air carrier's liability? Both questions were discussed in ethical and economic contexts.

The two pole positions on the limits of liability seem to be stated best by the delegates of Mexico and Portugal. Enrique M. Loaeza, Mexico, stated that

> ... the question of the limits of liability had caused his Government much concern because it considered that these limits would have a direct and immediate effect on the operating costs of air transport. While it ... [is] true that the Mexican Government ... [is] concerned with the public well-being and ... [tries] to contribute to it as much as possible — and the protection of the victims on the surface ... [is] part of the public well-being — it ... [is] no less certain that air transport ... [has] to be maintained in a satisfactory condition from the economic point of view and that, also, ... [is] for the public good.[64]

Loaeza argued that raising the limit of liability would increase the cost of insurance. In turn, such an increase would adversely affect Mexican operators of international air transport.

> If the limits ... [are] considerably increased, as proposed by the Delegation of the United States, the practical result ... [will] be the prevention of the development of international aviation for countries which ... [do] not have sufficient financial means in comparison with other countries.[65]

Manual Antonio Fernandes of Portugal disagreed with Loaeza. He argued that

> ... the general principle of civil liability ... [implies] total compensation for damage caused, and it would be legitimate to make exceptions to this principle only in the case of important reasons which were in

the public interest. The public interest in the operation of air transport
. . . [justifies] the exception whereby a limit of the liability of the
operators . . . [is] established, but the development of air transport
should not be protected at the expense of the innocent victims on the
surface.[66]

He went on to say that there was no reason to fear that insurance premiums
would increase by any large amounts. In fact, he argued, the cost of insurance in relation to all operating costs would be negligible. "The public
interest in the development of civil aviation [will] not, therefore, be affected by an increase in the limits [of liability]."[67]

Emory T. Nunneley, Jr., a delegate of the United States, argued for a system of liability based on a presumption of fault rather than the proposed
system of absolute liability.

The United States . . . [believes] this to be a just and equitable rule,
and that it . . . [establishes] the proper relation between the responsibility of the operator, and the development of aviation and the right of
the public.

Air transportation, whether commercial or private, . . . [serves] a great
public purpose, both national and international. It . . . [is] proper to
take every reasonable step to encourage its development, bearing in
mind that the development of aviation . . . [includes] a proper relation
between the responsibility of the operator and the third parties who
might be damaged as a consequence of an aviation accident. The opinion of the United States . . . [is] that there . . . [is] no necessity of im-
posing on aviation a heavier burden than that imposed on other means
of transportation.[68]

He concluded, therefore, that a system of absolute liability would be an unwarranted burden on aviation. Furthermore, it was a burden not necessary
for the proper protection of the public.[69]

Antonia Ambrosini, the delegate of Italy, countered the United States argument by contending that aviation is a very exceptional case which should
not be compared to that of other means of transportation on the surface.
"In the case of aviation, by the very nature of things, the public . . . [is]
exposed to a danger against which it . . . [can] not be protected."[70]

Dr. D. Saturnino Sal of Argentina agreed with the Italian delegate. Aviation is a special case.

. . . [A]bsolute liability . . . [entails] the system of compulsory insurance which . . . [is] a form of social insurance. The fact of taking
measures necessary to prevent difficulties of an economic nature which
might be created by international airlines should in no way hinder the
development of aviation.[71]

The limit of liability was also a central issue discussed at the International Conference on Private Air Law which met at the Hague in 1955. The United States delegate, G. Nathan Calkins, Jr., took the position that when amounts of liability are discussed, the discussion ceases to be a consideration of the legal aspects of the problem and focuses on economic considerations. He maintained that

> in 1929, limited liability had been accepted by the delegates who drafted the Warsaw Convention because they believed that it was necessary for the development of aviation, given the situation in which aviation found itself at that time, it being an infant industry with a rather dangerous safety record, and, in order to promote aviation, it was necessary to put a rather low limit on the liability of the carriers for death and personal injury.[72]

According to Calkins, the situation in 1955 was radically different from that of 1929 and none of these same justifications existed.

Many other delegates also took the position that the limits established by the 1929 Warsaw convention were too low.[73] However, two delegations — Australia and India — were generally opposed to any increase. Harold William Poulton, Australia, indicated a willingness to accept a compromise, but he argued that there is no justification for having poor passengers pay higher fares which are meant to provide higher liability coverage for all passengers. He contended that wealthy passengers, the ones particularly desirous of higher coverage, always take out additional coverage anyway.[74]

The Indian delegate, Shri Dalject Singh Bhatti, also based his opposition on economic grounds. He argued that ". . . any radical change in the limits prescribed in . . . the Convention would render the Convention unstable and that any instrument incorporating such a change would not be acceptable to countries like his own, particularly if the limit were raised to an unduly high figure."[75] Bhatti pointed out that the states which provide for unlimited liability are the most prosperous countries in the world and possess the highest living standards. Any increase in the liability limits, he said, would lead to higher insurance charges and thus to higher fares "which would not be conductive to the development of air transport."[76]

It is evident, then, on the basis of the analysis here, that the primary interest which states seek to protect in formulating particular rules concerning the liability of air transport carriers is an economic interest. However, there obviously is also an underlying ethical or moral concern centering on a respect for the value of human life. This latter interest is perhaps the motivation for accepting the principle of liability. At the level of specific rules, however, it is clearly the economic interest which predominates.

DEVIATIONS OR EXCEPTIONS TO EXCLUSIVE OR INCLUSIVE AUTHORITY

SEA

INNOCENT PASSAGE

An almost universal acceptance of the general principle of the right of innocent passage is evident in the records of the First Committee of the 1958 Conference on the Law of the Sea. It may be recalled that the voting records examined in Chapter 3 support this interpretation as each of the articles concerning innocent passage was accepted by large majorities in both the First Committee and in plenary sessions.[77]

Few delegates explicitly indicated their reasons for supporting the adoption of the principle beyond a simple acknowledgment that the right is firmly established as a principle of international law.[78] Perhaps G. I. Tunkin, chairman of the Soviet Union's delegation, expressed what was implicitly the majority viewpoint when he said that the right of innocent passage is one of the essential conditions of normal navigation.[79] Sir Reginald Manningham-Buller, United Kingdom, stated that the right of innocent passage is a right ". . . necessary to navigation which it . . . [is] in the interest of the coastal State itself to afford."[80] New Zealand's chairman, J. V. Wilson, stressed the interdependence of states and pointed out that recognition of the right of innocent passage is a balance ". . . of rights and obligations between the coastal State and States whose ships . . . [exercise] the right of passage."[81] In his statement, Arthur H. Dean, chairman of the United States Delegation, also explicitly related freedom of navigation as an essential freedom for maritime transport and communications to the right of innocent passage.[82]

It seems safe to assume that the interrelatedness of the right of innocent passage and the freedom of the high seas was generally recognized by the delegates to the 1958 conference. The basically economic interests which these delegates had identified in their consideration of the question of the freedom of the high seas for communication or transport and fishing applied also to a consideration of the right of innocent passage through territorial waters.

It should be recalled that delegates identified conservation, economic, and security interests as their basic concerns when discussing the territorial sea and contiguous zones. The discussion and debate on the right of innocent passage focused on balancing these latter interests with the interests in the freedom of the high seas. The interests in freedom of navigation were emphasized in the statements cited above. Protection of conservation, economic, and security interests were stressed by the delegates who questioned the right of warships and/or fishing vessels to pass through territorial waters without either authorization or prior notification. For example, Dhimitri Lamani of Albania identified a security interest when he stated that in his view ". . . foreign warships had no right of passage without the prior authorization of the State to which the territorial sea belonged."[83] He contended that there were many examples of ". . . foreign Powers using sea routes for other than peaceful ends."[84] Ahmed Shukairi, chairman of the Saudi Arabian Delegation, took a similar position when he argued that "the right of innocent passage must be subject to the security of the State, since that . . . [is] the basis of international law."[85] As for the right of fishing vessels, Natko Katcic, Yugoslavia, stated that there had been incidents ". . . caused by fishing vessels which, under the pretext of innocent passage, had fished in the territorial sea."[86]

Interests in the right of innocent passage through the territorial sea are not new interests, then; rather, these interests are primarily economic and security interests which have been identified previously. It is clear that the economic and security interests related to the right of innocent passage must be identified by balancing the exclusive interests of the particular coastal state in its territorial waters and the inclusive interest of all states in the freedom of navigation. Although not universally binding legal rules, the innocent passage provisions in the 1958 Convention on the Territorial Sea and the Contiguous Zone are widely recognized as the most comprehensive and acceptable contemporary explicit statement of the balance of these interests.

AIR

INNOCENT PASSAGE

The technological developments within aviation during World War II were spectacular. Delegates to the 1944 Chicago conference were well aware of the implications of these developments for post-war commerce. They were aware also that the potential of post-war civil aviation could not be realized if territorial boundaries prevented friendly aerial intercourse. Adolph Berle stressed this point when he articulated the United States' position.

> It is the view of my Government that, in the matter of passage through the air, we are in a stage in which there should be developed, established and settled customs of friendly permission as between friendly nations. Indeed, failure to establish such customs would burden many countries and would actually jeoparidze the situation of most of the smaller nations of the world, especially those without seacoasts. For, if the custom of friends did not permit friendly communication and com-

merce and intercourse through the air, these countries could at any time or at all times be subjected, even in peace, to air blockade.

Clearly this privilege of friendly passage accorded by nations can only be availed of or expected by nations which themselves are prepared to accord like privileges and permissions.

It is, therefore, the view of the United States that, without prejudice to full rights of sovereignty, we should work upon the basis of exchange of needed privileges and permissions which friendly nations have a right to expect from each other.[87]

Other delegates expressed similar viewpoints. For example, Sir Burunath Bewoor, chairman of the Indian Delegation, stated that

India recognizes that it is essential, if air services are to develop rationally, that a high degree of freedom of the air has to be granted. She is prepared to endorse the principles of freedom of flight and freedom to land for refueling and other non-traffic purposes for all civil aircraft, including regular air-transport services on a non-discriminatory basis.[88]

However, he continued, such freedoms of flight must be associated with the establishment of an authority to regulate such rights.[89]

A general recognition of the functional need for certain rights of freedom of passage was tempered by economic and security interests. Colonel Pedro A. Chapa, chairman of the Mexican Delegation, stated that his government

. . . applauds the idea sustained by other countries to concede the maximum facilities for the free passage of aircraft, whatever their nationality, over the airspace of the underlying countries, because it considers that it is the only way humanity can obtain the benefits that aviation will bring. However, it seems convenient to indicate from the start that this principle must have the natural limitations that the sovereign rights and security of a country shall dictate.[90]

The chairman of the Brazilian Delegation, Hahnemann Guimraes, noted that his country's aviation code established the freedom of transit, ". . . with a provision for the safeguard of the sovereign rights of underlying states, as a guaranty to their political, economic, and military interests."[91] This position was not unlike that taken by Carlos Icaza, chairman of the Panamanian Delegation who stated that "in permitting flights over its territory, . . . [Panama] must . . . take into consideration the importance of protecting installations which are vital to Panama and to world trade and which may be jeopardized by uncontrolled flying."[92]

It appears, then, that the primary interests which decision-makers identify in formulating rules of innocent passage through territorial airspace are economic and security interests.

CONCLUSIONS AND HYPOTHESES

When particular rules are formulated to regulate activities within the air and sea environments, decision-makers apparently seek to protect or enhance economic, conservation, humanitarian, and/or security interests. This appears to be the case whether the problem area is characterized as primarily exclusive, primarily inclusive, or as a deviation or exception.

Which of these interests or which combination of these interests is emphasized varies with the particular activity being regulated. For example, it is clear from the preceding analysis that security is emphasized much more frequently in connection with the territorial sea, territorial airspace, and innocent passage than it is in formulating rules relating to the high seas or to the airspace over the high seas. Decision-makers seem to demand that their perceived security interests be protected as a precondition to their acceptance of rules in the former problem areas.

On the other hand, it is evident that an economic interest is pervasive. Economic considerations are influential if not decisive in rule-making in all problem areas. Yet, there does seem to be a variable intensity of interest; that is, the economic interest appears to be more intense in exclusive interest areas such as in controlling resources in closely adjacent sea and shelf areas or in controlling cabotage in territorial airspace.

Conservation, though identified as a separate interest by some decision-makers, is so closely related to the more general economic interest as to be almost indistinguishable from it. However, timing may distinguish conservation from the more general economic interest in that the conservation claim may be seen as a claim to protect resources so that they may either continue to be exploited economically or be exploited economically in the future.

The humanitarian interest also is a very real interest. There obviously is an inclusive community value to protect human life and to compensate for certain kinds of damages. Of course, this interest must compete, as must all interests when particular rules are being formulated. In this, international decision-making is very akin to domestic decision-making. In both processes, decisional outputs apparently are a compromise among competing political actors and interests.

Since most decision-makers have identified identical general interests when commenting on particular international rules and principles, these general interests are not by themselves useful in explaining differences in rule acceptance and rejection. It is evident that identical general interests have difference meanings for different decision-makers. Japan and Peru are examples. Delegates of both states take their positions on sea law rules primarily on the basis of economic considerations, yet it may be recalled that their policy positions are quite different: one favors a narrow territorial sea and no exclusive fishing zone, and the other favors an expansive territorial sea and comprehensive conservation and exclusive fishing rights. Another example is the difference in what a security interest in the sea environment means to the United Arab Republic as opposed to what a security interest means to the United States: one favors a broad territorial sea to prevent showing the flag, and the other favors a narrow territorial sea to maintain freedom of access and movement. A basic problem, then, is to refine these general interest categories so that they become meaningful in clarifying why there are differences between states in rule acceptance and rejection.

The analysis in this chapter suggests that conservation, economic, and security interests are perceived differently by decision-makers based at least in part on the different economic, political, and social profile of their states. This is not to argue in support of an environmental determinism.[93] Yet it seems evident that interest perceptions do vary somewhat on the basis of objectively definable criteria such as state age, wealth, and location, for example.

Differences in interpretation of what constitutes a conservation, economic, and security interest appear to be based, at least in part, on a perceived needs and capabilities relationship. The needs may be either real or imagined, rational or irrational, functional or dysfunctional; yet, needs as perceived by national decision-makers apparently affect acceptance and rejection of particular international legal rules and principles.[94]

A security interest was evident in the statements of several decision-makers cited above. Some of these decision-makers perceived a need for a broad territorial sea and a more extensive territorial airspace in order to provide for their state's security. In the contemporary world, this may be an irrational policy position since a broader territorial sea and a more extensive territorial airspace afford no protection against such weapons as the ICBM and the missile-carrying nuclear submarine. In fact, it might be argued that this policy position is somewhat dysfunctional to the perceived need since the states asserting such claims are probably unable to police and effectively control these extensions to their territory. However, these claims are functional to the fulfillment of what is primarily a psychological need — a need to prevent showing of the flag by foreign naval and/or aerial maneuvers within visual range of the state. In this sense, of course, the need is also rational and real since the security threat or possible intimidation can be at least kept out of sight. The relationship between needs and capabilities is, then, essentially a negative one. Not possessing the military capability for competing in the contemporary international system, these decision-makers seek a solution which is at least psychologically satisfying.

On the other hand, decision-makers of states which possess large military forces capable of defending "national interests" seek solutions which satisfy different security needs. Since most of these latter states either possess or are allied with possessors of ICBMs and other advanced weapons systems, rules are sought which are rational and functional in the employment of these weapons systems. Maintaining accessibility and large open areas for maneuverability are, therefore, rational and functional policies.

Much the same analysis apples to conservation and economic interests. Decision-makers from the underdeveloped states favor policies which give them exclusive control over resources adjacent to and over their land territory. Again the need may be primarily psychological, in this case in reaction perhaps to what is perceived to be exploitation in the past. The desire is to guard resources which can contribute to their state's development. As some of the statements examined above indicate, these states do not have the capabilities for competing in international air commerce, fishing, and shipping. The decision-makers of these states work, therefore, to ensure that resources in adjacent areas — such as fish, minerals, and passengers and cargo in air and sea commerce — are conserved or exploited for the benefit of their underdeveloped states.

Developed states, on the other hand, generally seek to formulate rules which are functional to their continued exploitation of resources in what has been a common domain. Decision-makers of these states also are interested in conservation and in sustaining maximum yields. However, these decision-makers intend for their states to continue to participate in the liberation of these resources on a competitive basis. These states possess the capabilities for competing in international air commerce, fishing, and shipping, and seek to formulate rules which regulate rather than deny this competition.

A large number of specific hypotheses concerning combinations of explanatory variables are implicit in the preceding analysis. For example:

1. Economically underdeveloped states with limited military naval capabilities are more likely to favor a rule establishing a broad territorial sea than are economically developed states which possess a large military naval force;

2. Economically developed states are more likely to accept detailed rules on the freedom of navigation than are economically underdeveloped states;

3. The smaller a state's merchant fleet, the less active its ports, the

smaller its fishing catch, and the smaller number of large and small combatant naval vessels which it possesses, the more likely it is to favor a broad territorial sea, an extensive exclusive fishing zone, and comprehensive exclusive rights in an extended continental shelf; and

4. The more active a state is in international civil aviation the more likely that state is to accept rules limiting liability in international civil aviation.

Many other specific hypotheses could be formulated asserting relationships between rule acceptance and rejection and the predictor variables which have been collected. However, the more general proposition to be tested is this: In an analysis of rule acceptance and rejection, the greatest proportion of variance between states will be explained by a combination of variables which objectively define economic and defense capabilities and interests. The expectation is, then, that such variables as geographical location, size, social composition, date of independence, governmental stability, bloc alignment, and other such profile variables will be explantory at a secondary level.

The analysis of variance which follows is designed to select the optimal combination of explanatory variables from among the variables which have been collected. This analysis, then, will be a test of the general proposition as well as of the explicit and implicit hypotheses already discussed.

ANALYSIS OF VARIANCE

This section is a continuation of the analysis of *why* national decision-makers accept or reject selected international legal rules and principles. In the preceding section, what decision-makers *say* their reasons are has been analyzed; now a statistical analysis of variance in rule acceptance and rejection is undertaken. The specific statistical question to be answered is: Given states as the units of analysis under consideration, what single predictor variable gives a maximum improvement in ability to predict whether a state will accept or reject a particular legal rule or principle?[95]

The Inter-University Consortium's Automatic Interaction Detector (AID) (3) variance reduction program, which is used in the following analysis of variance, is designed to deal with this kind of specific statistical question. John A. Sonquist and James N. Morgan, developers of the program, describe their approach as follows:

> The program divides the sample, through a series of binary splits, into a mutually exclusive series of subgroups. Every observation is a member of exactly one of these sub-groups. They are chosen so that at each step in the procedure, their means account for more of the total

sum of squares (reduce the prediction error) than the means of any other equal member of subgroups.[96]

In this analysis, the sample is the 121 states which comprise the 1964 international political system. Dependent variables are the rules and principles of international air and sea law analyzed in Chapters 3 and 4; and independent or predictor variables have been selected on the basis of the findings of the analysis of rule acceptance and rejection in the preceding section of this chapter.

Certain of the predictor variables are primarily objective definitions and identifiers of what decision-makers perceive to be their states' capabilities or interests — specifically the conservation, economic, and security capabilities and interests which have been identified by the decision-makers themselves. A number of these definitions and identifiers were suggested in the statements cited above. Recall, for example, the statements made concerning fishing catches (Japan and Peru), defense capabilities (Bulgaria and India), and food supplies (Japan and Peru). Other predictor variables have been selected primarily for constructing economic, political, and social profiles of states which accept and reject the international legal rules and principles — the dependent variables — being analyzed.[97]

On the basis of the preceding analysis, it has been hypothesized that those predictor variables which are intended objectively to define security and economic interests will give a maximum improvement in predicting values of the dependent variable. Of course, this general hypothesis has not yet been tested. Furthermore, the variables purported objectively to define security and economic capabilities and interests have not been used previously and there is no way to ascertain in advance which from among all the variables collected will provide the most reliable definitions of these capabilities and interests. Given the exploratory character of the study, the strategy adopted is to use the maximum number of predictor variables permitted by the program.[98]

CLAIMS PRIMARILY IN SUPPORT OF AN EXCLUSIVE INTEREST

SEA

TERRITORIAL SEA

TWELVE-MILE TERRITORIAL SEA

At the Second United Nations Conference on the Law of the Sea in 1960 the eighteen-power proposal would have permitted states to claim a terri-

torial sea of up to twelve miles. In plenary session the vote on this proposal
was 36 in favor, 39 against, and 13 abstentions.[99]

Expenditure on Defense as a Percentage of Gross National Product is the
single variable which explains the greatest proportion of variance in voting
on the eighteen-power proposal — a .464 reduction in prediction error. That
is, knowing what a state spends on defense as a percentage of its GNP explains 46 percent of the variance between states voting on the eighteen-
power proposal at the 1960 conference.

Within the first group (the total 121 states comprising the 1964 international political system), the next most explanatory predictor variables are
Military Personnel as a Percentage of Total Population (.409) and Areal
Grouping (.355). As hypothesized, the most explanatory variables are
generally those which objectively define security and economic capabilities
or interests, Areal Grouping being the only exception among the three
most explanatory variables in the first step of the analysis.

The first binary split is made on the most explanatory variable, Expenditure on Defense as a Percentage of Gross National Product (see below).
The 121 states are divided into two new groups on the basis of whether defense expenditure data are ascertained.

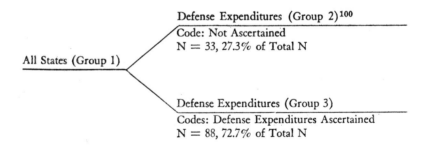

Defense Expenditures (Group 2)[100]

Code: Not Ascertained
N = 33, 27.3% of Total N

All States (Group 1)

Defense Expenditures (Group 3)
Codes: Defense Expenditures Ascertained
N = 88, 72.7% of Total N

In the analysis of Group 2, that is the thirty-three states for which Defense Expenditure data are not available, Date of Independence explains the
greatest proportion of the remaining variance (.553). Government Stability
(.499) and Former Colonial Ruler (.433) are the next most explanatory
variables in this group. Group 2 is divided, then, on the predictor Date of
Independence (see below). One of the new groups includes those states
within Group 2 which became independent after 1945 or whose date of independence is ambiguous; the other group is comprised of the states within
Group 2 which became independent between 1914 and 1945.

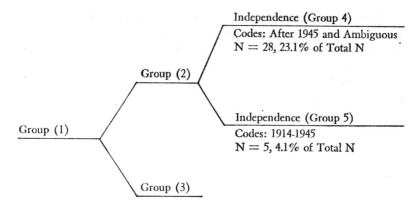

That data on defense expenditure were not available for the states included within Group 2 is a good indication of what kind of states these are. Data are generally not available for small, new underdeveloped states which have little or no self-defense capability. The explanatory power of the second step variables — Date of Independence, Governmental Stability, and Former Colonial Ruler — emphasizes this. And it may be recalled that these are the same kinds of states whose delegates identified economic, conservation, and security interests in support of an extended territorial sea at both the 1958 and 1960 conferences.

Group 4 splits on the Territorial Sea Claimed (1.00) — the next most explantory predictor is Military Personnel as a Percentage of Total Population (.309) (see below). One group is comprised of all states which claim not more than twelve miles and the other group is comprised of a state which claims in excess of twelve miles.

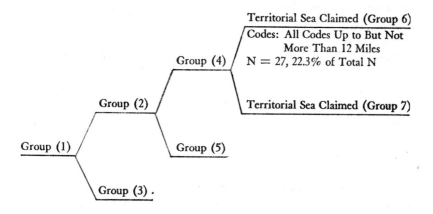

The binary split for Group 3, states for which Defense Expenditure data are available, occurs on the predictor Financial Status (.179) (see below). However, the split helps very little in prediction, primarily because one group consists of four states for which no Financial Status data are available. Military Personnel (.164) and Constitutional Status (.164) are only slightly less explanatory.

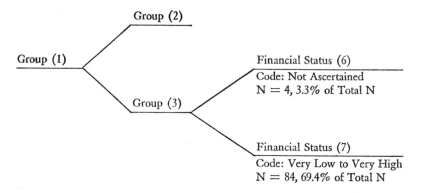

Successive splits are made on Constitutional Status, Fishing Activity, Independence, Aerial Grouping, and Former Colonial Ruler. However, none of these splits is particularly helpful because of the way in which the codes are grouped. In each successive split, it seems that a small number of states similar to those initially split into Group 2 are sorted out. While this seems to emphasize the correctness of that first binary split, it does not add significantly to the initial predictive capability.

It has been found that at the 1958 and 1960 conferences, economic, conservation, and security interests were stressed by both delegates favoring and opposing a twelve-mile territorial sea. Generally the delegates of young, small, underdeveloped states favored extension to that breadth while the delegates of relatively older, larger, more developed states generally opposed such an extension. Overall the AID analysis of the dependent variable Twelve-Mile Territorial Sea supports that analysis of the conference records. And, as expected, the single most explanatory variable is an objective definition of a security interest.[101]

SIX-MILE TERRITORIAL SEA

The following analysis of acceptance or rejection of a six-mile territorial sea is based on the vote in plenary session at the 1960 conference on the United States-Canadian proposal which provided for a six-mile territorial sea together with a six-mile contiguous zone. The vote on that proposal was

54 in favor, 28 against, and 5 abstentions.[102] Thirty-nine states are coded as not applicable, either because they were not represented at the conference or did not vote on this proposal.

As in the case of the eighteen-power proposal, the single variable which explains the greatest proportion of variance in voting on this proposal is Expenditure on Defense as a Percentage of Gross National Product — in this instance a .500 reduction in prediction error. Military Personnel as a Percentage of Total Population (.387) and Areal Grouping (.361) are the next most explanatory variables within this first group.

The split on Defense Expenditures places states with very low or not ascertained expenditures in one group and all other states in the second group (see below).

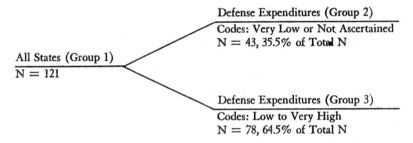

The most explanatory variable in Group 2 is Date of Independence (.537) (see below). Governmental Stability (.467), Former Colonial Ruler (.462), and Areal Grouping (.431) are next, and in that order. However, the meaning of this split is somewhat ambiguous since one of the new groups is comprised of states which gained their independence before the nineteenth century, after 1945, or whose date of independence is ambiguous; and the other group is comprised of states which gained their independence between 1800 and 1945. The remaining two splits, on Population Growth Rate and Territorial Sea Claimed, are equally as ambiguous.

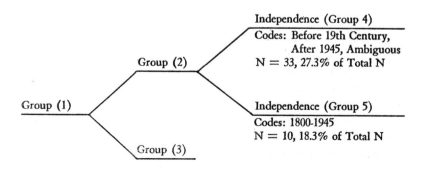

Splits from Group 3 seem more helpful. Group 3 splits on Areal Grouping (.215) (see below); the next most explanatory variable is Fishing Activity (.193). One of the new groups is states in Africa, East Europe, East Asia, and the Middle East; the other group includes the states in all the remaining areal groupings.

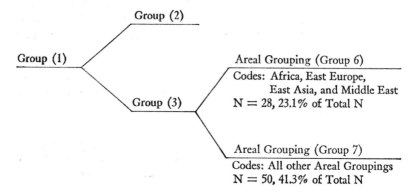

Group 6 in turn splits on the predictor Fishing Activity (.336) (see below) with Military Personnel as a Percentage of Total Population (.244) and Port Activity (.229) as the next most explanatory variables. States which are very active, not ascertained, or have no fishing activity are split into Group 8 and all others into Group 9.

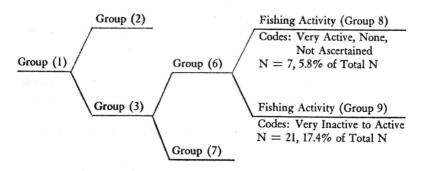

The results of the analysis of variance of the dependent variable Six-Mile Territorial Sea are very comparable to those obtained in the case of the Twelve-Mile Territorial Sea. That is, once again the single most explanatory variable is an objective definition of a security interest and when the remaining splits are interpretable at all they seem to be sorting states primarily into new, small, underdeveloped and relatively older, larger, and more developed categories. Overall, then, the AID analysis and the analysis of delegates statements appear to be consonant.

CONTIGUOUS ZONE

Seventy-eight states either have signed, ratified, or otherwise adhered to the 1958 Convention on the Territorial Sea and the Contiguous Zone and/or have made an unilateral claim to one or more special purpose contiguous zone. The AID analysis does not help in explaining the variation between these seventy-eight states and the forty-three states which apparently reject a contiguous sea zone rule. The most explanatory variable is Constitutional Status of Current Regime. One of the two groups which result from a split on this variable includes the fourteen states which were coded Not Ascertained; the other group is comprised of all other states.[103]

CONTINENTAL SHELF

Seventy states either have signed, ratified, or otherwise adhered to the 1958 Convention on the Continental Shelf and/or have made an unilateral claim to the adjacent continental shelf. The single predictor variable which explains the greatest proportion of variance in support of a rule concerning the continental shelf is Territorial Sea Claimed — a .519 reduction in prediction error (see below). Miles of Sea Coast (.519) is only slightly less explanatory, and Port Activity (.326) and Merchant Marine Fleet (.275) are the next most explanatory variables. Certainly the point is made and emphasized that knowing whether a state is a coastal state helps in explaining its position on a continental shelf rule.

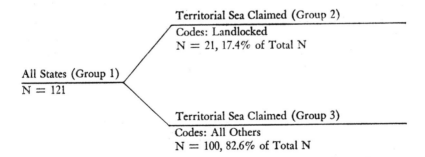

Territorial Sea Claimed (Group 2)
Codes: Landlocked
N = 21, 17.4% of Total N

All States (Group 1)
N = 121

Territorial Sea Claimed (Group 3)
Codes: All Others
N = 100, 82.6% of Total N

The second binary split is made in Group 3, that is, the group comprised of all coastal states. Areal Grouping is the single most explanatory variable (see below). One of the new groups is comprised of African, East Asian, East European, and Middle Eastern states; the second group includes the states in Group 3 from all other Areal Groupings. Areal Grouping provides a .224 reduction in prediction error with Westernization being only slightly less explanatory — a .222 reduction in prediction error.

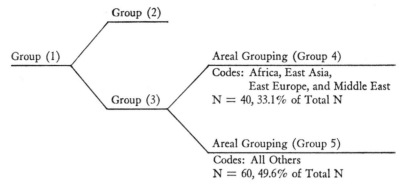

In this analysis there is altogether a .529 reduction in prediction. In short, in this case it does not add appreciably to predictive capability to go beyond a division of states into coastal and non-coastal categories.

AIR

TERRITORIAL AIRSPACE

One-hundred-seventeen states either have signed, ratified, or otherwise adhered to the 1944 Chicago Convention on Civil Aviation and/or have domestic legislation which asserts a claim either to comprehensive jurisdiction or sovereignty over superjacent airspace. Bloc Alignment is the single predictor variable which explains the greatest proportion of variance among states on this dependent variable — a reduction in prediction error of .261 (see below). It is well known, of course, that several Communist states have not accepted the Chicago convention, and, in fact, the split divides state into Communist and non-Communist groups. Of the fourteen Communist states, the total and international civil aviation activity of nine has not been ascertained. Only one of the remaining five states is even moderately active in either total or international civil aviation.

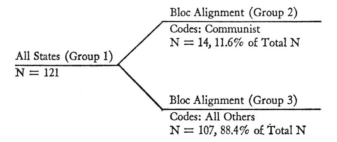

Support for a rule establishing state sovereignty in superjacent airspace is so widespread that the AID analysis of variance proceeds no further. That is, no further binary split is made since no other candidate group meets the established split eligibility criteria.

CLAIMS PRIMARILY IN SUPPORT OF AN INCLUSIVE INTEREST

SEA

HIGH SEAS

Two measures of acceptance of a rule or general principle concerning the freedom of the high seas are used in this analysis. The first is the support in plenary session at the 1958 conference for Articles 1 and 2 of the High Seas Convention; the second is whether a state has signed, ratified, or otherwise adhered to this convention.

Eighty-one states supported Articles 1 and 2 in plenary session at the 1958 conference. Since support for the principle is so widespread, there is no point in making a detailed analysis of the variance. However, it is of some interest to find that the first binary split is made on Defense Expenditure with a .509 reduction in prediction error. Areal Grouping (.484) and Military Personnel (.429) are the next most explanatory variables within Group 1.[104]

Sixty states either have signed, ratified, or otherwise adhered to the 1958 Convention on the High Seas. In explaining the difference between these sixty states and all others, the single most explanatory variable is Areal Grouping (see below). However, this variable reduces prediction error by only .139. The next most explanatory variable within Group 1 is Economic Development which reduces prediction error by .125.

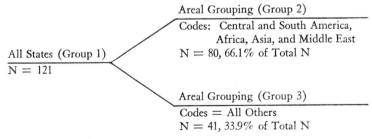

Areal Grouping (Group 2)
Codes: Central and South America,
        Africa, Asia, and Middle East
N = 80, 66.1% of Total N

All States (Group 1)
N = 121

Areal Grouping (Group 3)
Codes = All Others
N = 41, 33.9% of Total N

Group 2 is split on Constitutional Status of Current Regime (see below). Totalitarian states and those states either not ascertained or unascertainable comprise one group; all the other states in Group 2 comprise the other. Again the level of explanation is low, a .127 reduction in prediction error. Economic Development (.100) is the next most explanatory variable.

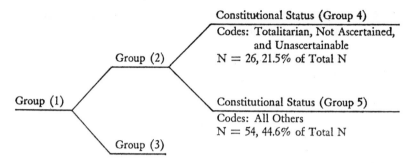

Within Group 4, Areal Grouping (.307) is the most explanatory variable (see below). One of the new groups includes Central and South African, East and Southeast Asian, Middle Eastern, and South American states. The other *group* is one Central American state.

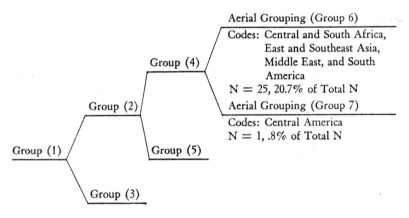

Group 5 splits on Territorial Sea Claimed (.185). Because of the code splits, however, this step is uninterpretable — one group unexplainably includes states which claim more than three but not more than six miles and landlocked states and the other group all other states. Successive splits on Military Personnel, Fishery Products (Smoked), and Defense Expenditures are also uninterpretable for the same reason. And the same problem is encountered on the other main branch of the tree diagram. That is, Group 3 splits on Miles of Sea Coast, but in an uninterpretable way since three of the codes grouped together are less than 100 miles, 1,000-1,499, and 1,500-1,999.

This AID analysis of a rule on the freedom of the high seas based on acceptance of the 1958 Convention on the High Seas does not add to predictive capability. It may be recalled that an economic interest was the basic interest in the high seas identified by delegates to the 1958 conference. The

AID analysis does not seem to support this; however, in at least three of the analysis steps Economic Development is the second most explanatory variable.

NATIONALITY AND REGISTRATION OF SHIPS

The following analysis of acceptance or rejection of rules concerning nationality and registration of ships is based on acceptance of the 1958 Convention on the High Seas and domestic legislation on nationality and registration. Eighty-one states either have signed, ratified, or otherwise adhered to the convention and/or have domestic legislation concerning nationality and registration of ships.

Defense Expenditure is the single most explanatory variable, providing a .243 reduction in prediction error (see below). Date of Independence is almost as explanatory (.241).

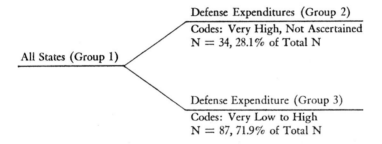

All States (Group 1)

Defense Expenditures (Group 2)
Codes: Very High, Not Ascertained
N = 34, 28.1% of Total N

Defense Expenditure (Group 3)
Codes: Very Low to High
N = 87, 71.9% of Total N

Group 2 splits on Constitutional Status (.309) (see below). The next most explanatory variables are Areal Grouping (.173) and Port Activity (.159). One of the two new groups is comprised of authoritarian and totalitarian states together with those states for which Constitutional Status is unascertainable. The other new group is comprised of ten states within which government is conducted with reference to recognized constitutional norms.

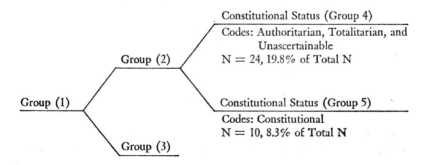

Group (1)

Group (2)

Group (3)

Constitutional Status (Group 4)
Codes: Authoritarian, Totalitarian, and Unascertainable
N = 24, 19.8% of Total N

Constitutional Status (Group 5)
Codes: Constitutional
N = 10, 8.3% of Total N

Within Group 3, the single most explanatory variable is Date of Independence (.169) (see below). States which gained their independence after 1945 or whose date of independence is ambiguous split into one group; states which gained their independence before 1945 comprise the second group. And Areal Grouping (.137) is the next most explanatory variable in Group 3.

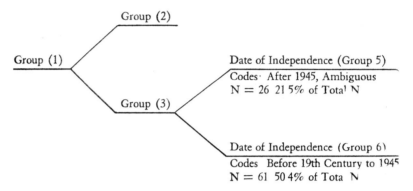

The single most explanatory variable, then, is one objective definition of security. However, the fundamental interests which states seem to have in rules concerning nationality and registration are economic and humanitarian. Defense Expenditure in this case seems then to be used as an identifier of an economic, political, or social profile. Recall that within Group 1, Date of Independence reduces prediction error by only .002 less than does Defense Expenditure. Moreover, the most explanatory variables in both Groups 2 and 3 are primarily identifiers of political or social profiles — Constitutional Status and Date of Independence.[105]

SAFETY AT SEA

Two indications of acceptance of rules concerning safety at sea are used in this analysis. The first measure of rule acceptance is whether a state has signed, ratified, or otherwise adhered to the 1948 and/or 1960 Safety of Life at Sea Convention — seventy-five states have. The second measure is whether a state has signed, ratified, or otherwise adhered to the 1929 Load Line Convention as modified in 1938 and 1957. Seventy-three states have accepted the latter rules.

1948 AND/OR 1960 SAFETY OF LIFE AT SEA CONVENTIONS

In the case of the 1948 and 1960 conventions, the single most explanatory variable is Merchant Marine Fleet (see below). This predictor variable reduces prediction error by .232. Next in order of explanatory power are Net Food Supplies (.206), Economic Development (.189), and Gross National Product (.188). All these variables seem to be primarily descriptive of an economic profile of the states being categorized.

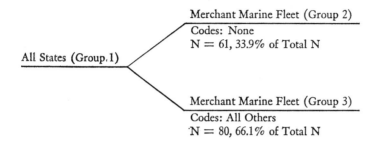

Merchant Marine Fleet (Group 2)
Codes: None
N = 61, 33.9% of Total N

All States (Group 1)

Merchant Marine Fleet (Group 3)
Codes: All Others
N = 80, 66.1% of Total N

Group 2 splits on the predictor Former Colonial Ruler. Former British colonies and the former colonies of other than France and Spain comprise the other. This knowledge does not add appreciably to predictive capability. Group 3 splits on Governmental Stability (see below). (Net Food Supplies is almost equally explanatory — a reduction in prediction error of .188). The moderately stable and unstable states comprise one group and all other states from Group 3 comprise the other.

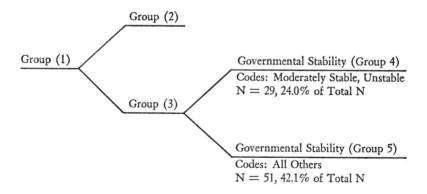

Group (2)

Group (1)

Group (3)

Governmental Stability (Group 4)
Codes: Moderately Stable, Unstable
N = 29, 24.0% of Total N

Governmental Stability (Group 5)
Codes: All Others
N = 51, 42.1% of Total N

An uninterpretable split in Group 4 is made on Date of Independence — for example, states which became independent between 1800 and 1913, and after 1945 comprise one group. The split in Group 5 is made on the predictor International Financial Status (.309) (see below). The next most explanatory variables are Miles of Sea Coast (.299) and Economic Development (.235).

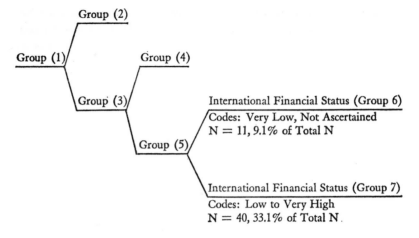

There is widespread support for the safety at sea rules embodied in the 1948 and 1960 Conventions on Safety of Life at Sea. Since support is widespread it is especially difficult to distinguish differences between states which accept and those which reject the safety at sea rules. That this is the case is evident in the small reduction of prediction error made in each of the successive analysis steps just described. As hypothesized, the most explanatory variable is an objective definition of an economic interest in the sea, and socalled profile variables are explanatory at a secondary level. In general therefore, the AID analysis tends to support findings based on the earlier analysis of decision-makers' statements.

THE 1929 LOAD LINE CONVENTION

The AID analysis of acceptance or rejection of safety of sea rules on the basis of the Load Line Convention generally follows the pattern established in the analysis of the 1948 and 1960 Safety of Life at Sea Conventions. The single most explanatory prediction in the case of the Load Line Convention is Security Forces: Navy (total vessels) (.362). Again, as with the 1948 and 1960 conventions, the AID analysis builds economic, political, and social profiles which tend generally to support the findings of the earlier analysis of what decision-makers say their interest in safety at sea rules is.

AIR

NATIONALITY AND REGISTRATION OF AIRCRAFT

One-hundred-fifteen states either have signed, ratified, or otherwise adhered to the 1944 Chicago convention and/or have domestic legislation providing for registration and/or nationality of aircraft. It has not been possible to ascertain whether the remaining three states — East Germany, Hungary, and North Korea — have domestic legislation, however, neither of the three has accepted the Chicago convention.

The most explanatory variable within Group 1 is Bloc Alignment (.263) (see below). This split is identical to that which occurred when rules concerning sovereignty in territorial airspace were analyzed. It may be recalled that the extent of civil aviation activity of nine of the fourteen Communist states has not been ascertained and that only one Communist state is even moderately active in either total or international civil aviation.

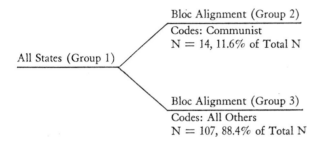

Bloc Alignment (Group 2)
Codes: Communist
N = 14, 11.6% of Total N

All States (Group 1)

Bloc Alignment (Group 3)
Codes: All Others
N = 107, 88.4% of Total N

Group 3 splits on the predictor Port Activity (.058), one of the new groups being comprised of landlocked states and the other group of all other states included within Group 3. Many of the land-locked non-Communist states are small, and relatively inactive in civil aviation: Afghanistan, Austria, Bolivia, Burma, Central African Republic, Chad, Laos, Luxembourg, Malawi, Mali, Uganda, Upper Volta, Uruguay, and Zambia fit into this category. In fact, Switzerland is the only landlocked non-Communist state active in international civil aviation. Both Bloc Alignment and Port Activity, then, are apparently in this case measures of aviation activity.

LIABILITY

Both the 1929 Warsaw and the 1952 Rome conventions are used as measures of the extent of acceptance of rules or principles of liability in international air law. Eighty-six states either have signed, ratified, or otherwise adhered to the 1929 Warsaw convention as modified by the 1955 Hague Protocol; only thirty-eight states have signed, ratified, or otherwise adhered to the 1952 Rome Convention on Damage Caused by Foreign Aircraft to Third Parties on the Surface.

When the Warsaw convention is used as the basis of analysis, the single variable which explains the greatest proportion of variance is Areal Grouping (.222) (see below). Former Colonial Ruler, the next most explanatory predictor variable within Group 1, reduces prediction error by .174. One of the two Areal Groupings is comprised of Central and South American, Caribbean, and Middle Eastern states; the other group includes the Group 1 states from all other Aerial Groupings.

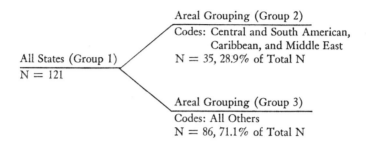

Areal Grouping (Group 2)
Codes: Central and South American,
        Caribbean, and Middle East
N = 35, 28.9% of Total N

All States (Group 1)
N = 121

Areal Grouping (Group 3)
Codes: All Others
N = 86, 71.1% of Total N

Within Group 2, the most explanatory variable is Total Aviation Activity which reduces prediction error by .384 (see below). The next most explanatory variables within Group 2 are Per Capita Gross National Product (.243), International Aviation Activity (.218), and Air Power (.218). Group 3 includes states which are inactive in aviation or whose activity in aviation has not been ascertained; Group 4 includes states which are active, moderately active, and very inactive. Of course, it is not at all clear why very inactive states are included in Group 4. However, the other group which results from the split, Group 3, seems to be a homogeneous grouping. There does, then, seem to be some explanatory power in a predictor variable which objectively identifies an interest in civil aviation. It is somewhat unexpected, however, to find that Areal Grouping is the best initial identifier of this kind of interest.[106]

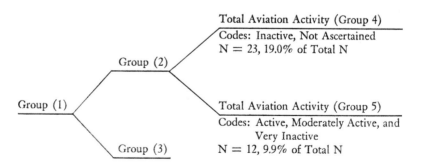

Total Aviation Activity (Group 4)
Codes: Inactive, Not Ascertained
N = 23, 19.0% of Total N

Group (2)

Group (1)

Total Aviation Activity (Group 5)
Codes: Active, Moderately Active, and
        Very Inactive
N = 12, 9.9% of Total N

Group (3)

DEVIATIONS OR EXCEPTIONS TO EXCLUSIVE OR INCLUSIVE AUTHORITY

SEA

INNOCENT PASSAGE

Fifty-two states have either signed, ratified, or otherwise adhered to the 1958 Convention on the Territorial Sea and the Contiguous Zone. The basis for this analysis for acceptance or rejection of a rule on innocent passage through the territorial sea is whether a state has signed, ratified, or otherwise adhered to this convention.

The single most explanatory predictor variable is Areal Grouping (.137) (see below). One of the groups which results from the split is comprised of African, Central and South American, East and Southeastern Asian, and Middle Eastern states; the other group includes the states from all other Areal Groupings.[107]

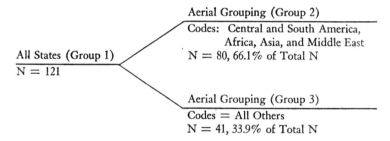

Aerial Grouping (Group 2)

Codes: Central and South America,
Africa, Asia, and Middle East
N = 80, 66.1% of Total N

All States (Group 1)
N = 121

Aerial Grouping (Group 3)

Codes = All Others
N = 41, 33.9% of Total N

The most explanatory variable within Group 3 is Fishery Products (Fish Meals and Solubles) (.277) (see below). States which are small producers comprise one group, all other Group 3 states comprise the other. Group 7 divides on the predictor Date of Independence, and one of the resulting groups divides on Security Forces: Air Force. Neither split adds to predictive capability, again because of the way in which codes are grouped.

In general, then, the AID analysis of rules concerning innocent passage through the territorial sea is unproductive. No appreciable increase in capability to predict rule acceptance or rejection is gained and what decision-makers say their reasons are for accepting a right of innocent passage remain the best indication of why these rules are or are not acceptable.

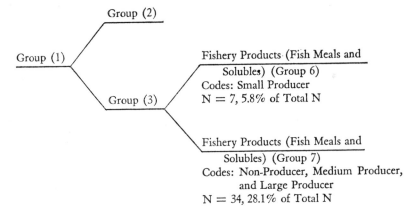

Group (2)

Group (1)

Group (3)

Fishery Products (Fish Meals and
Solubles) (Group 6)
Codes: Small Producer
N = 7, 5.8% of Total N

Fishery Products (Fish Meals and
Solubles) (Group 7)
Codes: Non-Producer, Medium Producer,
and Large Producer
N = 34, 28.1% of Total N

AIR

INNOCENT PASSAGE

One hundred nine states have signed, ratified, or otherwise adhered to the 1944 Chicago Convention on Civil Aviation; seventy states have signed, ratified, or otherwise adhered to the International Air Services Transit Agreement. Acceptance of one or both of these conventions is used here as a measure of the extent of applicability of rules concerning innocent passage through territorial airspace.

The results of the AID analysis of variance in this case is almost identical to those obtained when rules concerning sovereignty in territorial airspace and nationality and registration of aircraft were analyzed. That is, the single most explanatory variable when the analysis is based on acceptance of the Chicago convention is Bloc Alignment (.554) (see below). The next most explanatory variables within Group 1 are Areal Grouping (.397) and Constitutional Status (.339).

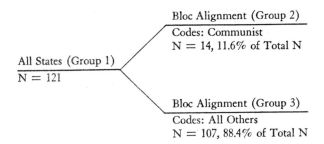

Bloc Alignment (Group 2)
Codes: Communist
N = 14, 11.6% of Total N

All States (Group 1)
N = 121

Bloc Alignment (Group 3)
Codes: All Others
N = 107, 88.4% of Total N

Group 3 splits on Port Activity (.117), one of the new groups being comprised of landlocked states and the other group of all other states included within Group 3. This, of course, is identical to what occurred in the analysis of the nationality and registration of aircraft. Again, as in that case, Bloc Alignment and Port Activity are apparently measures of aviation activity.[108]

CONCLUSIONS

The use of the AID program has been exploratory in this analysis of variance in rule acceptance and rejection. One consequence is that the findings are tentative and suggestive rather than conclusive. Several of the problems encountered have been indicated in the discussion above. For example, the findings make it quite obvious that a number of refinements will have to be made before the desired level of explanatory power and predictive capability can be obtained. Codes will have to be reconsidered in an attempt to make distinctions between groupings more interpretable. And it will be possible, on the basis of this exploratory use of AID, to be more selective in sorting out which predictor variables to use in each individual analysis of a particular rule. That is, not only may fewer predictors be used, but, as has been demonstrated, those which are used can be better focused for the legal problem area being analyzed.

Despite these limitations, however, the overall results of the AID analysis tend to support the findings obtained from the analysis of the records of various international conferences. In the analysis of the records of the 1958 and 1960 Conferences on the Law of the Sea, it was found that delegates emphasize conservation, economic, and security interests when discussing the breadth of the territorial sea. Generally delegates from young, small, underdeveloped states advocate a broader territorial sea than do delegates from the relatively older, larger, and more developed states. In the AID analysis of both the six- and twelve-mile territorial sea proposals, the single most explanatory variable is an objective indicator of security capabilities. Moreover, at each successive step in the AID analysis, states are divided into young, small, underdeveloped and relatively older, larger, and more developed categories.

Bloc Alignment is the single most explanatory variable in the AID analysis of: (1) acceptance of state sovereignty in territorial airspace; (2) nationality and registration of aircraft; and (3) innocent passage through territorial airspace. However, in this instance Bloc Alignment appears to be primarily an indication of extent of civil aviation activity rather than an ideological or political categorization. It has not been possible to ascertain the civil aviation activity of nine of fourteen Communist states, and only one of the remaining five is even moderately active in either total or international civil aviation (see the analyses of these three problem areas above).

Extent of civil aviation activity seems, then, to be a useful indicator in clarifying why states accept or reject rules concerning civil aviation activity.

Merchant Marine Fleet is the predictor variable which explains the greatest proportion of variance in safety at sea rules. Moreover, economic indicators are the next most explanatory variables. These findings are congruent with the results of the analysis of conference records.

The AID analyses of the other selected air and sea law rules are less productive. In the case of support for a rule or general principle concerning the freedom of the high seas, Defense Expenditure is the most explanatory variable. However, at the 1958 conference, economic interests were the most frequently identified interests in discussions of the freedom of the high seas. And in at least three steps in the AID analysis, Economic Development is the second most explanatory variable. It is quite possible, then, that, in this instance, Defense Expenditure is an indicator of economic status.

A similar ambiguity exists in the AID analysis of rules concerning nationality and registration of ships. Again the single most explanatory variable is Defense Expenditure. Yet, the fundamental interest which decision-makers identify in connection with rules regulating nationality and registration are economic and humanitarian.

The most unproductive analyses deal with contiguous zones and the continental shelf. In the case of contiguous zones, the results are totally uninterpretable; and in the case of the continental shelf, the greatest proportion of variance is explained by knowing whether a state borders the sea or is landlocked.

It is evident, on the basis of this analysis, that AID analyses of rules concerning the territorial sea, nationality and registration of aircraft, innocent passage through territorial airspace, and safety at sea, in particular, illustrate that the basic capabilities and interests which are identified by national decision-makers can be objectively defined. There is, of course, a need to refine these objective definitions, but finding that these interests can be objectively defined with any degree of reliability demonstrates the feasibility of using an analysis of variance as an approach in explaining and/or predicting rule acceptance and rejection.

SUMMARY

When particular rules are formulated to regulate activities within the air and sea environments, decision-makers seem to attempt to protect or enhance economic, conservation, humanitarian, and/or security interests. Which particular interest or which combination of interests must be protected or enhanced as a precondition of rule acceptance or rejection varies with the particular activity and/or area for which rules are being formulated. In general, however, economic and security seem to be the most pervasive interests.

The interests which decision-makers identify can be objectively defined in terms of capability measures or indicators. And the tentative findings, in an analysis of variance, are that some explanatory and predictive capability can be achieved by using these objective definitions of interests as predictors of rule acceptance or rejection. However, it must be emphasized that these findings are tentative and suggestive and the use of the AID variance reduction routine must be refined considerably before a significant and reliable explanatory and predictive capability can be achieved.

NOTES

1. While most social science research is clearly nonexperimental, the proponents of simulation contend that theirs is a quasi-experimental method. See, for example, Richard C. Snyder's argument in Harold Guetzkow, et al., *Simulation in Social Science: Readings* (Englewood Cliffs: Prentice-Hall, Inc., 1962). The contention is that simulation more closely approaches the laboratory methods of the natural sciences than does any other contemporary social science research method. (Of course, the crucial question is whether properties and behavior of the "real object" can be inferred from the simulation.) This writer knows of no similar claim made for any other technique or method being used by contemporary social scientists.

2. *Models of Man* (New York: John Wiley and Sons, 1957) and *Causal Interferences in Nonexperimental Research* (Chapel Hill: University of North Carolina Press, 1964).

3. Ibid, p. 14. Blalock makes a number of assumptions in addition to those relating to the selection of variables. For example, in his system of simultaneous linear equations, he must make an assumption as to the direction of causation. He chooses to use a recursive system, i.e., he rules out two-way causation. See further the work of both Simon and Blalock for details on how social scientists may approach the question of causation with a rather high degree of system and rigor.

This writer is indebted to Professors Phillip Converse and Donald Stokes for even his very limited understanding of the complexities of causation. One of the high points of graduate training was the opportunity to attend the Inter-University Consortium courses conducted by Professors Converse and Stokes in the summer of 1965.

4. Ibid., p. 15.

5. On motivation as used by political scientists, see, for example, Gabriel Almond, et al., *The Appeals of Communism* (Princeton: Princeton University Press, 1954). For an interesting application of this approach, see Jorgen Scott Rasmussen, *Retrenchment and Revival: A Study of the Contemporary British Liberal Party* (Tucson: The University of Arizona Press, 1964), Part II, pp. 173-273.

6. Jurisdiction in such matters as customs, fiscal matters, immigration, and sanitation appears to have been accepted without serious question. In any case, these matters were mentioned infrequently.

7. See United Nations Conference on the Law of the Sea, *Official Records, 2*, op. cit., p. 36; and 3, op. cit., pp. 25-26; and Second United Nations Conference on the Law of the Sea, *Official Records, Summary Records of Plenary Meetings of the Committee of the Whole*, op. cit., p. 45. These basic points were made by the United States Delegation at both conferences.

Shipping safety was also stressed by Dean. He maintained that

> many landmarks still used for visual piloting by small craft . . . [are] not visible at a range of twelve miles; only 20% of the world's lighthouses . . . [have] a range exceeding that distance; radar navigation . . . [is] of only marginal utility beyond twelve miles; and many vessels (which frequently . . . [do] not wish to enter the territorial sea) . . . [do] not carry sufficient cable or appropriate equipment to anchor at the depths normally found outside the twelve-mile limit (United Nations Conference on the Law of the Sea, *Official Records*, 3, op. cit., p. 26)

8. Second United Nations Conference on the Law of the Sea, *Official Records, Summary Records of Plenary Meetings and of Meetings of the Committee of the Whole*, op. cit., p. 73.

9. Idem.

10. Ibid., p. 57. France and Italy made similar claims, ibid., pp. 24 and 64. The French delegate also argued that the proposal for a twelve-mile territorial sea or a zone of exclusive fishing rights out to twelve miles did not take into account the contribution which distant-water fishing states make in supplying the world's rapidly increasing demand for food (idem.).

11. For 1958, see United Nations Conference on the Law of the Sea, *Official Records*, 3, op. cit.; p. 60 (Australia); p. 51 (Belgium); p. 51 (Canada); p. 172 (West Gemrany); p. 21 (Greece); p. 24 (Japan); p. 28 (Liberia); p. 11 (Netherlands); p. 19-20 (New Zealand); p. 50 (Pakistan); p. 57 (Paraguay); p. 183 (Portugal); p. 136 (Sweden); p. 46 (Switzerland); and p. 104 (United Kingdom). For 1960, see Second United Nations Conference on the Law of the Sea, *Official Records, Summary Records of Plenary Meetings and of Meetings of the Committee of the Whole*, op. cit.: pp. 15 and 82 (Australia); p. 73 (West Germany); p. 72 (Japan); and pp. 56-67 (United Kingdom).

It should be noted that certain of these states did favor certain exclusive fishing rights for coastal states. The Canadian delegate, for example, clearly favored such a right. An extension of fishing rights generally was preferred to an extension of the territorial sea itself.

12. The three which do not possess such a special interest are New Zealand, Paraguay, and Switzerland. Paraguay and Switzerland are landlocked.

13. Second United Nations Conference on the Law of the Sea, *Official Records, Committee of the Whole, Verbatim Records of the General Debate* (United Nations: United Nations, 1960) (U.N. Doc. No. A/Conf. 19/9), p. 190.

14. Idem.

15. Second United Nations Conference on the Law of the Sea, *Official Records, Summary Records of Plenary Meetings and of Meetings of the Committee of the Whole*, op. cit., p. 25.

16. Ibid., p. 102.

17. Idem.

18. Idem.

19. Ibid., p. 18.

20. Ibid., p. 48. See also United Nations Conference on the Law of the Sea, *Official Records*, 5 (United Nations: United Nations, 1958) (U.N. Doc. No. A/Conf. 13/41), passim. This is the record of the Third Committee, the committee which considered fishing and conservation of living resources on the high seas.

21. Three of the 36 states which mentioned these interests are landlocked. Three claim a territorial sea of three miles. Nine claim more than three miles but not more than six miles. Fifteen claim more than six but not more than twelve miles, and five claim more than twelve miles. One, the Philippines, makes a special claim as an archipelago. Seventeen of the 36 possess a special interest in the law of the sea as such an interest is objectively defined in Chapter III.

In addition to the statements already cited, see, for 1958, United Nations Conference on the Law of the Sea, *Official Records*, 3, op. cit.: p. 122 (Burma); pp. 27-28 (Ceylon); p. 33 (Chile); p. 48 (Colombia); p. 56 (Costa Rica); p. 62 (Ecuador); p. 63 (Hungary); p. 59 (Iceland); p. 14 (Indonesia); p. 34 (Israel); p. 18 (Jordan); p. 44 (South Korea); p. 53 (Libya); p. 34 (Romania); p. 30 (Spain); p. 41 (Turkey); pp. 31 and 106 (the Soviet Union); p. 22 (Uruguay); p. 23 (Venezuela); p. 53 (Vietnam); and p. 16 (Yeman). For 1960, see Second United Nations Conference on the Law of the Sea, *Official Records, Summary Records of Plenary Meetings of the Committee of the Whole*, op. cit.: p. 101 (Albania); p. 91 (Argentina); pp. 25 and 48 (Bulgaria); p. 108 (Ecuador); p. 108 (Ethiopia); pp. 92 and 135 (Ghana); pp. 26 and 79-81 (Iceland); pp. 76-77 (India); p. 100 (Israel); p. 85 (Jordan); p. 103 (South Korea); p. 84 (Norway); p. 46 (Panama); pp. 17, 67, and 149 (Peru); p. 51 (Philippines); p. 148 (Spain); p. 112 (Sudan); p. 111 (Tunisia); p. 39 (the Soviet Union); p. 15 (Uruguay); and pp. 42-43 (Vietnam).

22. United Nations Conference on the Law of the Sea, *Official Records*, 4 (United Nations: United Nations, 1958) (U.N. Doc. No. A/Conf. 13/42), pp. 8, 11, and 71 (West Germany) and p. 14 (Japan).

23. Ibid., p. 14.

24. Ibid., p. 8. Both West Germany and Japan accepted the inevitability of the majority view prevailing and acted to help to shape the resulting Convention on the Continental Shelf. See, for example, p. 60 and passim.

25. See, for example, ibid.: p. 48 (Argentina); p. 13 (Ceylon); p. 16 (Chile); pp. 25 and 74 (Cuba); pp. 14-15 (Mexico); p. 8 (Philippines); p. 20 (the Soviet Union); and p. 21 (Venezuela).

26.   See, for example, ibid.: p. 4 (Nationalist China); p. 3 (Sweden); and the general discussion pp. 68 and 71-72. See also United Nations Conference on the Law of the Sea, *Official Records,* 2, op. cit., pp. 13-15. It may be recalled that in analyzing the rules on the continental shelf in Chapter III, it was determined that while the definitions included in the conventional rule are universally recognized, they apparently are not universally binding.

27.   See United Nations Conference on the Law of the Sea, *Official Records,* 6, op. cit., passim. The delimitation question in this instance was to determine the extent of the continental shelf which could be claimed by establishing a limiting depth of superjacent waters. Proposals ranged from 200 to 1,000 meters or to a depth permitting exploration or exploitation. The conventional provision eventually accepted by the conference was a depth of 200 meters or to a depth permitting exploitation.

28.   Ibid., p. 40.

29.   Ibid., p. 11.

30.   Idem.

31.   Ibid., p. 34.

32.   Ibid., p. 24. On these two interests generally, see ibid.: p. 2 (Argentina); p. 29 (Canada); p. 13 (Ceylon); p. 16 (Chile); pp. 9, 10, and 40 (Colombia); pp. 25 and 74 (Cuba); p. 43 (Guatemala); p. 28 (Iceland); p. 14 (Lebanon); p. 11 (Peru); p. 8 (Philippines); p. 7 (Spain); p. 20 (the Soviet Union); p. 19 (United States); pp. 5 and 34 (Uruguay); pp. 21 and 56 (Venezuela); and p. 11 (Yugoslavia.)

Some delegates wished to include discussions of natural resources in the superjacent waters. See statements by the delegates of Peru and Iceland, for example (ibid., pp. 11 and 28). In this sense, the conservation interest of coastal states was considered by the committee.

33.   The wealth of the sea and the continental shelf are themselves fascinating subjects. One of the most complete works on the subject is John L. Mero's *The Mineral Resources of the Sea* (Amsterdam, London, and New York: Elsevier Publishing Co., 1965). Mero says that the oil potential of the continental shelf of the world is approximately equal to that of the land area. He states that in 1964 non-living materials were being extracted from the sea at an annual rate of about $1¼ billion. Sodium chloride, magnesium metal, magnesium compounds, bromine, potash, soda, sulphur, and gypsum are now being extracted from the sea. Phosphorite and manganese nodules are found in abundance on the continental shelves of numerous states. Diamonds are being taken from the shelf off Southwest Africa, iron sands are being dredged in Japan, tin concentrates are being dredged off the coasts of Indonesia, Thailand, and Malaysia, and coal is being mined from under the sea in a number of locations including Nova Scotia, Peru, and Great Britain. Of course, petroleum is being taken from the shelf in several parts of the world.

See further the comprehensive four-part series in *Engineering and Mining Journal,* 146 (May, June, July, and August, 1965). In Part IV of this series, "The Ocean: Mining's Newest Frontier," [(August, 1965), pp. 79-96], H. D. Hess states that "it is estimated that oceans contain more than 50-quadrillion metric tons of dissolved minerals including virtually all the natural chemical elements known to man" (p. 80). These non-living riches are, of course, in addition to the living resources. In 1964, a total fishing catch of more than 51 million metric tons was reported to the United Nations.

National decision-makers are — and were in 1958 — becoming increasingly aware of the potential wealth *in* the adjacent sea and *on* and *in* the adjacent continental shelf. Existing or soon to be available technological developments make it possible to liberate greater proportions of this wealth. Little wonder that decision-makers act to protect or to enhance what they perceive to be their conomic interests in "their" adjacent sea and shelf areas.

34.   United States Department of State, *Proceedings of the International Civil Aviation Conference, Chicago, Illinois, November 1 - December 7, 1944,* (Washington: Government Printing Office, 1948), p. 55.

35.   Ibid., p. 83. D. G. Sullivan, New Zealand, also spoke in favor of international ownership. See pp. 77-80.

36.   Ibid., p. 84.

37.   Ibid., p. 75.

38.   Idem.

39   Ibid., p. 568.

40.   Ibid., p. 64.

41.   It should be recalled that when the Chicago conference was held, World War II was still being fought. At that time the United States was the only state which possessed a large fleet of transport aircraft which could be immediately put into civil air transport service when the war was ended. A number of states, and notably the United Kingdom, seemed to fear United States domination of post-war civil aviation; this despite the offer of the United States government to provide aircraft to those states which required them in order to develop peaceful civil air transport services.

42.   Ibid., p. 74. Hahnemann Guimaraes, chairman of the Brazilian Delegation, spoke in favor of the freedom of transit. Yet he, too, identified the need for the overflown state to be empowered to safeguard its soverign rights ". . . as a guaranty to their political, economic, and military interests" (p. 85). See the *Proceedings* of the Chicago conference passim. Although the records contained therein are extensive, fewer policy position statements are recorded there than in comparable records of the 1958 and 1960 Conferences on the Law of the Sea.

43. See, for example, United Nations Conference on the Law of the Sea, *Official Records*, 4 (United Nations: United Nations, 1958) (U.N. Doc. No. Conf. 13/40): p. 13 (Australia); p. 25 (Nationalist China); p. 24 (Czechoslovakia); p. 5 (Denmark); p. 11 (Japan); p. 23 (Nepal); p. 6 (Poland); p. 20 (Portugal); p. 16 (Romania); p. 21 (Tunisia); p. 9 (the Soviet Union); p. 31 (United Arab Republic); p. 3 (United Kingdom); p. 15 (United States); and p. 8 (Yugoslavia).

44. Ibid., p. 20.

45. Ibid., p. 21.

46. Ibid., p. 31.

47. Ibid., p. 3.

48. Ibid, p. 15.

49. Ibid., p. 26.

50. Ibid.: p. 40 (Peru) and p. 31 (Chile).

51. Ibid., p. 31. In part, this is an argument based on a conservation interest. See the section on the territorial sea and contiguous zones. See also the general debate in the First and Third Committees.

52. See United Nations Conference on the Law of the Sea, *Official Records*, 3, op. cit., pp. 25-26, for the United States' delegate's statement on economic effects.

53. See United Nations Conference on the Law of the Sea, *Official Records*, 4, op. cit., passim, especially pp. 28-30 and pp. 60-67. The delegates of Panama and Liberia did argue, apparently not persuasively, that it is a contradiction to say that each state is authorized to establish its own conditions for registering or granting its nationality and to say at the same time that such registration and/or nationality need not be recognized in the absence of a "genuine link." See pp. 29-30 and 62-63 (Panama) and p. 22 (Liberia).

54. Ibid.: p. 13 (Australia); p. 25 (Nationalist China); p. 5 (Denmark); p. 10 (Japan); p. 22 (Liberia); p. 3 (Netherlands); p. 8 (Pakistan); p. 64 (Sweden); p. 4 (United Kingdom); and p. 64 (United States).

55. Ibid., p. 64.

56. Ibid., p. 3.

57. Ibid., p. 25.

58. Ibid., p. 5.

59. Conference on Safety of Life at Sea, IMCO/SAFCON/Plenary/S.R. 7, 17 June 1960, p. 3. The mimeographed records of the 1960 conference were made available by the United States Maritime Administration.

60. Ibid., p. 5.

61. International Conference on Safety of Life at Sea, April 23 - June 10, 1948, *Report of the United States Delegation Including Final Act and Related Documents* (Washington: Department of State, Publication Number 3282, 1948), p. 1.

62. PIO Division, United States Coast Guard Headquarters, Washington, D. C., News Release No. 23-60, 15 July 1960. This release is among the records of the 1960 conference collected by the U. S. Maritime Administration.

63. International Conference on Safety of Life at Sea, April 23 - June 10, 1948, *Report of the United States Delegation,* op. cit., p. 17.

64. International Civil Aviation Organization, *Conference on Private International Air Law, Rome, September-October, 1952,* (Montreal: International Civil Aviation Organization, 1953) (Doc. 7379-LC/134), p. 123.

65. Idem. A similar position was taken by the delegate from Argentina. See ibid., p. 126.

66. Ibid., p. 132. See also the statement made by the Netherlands' delegate, p. 128.

67. Idem. See also the statements of the Australian delegate (p. 15) and the French delegate (p. 126).

68. Ibid., p. 13.

69. Idem. See also the statements made by the representatives of the International Union of Aviation Insurers (p. 14) and the International Air Transport Association (p. 82).

70. Ibid., p. 14.

71. Ibid., p. 126. Absolute liability was favored also by Australia. See p. 15.

72. International Civil Aviation Organization, *International Conference on Private Air Law, The Hague, September,* 1955, 1 (Montreal: International Civil Aviation Organization) (Doc. 7686-LC/140). p. 162.

73. See, for example, ibid.: p. 175 (France); p. 173 (Greece); p. 166 (Ireland); p. 187 (New Zeland); pp. 165-166 (Norway); p. 174 (Venezuela). Of course, not all of these delegations favored the large increases advocated by the United States. However, almost without exception these delegations recognized the changes in aviation safety, etc., which the United States delegate had referred to in his appeal for larger amounts.

74. Ibid., pp. 169-170.

75. Ibid., p. 166.

76. Ibid., p. 167. See also p. 274 (Costa Rica); p. 168 (Hungary); p. 169 (Mexico); and p. 177 (Spain).

77. See again the section of Chapter 3 on innocent passage.

78. See, for example, United Nations Conference on the Law of the Sea, *Official Records, 3, op. cit.*: p. 18 (Afghanistan); p. 34 (Dominican Republic); p. 13 (Guatemala); and p. 28 (Liberia). See more generally, ibid., pp. 75-88, 93-103, and 111-118.

79. Ibid., p. 32.

80. Ibid., p. 9.

81. Ibid., p. 20.

82. At this point in the debate, Dean was arguing a case against an extension of the territorial sea. He contended that the right of innocent passage would not satisfactorily substitute for freedom of the high seas, for the right of passage is ". . . in itself . . . a recognition of the fact that the freedom of navigation . . . [is restricted by the coastal State's sovereignty over the territorial sea" (ibid., p. 25)].

Not all delegates agreed on the nature of the right. Some, Yugoslavia and Bulgaria, for example, argued that the coastal state's sovereignty is the rule and the right of innocent passage the exception (pp. 23 and 58). Others, United Kingdom and Bolivia, for example, maintained that the right of innocent passage is an independent right and not subordinate to any other right in any way (pp. 9 and 16). Article 16 of the Convention on the Territorial Sea and the Contiguous Zone seems to reflect the former rather than the latter viewpoint.

Implicit in all the debate was the notion that the right of innocent passage already was well protected by customary international law. In fact, as Myres S. McDougal has indicated to me, the conventional rule may introduce some ambiguities.

83. Ibid., p. 46. Recalling the *Corfu Channel Case* (I.C.J. *Reports*, 1949) one might have predicted Albania's position.

84. Idem.

85. Idem.

86. Ibid., p. 24. On these interests in general, see ibid.: pp. 130-131 (Albania); p. 61 (Cuba); p. 13 (Italy); p. 18 (Jordan); p. 44 (South Korea); pp. 11 and 128 (Netherlands); p. 34 (Romania); pp. 139-130 (Saudi Arabia); p. 129 (Turkey); p. 32 (the Soviet Union); and p. 129 (United Kingdom).

87. United States Department of State, *Proceedings of the International Civil Aviation Conference, Chicago*, 1, op. cit., p. 56.

88. Ibid., p. 76.

89. Idem.

90. Ibid., p. 75.

91. Ibid., p. 85.

92. Ibid., p. 65.

93. See Harold and Margaret Sprout, *Man-Milieu Relationships in the Context of International Politics* (Princeton: Center of International Politics, 1956), and their "Environmental Factors in the Study of International Politics," *International Politics and Foreign Policy: A Reader in Research and Theory* (New York: The Free Press, 1961), ed. James N. Rosenau, pp. 106-119.

94. It should be clear that there may be a difference in the way the participant and the observer perceive both the identified interests and the variables used to objectively define these interests.

95. The specific statistical question as stated in the general form by Sonquist and Morgan is: "Given the units of analysis under consideration, what single predictor variable will give us a maximum improvement in our ability to predict values of the dependent variable" (op. cit., p. 4).

96. Idem. See ibid., pp. 5-6 for a description of the algorithm. See Blalock, *Social Statistics* (New York, Toronto, and London: McGraw-Hill Book Co., Inc., 1960), Chapter 16, pp. 242-272, for an explanation and discussion of "Analysis of Variance."

97. Recall the previous caveat concerning the distinction between the perceptions of the observer and the participant.

98. This maximum is thirty-six. The predictor variables used are: Areal Grouping; Land Size; Population Size; Population Density; Population Growth Rate; Level of Urbanization; Agricultural Population as Percent of Total Popula-

tion; Gross National Product; Per Capita Gross National Product; International Financial Status; Staus of Economic Development; Date of Independence; Westernization; Former Colonial Ruler; Constitutional Status of Current Regime; Governmental Stability; Bloc Alignment; Merchant Marine Fleet; Port Activity; Total Scheduled Civil Aviation Services; International Civil Aviation Activity; Summary of Balance of Payments; Fishing Activity; Fishery Products (Canned); Fishery Products (Salted); Fishery Products (Fish Meals and Solubles); Net Food Supplies; Claims to Territorial Sea; Miles of Sea Coast; Security (Navy total vessels); Security Forces (Navy large and small combatants); Security Forces (Air Force); Military Personnel as a Percentage of Total Population; Expenditures on Defense as a Percentage of Gross National Product; Major Maritime Power; and Major Air Power.

99.   When only the votes of states included within the 1964 international political system are considered, the vote was 34-37-12. Recall that certain entities less than states were represented at the conference.

100.   The group numbers used in the diagrams in this chapter do not correspond to the group numbers assigned in the AID computer analysis. The analysis would be unnecessarily difficult to follow if the assigned numbers were used.

101.   It must be emphasized that the findings which are being reported in this chapter are based on a very preliminary and exploratory use of a sophisticated statistical data analytic technique.

102.   The vote by the states included within the 1964 international political system was 51-26-5.

103.   This result indicates a need to lessen the number of possible codes, at least for this variable.

104.   This, of course, closely parallels the findings on the six- and twelve-mile territorial seas.

105.   This analysis further illustrates the need to refine codes and illustrates the care which must be exercised in selecting predictor variables. Of course, support for rules concerning nationality and registration is widespread — 81 of 121 states included in the 1964 international political system — and this makes more difficult the task of identifying the differences between supporters and non-supporters.

106.   The split in Group 3 is made on Net Food Supplies, but the codes are grouped in an uninterpretable way.

When the 1952 Rome convention is used as the basis of analysis, the single most explanatory predictor variable is Areal Grouping — a .328 reduction in prediction error. And International Aviation Activity is the next most explanatory variable (.195). Because of the way in which codes are grouped, however, the AID analysis of the 1952 Rome convention is not helpful in developing an explanatory or predictive capability.

107.   Only twenty-two of the eighty states included in Group 2 have accepted the convention.

108.   The AID analysis of the Air Services Transit Agreement is not helpful. The first split is made on Areal Grouping, but again the splits are uninterpretable.

6: THE APPLICABILITY OF
INTERNATIONAL AIR AND SEA LAW
TO LEGAL PROBLEMS OF
OUTER SPACE

INTRODUCTION

In Chapter 2, it was determined that there are twenty-two outer space legal and political problems or problem areas discussed in space law literature. The United Nations, which has been the principal international political forum for processing these problems, focused discussion on them beginning with the General Assembly's Twelfth Session which met in 1958.[1] At this session, in recognition of the numerous potential legal and political problems which might arise as space is explored and exploited, the General Assembly established an *Ad Hoc* Committee on the Peaceful Uses of Outer Space.[2] However, because of a cold-war-inspired dispute over representation on the eighteen-member committee, three Communist nation-states — the Soviet Union, Czechoslovakia, and Poland — refused to participate. Moreover, India and the United Arab Republic also decided not to participate, apparently basing their decision on the assumption that the committee could not constructively accomplish its assigned tasks without the full participation of both the major space explorers.

The *Ad Hoc* Committee did meet despite the nonparticipation of these five member nation-states; and by June 1959, the committee produced a final report which subsequently was adopted by the General Assembly.[3] This report is an important document in the history of the development of a law of outer space since the committee not only surveyed the potential scope of space activities, but also considered the possibilities for international cooperation and made recommendations concerning priority treatment for several of the problems which it identified.

A permanent Committee on the Peaceful Uses of Outer Space was established in 1959.[4] As with its predecessor, the *Ad Hoc* Committee, there was a problem in obtaining full participation and the committee did not begin its work until March 1962, when the Soviet Union and the several other nonparticipants agreed to cooperate. Since 1962 the permanent committee together with its subcommittees has produced annual reports; and these reports have been among the principal bases for the several General Assembly resolutions and the two treaties treating problems related to space exploration and exploitation.

The General Assembly resolutions have stressed: (1) that outer space should be used only for peaceful purposes; and (2) the desirability of maximizing international cooperation in developing these peaceful uses. In addition in General Assembly Resolution 1884 (XIII), member nation-states were requested to refrain from placing into earth orbit nuclear weapons or any weapons of mass destruction; member nation-states also were requested not to install such weapons on celestial bodies.[5] But there really have been only two resolutions which have stated a general agreement on more specific application of legal principles to the legal and political problems in outer space; these are Resolutions 1721 (XVI) and 1962 (XVIII).

General Assembly Resolution 1721 (XVI), International Co-operation in the Peaceful Uses of Outer Space, commended three additional general principles to member nation-states, as follows: international law, including the United Nations Charter, applies to outer space and celestial bodies; outer space and celestial bodies are not subject to national appropriation; and outer space and celestial bodies are free to be explored and used by all nation-states in conformity with international law. This same resolution called upon nation-states launching objects into space to furnish information concerning the object launched to the Secretary General. In turn the Secretary General was requested to maintain a public registry of launchings.[6]

The second principal statement of agreement on the legal principles applicable to the space environment, General Assembly Resolution 1962

(XVIII), was unanimously adopted on December 13, 1963. This resolution is a Declaration of Legal Principles Governing the Activities of States in the Exploration and Use of Outer Space. In addition to restating the principles commended to member nation-states in Resolution 1721 and in the resolutions which preceded it, the General Assembly solemnly declared that nation-states engaged in the exploration and use of outer space should be guided by the following principles: (1) nation-states are internationally responsible for national activities in outer space; (2) nation-states should consult when any nation-state intends to conduct some outer space activity which might cause harm to another nation-state or when they plan to engage in some activity which might interfere with other space experiments; (3) the launching nation-state retains jurisdiction and control over objects of its registry, and such objects should be returned to the launching nation-state when return is requested; (4) both the launching nation-state and the nation-state from whose territory or facility an object is launched are internationally liable for damages; and (5) astronauts should be regarded as envoys of all mankind, should be rendered all possible assistance when assistance is required, and should be returned promptly to the nation-state of registration of their space vehicle.

It seems significant that Resolution 1962 was entitled a declaration, and, in fact, it is obvious from the records of the Committee on Peaceful Uses that delegates intended 1962 to be more than simply another General Assembly resolution. Yet, comments made within the Committee on Peaceful Uses before the draft declaration was transmitted to the General Assembly make it equally clear that delegates to the committee also considered the declaration to be only an initial step: that is, the declaration was considered a statement of those principles upon which there was unanimous agreement rather than a codification of all legal principles which are or might be applicable to outer space.[7] Despite the fact that "the United States is on record as stating that these principles reflect international law as accepted by Members of the United Nations,"[8] the legal character of a resolution or declaration passed by a unanimous vote in the General Assembly is far from settled. A number of delegations, therefore, advocated that a formal treaty be concluded so that general agreement on these particular legal principles might be recorded in a more traditional way. Subsequently two treaties were drafted. Both were recommended to member nation-states by unanimous vote: the first, the Treaty on Principles Governing the Activities of States in the Exploration and Use of Outer Space, Including the Moon and Other Celestial Bodies, in December 1966;[9] the second, the Agreement on the Rescue of Astronauts, the Return of Astronauts, and the Return of Objects Launched into Outer Space, in December 1967.[10]

The 1967 treaty deals specifically and in detail with the problem Rescue and Return. Several of the other twenty-one problems determined in Chapter 2 are dealt with to some extent in the 1966 treaty (see Table 21).[11] Some of the problems are considered in very specific terms — Destructive Weapons, for example (see Table 21).[12] Some problems — for example, Reconnaissance — are not included at all. The 1966 and 1967 treaties, even if universally accepted, do not therefore deal comprehensively with the legal and political problems of outer space. Indeed, there still is a need to continue to seek solutions, and international air and sea law seem to be particularly promising analogies.

TABLE 21

OUTER SPACE LEGAL PROBLEMS INCLUDED WITHIN THE 1966 SPACE LAW TREATY

Problem	Treaty Provision
Claims to Celestial Bodies	Article II. "Outer space, including the moon and other celestial bodies, is not subject to national appropriation by claims of sovereignty, by means of use or occupation, or by any other means."
Communications Satellites	No specific reference to this problem.[a]
Contamination or Pollution	Article IX. . . . "States Parties to the Treaty shall pursue studies of outer space, including the moon and other celestial bodies, and conduct exploration of them so as to avoid their harmful contamination and also adverse changes in the environment of the earth resulting from the introduction of extraterrestrial matter and, where necessary, shall adopt appropriate measures for this purpose."
Definitions	No definitions.
Delimitation	No applicable provision.
Destructive Weapons	Article IV. "States Parties to the Treaty undertake not to place in orbit around the earth any objects carrying nuclear weapons or any other

TABLE 21, Continued

Problem	Treaty Provision
	kinds of weapons of mass destruction, install such weapons on celestial bodies, or station such weapons in outer space in any other manner."
Electro-Magnetic[b]	No applicable provision.
Exploration and Exploitation	Article I. "The exploration and use of outer space, including the moon and other celestial bodies, shall be carried out for the benefit and in the interests of all countries, irrespective of their degree of economic or scientific development, and shall be the province of all mankind."
	Article III. "States Parties to the Treaty shall carry on activities in the exploration and use of outer space, including the moon and other celestial bodies, in accordance with international law, including the Charter of the United Nations, in the interest of maintaining international peace and security and promoting international co-operation and understanding."
	Article XI. "In the exploration and use of outer space, including the moon and other celestial bodies, States Parties to the Treaty shall be guided by the principle of co-operation and mutual assistance and shall conduct all their activities in outer space, including the moon and other celestial bodies, with due regard to the corresponding interests of all other States Parties to the Treaty."
	Article X. "In order to promote international co-operation in the exploration and use of outer space, including the moon and other celestial bodies, in conformity with the purposes of this Treaty, the States Parties to the Treaty shall consider on a basis of equality any requests by other States Parties to the Treaty to be afforded an opportunity to observe the flight of space objects by those States."
	Article XI. "In order to promote international co-operation in the peaceful exploration and use

TABLE 21, Continued

Problem	Treaty Provision

of outer space, States Parties to the Treaty conducting activities in outer space, including the moon and other celestial bodies, agree to inform the Secretary-General of the United Nations as well as the public and the international scientific community, to the greatest extent feasible and practicable, of the nature, conduct, locations, and results of such activities."

Article XIII. "The provisions of this Treaty shall apply to the activities of States Parties to the Treaty in the exploration and use of outer space, including the moon and other celestial bodies, whether such activities are carried on by a single State Party to the Treaty or jointly with other States, including cases where they are carried on within the framework of international inter-governmental organizations."

Flight Rules

No applicable provision.

Freedom of Access and Passage

Article I. "Outer space, including the moon and other celestial bodies, shall be free for exploration and use by all States without discrimination of any kind, on a basis of equality and in accordance with international law, and there shall be free access to all areas of celestial bodies."

General Interference[c]

Article IX. "If a State Party to the Treaty has reason to believe that an activity or experiment planned by it or its nationals in outer space, including the moon and other celestial bodies, would cause potential harmful interference with activities of other States Parties in the peaceful exploration and use of outer space, including the moon and other celestial bodies, it shall undertake appropriate international consultations before proceeding with such activity or experiment. A State Party to the Treaty which has reason to believe that an activity or experiment planned by another State Party in outer space, including the moon and other celestial bodies, would cause potential harmful interference with activities in the peaceful explora-

TABLE 21, Continued

Problem	Treaty Provision

| | tion and use of outer space, including the moon and other celestial bodies, may request consultation concerning the activity or experiment." |

| General Military Problems[d] | Article IV. "The establishment of military bases, installation, and fortifications, the testing of any types of weapons and the conduct of military manoeuvres on celestial bodies shall be forbidden." |

| Inspection | Article XII. "All stations, installations, equipment, and space vehicles on the moon and other celestial bodies shall be open to representatives of other States Parties to the Treaty on a basis of reciprocity. Such representatives shall give reasonable advance notice of a projected visit, in order that appropriate consultations may be held and that maximum precautions may be taken to assure safety and to avoid interference with normal operations in the facility to be visited." |

| Jurisdiction/ Sovereignty | Article VI. "States Parties to the Treaty shall bear international responsibility for national activities in outer space, including the moon and other celestial bodies, whether such activities are carried on by governmental agencies or by non-governmental entities, and for assuring that national activities are carried out in conformity with the provisions set forth in the present Treaty. The activities of non-governmental entities in outer space, including the moon and other celestial bodies, shall require authorization and continuing supervision by the State concerned. When activities are carried on in outer space, including the moon and other celestial bodies, by an international organization, responsibility for compliance with this Treaty shall be borne both by the international organization and by the States Parties to the Treaty participating in such organization." |

| | Article VIII. "A State Party to the Treaty on whose registry an object launched into outer space is carried shall retain jurisdiction and con- |

TABLE 21, Continued

Problem	Treaty Provision
	trol over such object, and over any personnel thereof, while in outer space or on a celestial body." In a sense, of course, all the provisions of the treaty concern jurisdiction or sovereignty insofar as they establish rules or controls.
Liability	Article VII. "Each State Party to the Treaty that launches or procures the launching of an object into outer space, including the moon and other celestial bodies, and each State Party from whose territory or facility an object is launched, is internationally liable for damage to another State Party to the Treaty or to its natural or juridicial persons by such object or its component parts on the earth, in air space, or in outer space, including the moon and other celestial bodies." See also Article VI *supra.*
Legal Regime[e]	No specific provision concerning this problem; however, in general, the treaty seems to consider outer space, including the moon and other celestial bodies, *res communis.* See particularly Articles I and II.[f]
Metalaw	No applicable provision.
Peaceful/Non-peaceful	Article IV. "The moon and other celestial bodies shall be used by all States Parties to the Treaty exclusively for peaceful purposes." The whole treaty emphasized peaceful exploration and use of space.
Reconnaissance	No applicable provision.
Registration	No specific provision. However, registration is referred to in Articles V and VIII.[f]
Rescue and Return	Article V. 1966. "States Parties to the Treaty shall regard astronauts as envoys of mankind in outer space and shall render to them all possible assistance in the event of accident, distress or emergency landing on the territory of another State Party or on the high seas. When astronauts make such a landing, they shall be safely and promptly returned to the State of registry of their space vehicle.

TABLE 21, Continued

Problem	Treaty Provision
	"In carrying on activities in outer space and on celestial bodies, the astronauts of one State Party shall render all possible assistance to the astronauts of other States Parties."
	Articles I-X of 1967 treaty. See text of treaty in Appendix B.
Weather Satellites	No applicable provision.[a]

[a] The emphasis on cooperation and benefit of all mankind indirectly concerns such specific space activities as communications and weather satellites. The provisions on jurisdiction and control also apply to these problem areas.

[b] E.g., frequency interference.

[c] E.g., between aircraft and spacecraft or between space experiments.

[d] E.g., military operations, general references to disarmament or to rights of self-defense.

[e] E.g., *res nullius* or *res communis*.

[f] Full text of the treaty is reproduced in Appendix A.

ARE AIR, SEA, AND OUTER SPACE LEGAL PROBLEMS COMPARABLE?

In Part II, selected international air and sea law rules were determined. The question now posed is this: Are the selected air and sea legal problems or problem areas and certain outer space legal problems comparable and are similar interests or preconditions perceived by national decision-makers in the three environments?

SOVEREIGNTY AND DELIMITATION

In outer space, as in adjacent airspace and sea areas, the questions of delimitation and territorial sovereignty are interrelated. Both questions are related to the desire of national decision-makers to fix state boundaries. The late Adlai E. Stevenson argued that men are conditiond to think in terms of states ". . . defined by finite areas expressed in finite measurements . . . And especially . . . (men) are conditioned to think in terms of national sovereignties."[13]

This preoccupation with fixed boundaries and fixed territorial areas within which governments may exercise exclusive rights is generally evident in the discussions of air and sea legal rules and principles in Chapters 3 and 4, particularly in the discussion of the delimitation of adjacent sea areas. Numerous delegates to the 1958 Conference on the Law of the Sea stressed the importance of framing an acceptable rule establishing a uniform breadth for the territorial sea.[14] In fact, establishing a conventional rule was considered to be so important that failure of the 1958 conference to draft an acceptable rule resulted in a call for a second conference in 1960.[15]

In the case of airspace, Article I of the 1944 Chicago convention — and of the two civil aviation conventions which it supersedes — defines the area within which governments may exercise their authority. Apparently the future importance of defining an upper boundary did not occur to the framers of these three conventions, the presumption being that a state's area of complete and exclusive authority was adequately defined by the term "airspace."[16] However, with the arrival of the Space Age, the question of the upward extent of the sovereignty and jurisdiction of the subadjacent state has been reopened. The basic claims to sovereign rights in territorial airspace and adjacent sea areas concern the control of access into and of activities within these areas. In Chapter 5, it was determined that national decision-makers discuss these claims and counterclaims in terms of two primary interests, economic and security, although conservation and humanitarianism are sometimes identified as separate interests as well.

In air law, both the claims to control access into and activities within territorial airspace are functional to states' economic and security interests. For example, by exercising these controls a state can insure that it will benefit from the commercial air traffic within its airspace. It can insure that damages are paid for injuries to its citizens' person and property. And it can use its domestic controls as a bargaining lever when attempting to obtain or retain its share of international civil air traffic. By retaining complete and exclusive jurisdiction in its airspace, a state is able to deny entry to aircraft which are perceived to be a threat to state security. And the aircraft which are admitted may be required to follow prescribed routes, land at designated airports, and transport only specified kinds of cargoes.

States' claims in sea law are also functional to the protection and/or enhancement of economic and security interests. In the case of the sea, there is, in addition to an interest in common carriage, a direct economic and conservation interest in natural resources. In the analysis in Chapter 5, it was found that such claims and counterclaims as those to specific breadths of territorial sea, to rights of passage, and to the exploitation of resources were justified in terms of these three interests.

Claims concerning rights and activities in space also involve economic and security interests and are closely related to claims in territorial airspace. This should not be surprising since, as McDougal, Lasswell, and Vlasic point out, airspace and outer space are a physical continuum. To effectively use outer space also involves the use of airspace. Moreover, ". . . the conduct of activities in space may have important consequences for the internal value processes of the territorial communities on earth."[17]

For example, if spacecraft are to be used as a means of commercial transportation, rules concerning access to territorial airspace will have to be adopted — and the location of the airspace-outer space boundary will then become a practical problem. While states have not protested overflights by orbiting satellites engaged in the peaceful exploration of space,[18] states may very well protest overflights by spacecraft at less than orbit altitudes. And common carrier spacecraft might well operate at suborbital altitudes particularly when entering and leaving territorially small, non-coastal states.[19] Successful development of spacecraft systems for transporting cargo, mail, and passengers, therefore, will be possible only if satisfactory policies concerning delimitation of and access to territorial airspace are adopted.[20] When formulating these policies, there is no reason to expect that national decision-makers will not attempt to protect interests which are identical to those which they attempt to protect in granting access to adjacent territorial air and sea areas and in asserting claims to particular breadths of territorial sea.

National decision-makers, for example, presumably will perceive an economic interest in commercial spacecraft operations just as they do in commercial plane and ship operations. While it is difficult now to imagine any practical commercial uses for common carrier spacecraft, there are numerous cases in history when one age's fantasy has become another age's reality.[21]

There are also other activities which, when conducted in outer space, affect the economic well-being of states. The economic benefits which may result from programs in weather research and prediction are examples. Ambassador Stevenson spoke of these benefits at the 1210th meeting of the First Committee of the United Nations General Assembly on December 4, 1961.

> It . . . [is] now possible to keep the entire atmosphere under constant observation — which portend[s] a revolution in meterology that . . . [holds] special promise for the improvement of weather forecasting in the tropics and the southern hemisphere, where vast oceans . . . [can] not be covered by present methods. The accurate forecasting of ty-

phoons, floods, rainfall and drought . . . [will] save human life, reduce damage, make possible the efficient use of water resources, enable farmers to plant according to future rainfall, and benefit fishing, grazing and the transport and storage of fuels and raw materials. The resulting progress in industry, agriculture and health . . . [will] raise living standards throughout the world.[22]

Some of these benefits already are being realized. For example, United States weather satellites now carry an automatic picture-transmission system (APT) which provides pictures of cloud cover over wide areas and then transmits them to relatively inexpensive ground stations on Earth.

According to a December 1968 press report, "an APT Satellite will pass within range of any ground station two or three times during daytime. A receiving station can receive weather pictures taken over regions up to 2,000 miles away. Each satellite will yield up to five good pictures per pass."[23]

Recently two Mexican cities and a Mexican agricultural program were saved because of information obtained by a Mexican APT station from a United States weather satellite. The Mexicans had followed Hurricane Naomi (September, 1968) from its origin and were thereby alerted to take precautions before its passage over the Nazas River Valley. But their troubles weren't over when Naomi swept past; in fact, it was the heavy rains which lingered which caused Mexican officials to face up to a difficult decision. The Lazaro Cardenas Dam which was nearing completion on the Nazas River was threatened by increasing water pressure. Should they risk destruction of the dam and flooding the valley or should they open the dam to relieve the pressure? The critical variable was water; would there be more rain?

If the officials waited and additional rains came, the dam would break and two cities, Gomez Palacios and Torreon, would be flooded, and, of course, the water which the dam was being built to store would be lost. On the other hand, if they released the water and there was no more rain, not only would they needlessly flood the valley, but they would lose the water needed for the region's agricultural program.

APT pictures available to the officials indicated that the weather was clearing. As a consequence the officials were able confidently to decide to keep the dam closed; neither city was flooded and the water needed for the agricultural program was retained.[24]

Economic well-being also will be affected by the greatly increased volume and speed of communication traffic made possible by communications satellites. Some sixty-five nation-states already are members of a global communications satellite system, INTELSAT, developed by the United States. Satellites now operating as a part of this system are available for use for telephone, telegraph, radio, and television transmission.

While all the General Assembly resolutions and the two space law treaties have stressed that the benefits of space exploration and exploitation are to be shared by all mankind, it is clear that this principle already is in jeopardy. When INTELSAT was established in 1964[25] the United States assured its control by providing that voting rights would be in proportion to a nation-state's share in ownership and capital investment. Initially the United States owned sixty-one percent and the agreement provides that the United States' interest will never go below fifty-three percent. This majority control by one member is contrary to past practice in international cooperative programs in communications: that is, in the past, all such programs have provided for equality among the participants. Consequently, from the very beginning there was opposition to the unequal position of the United States in INTELSAT.

Apparently the Soviet Union was attempting to capitalize on this dissatisfaction when it proposed an INTELSPUTNIK system at the 1968 Conference on the Exploration and Peaceful Uses of Outer Space. The Soviets promised equal voting status to all members and indicated that their system would require less elaborate and less costly ground installations than those required for INTELSAT.

General dissatisfaction together with the Soviet proposal led to a conference being called in February and March 1969 to attempt to design a single satellite communications network which would satisfy everyone. Some eighty nations, including the Soviet Union and the Eastern European Communist nation-states, participated.[26]

In addition to weather and communications satellites, nation-states are likely to perceive an economic benefit from navigations satellites; in fact, when precisely positioned, such satellites will provide more exact navigational information than can be obtained using conventional methods. Moreover, space is important economically as an environment for research as well. There are, then, numerous activities which either are or can be conducted in outer space which affect the economic interests of states on Earth.[27]

Of course, activities in space can also pose a threat to the security interests of states. In fact, threats or potential threats to state security from outer space are perhaps even more frightening than are comparable threats from adjacent air and sea areas.[28]

A preoccupation with threats to the security of nation-states on Earth from certain activities in and uses of outer space are very evident in the 1959 Report of the *Ad Hoc* Committee on the Peaceful Uses of Outer Space. This interest was emphasized by the delegates' concentration on the peaceful uses of outer space.[29] The fundamental point which delegates stressed was ". . . that outer space might be used to benefit mankind or to increase the threat to the security of humanity."[30] and that United Nations action was necessary to forestall that threat. V. A. Zorin, Soviet Union, stated that "the problem [of banning military uses of outer space] . . . [will] not be solved unless account . . . [is] taken of the security of both the United States and the Soviet Union."[31] Oscar Pinochat, Chile, added that a major question is whether outer space can be used without restriction, ". . . in the same way as the high seas."[32] He did not think so, "Since there . . . [is] a very special character attaching to outer space, and its unrestricted use by interplanetary space-ships . . . [will] endanger the security of mankind."[33] Similarly, Silviu Brucan, a delegate of Romania, stated that "the mastering of outer-space missiles . . . [has] added a new and important dimension to the threat of all-out war and the problem for the United Nations . . . [is] to eliminate the possibility that destruction might come from or through outer space."[34] The Australian delegate, Dr. E. Ronald Walker said ". . . it [is] an unhappy fact that although the Committee . . . [is] discussing the peaceful use of outer space, mankind's space activities might also be directed to other than peaceful purposes; indeed the military possibilities opened by recent satellite and rocket experiments . . . [are] terrifying."[35]

The 1966 Space Law Treaty deals with several threats to nation-states' security. For example, nation-states are prohibited from: (1) orbiting nuclear weapons and other weapons of mass destruction; (2) basing such weapons on celestial bodies or in space; (3) establishing military facilities on celestial bodies; and (4) conducting military maneuvers on celestial bodies.[36] Provision is also made for on-site inspection of "all stations, installations, and equipment and space vehicles on the moon and other celestial bodies . . ."[37] on a basis of reciprocity. Of course, the whole treaty emphasizes cooperation and peaceful uses of outer space and celestial bodies and is apparently intended to minimize threats to the security of underlying states. However, some threats remain unchecked, reconnaissance, propagandizing, and electronic jamming, for example. These problems have been discussed most frequently by Soviet and Eastern European writers.[38] However, since the Soviets became engaged in their own reconnaissance program (their Cosmos series), they have ceased to complain about so-called spies-in-the-sky.[39]

Another facet of the airspace-outer space boundary and territorial sovereignty problems is the previously mentioned desire of decision-makers to know with some certainty which, if any, national or international controls or regulations are applicable in outer space. As an example of this, in 1959, Sweden's representative in the First Committee of the United Nations General Assembly, Rickard Sandler, spoke of the ". . . paramount importance of each sovereign State to know the exact limits within which its rights and responsibilities . . . [are] to be respected . . . ."[40] Spokesmen for Canada, Chile, France, Italy, and Spain have also stressed the importance of fixing the boundary.[41]

The problems of sovereignty and delimitation in adjacent air, sea, and outer space areas, while not identical, do seem to be reasonably comparable. A need for some degree of fluidity in transitional zones is evident in all the areas discussed.[42] In general, the fundamental interests concerning sovereignty and delimitation which national decision-makers perceive in the air, sea, and outer space environments do appear to be identical. However, it does not follow that particular air and sea rules are directly applicable. Situations and circumstances simply are too variable for specific analogies to be more than suggestive. Yet having clarified why rules concerning sovereignty and delimitation which national decision-makers perceive in the should be helpful to those formulating rules for the space environment.

There has not been any great pressure on decision-makers to formulate detailed rules on sovereignty and delimitation in outer space. Those who advocate immediate establishment of detailed rules hope to avoid conflict in the space environment by establishing rules before conflict situations can develop. And, of course, some of these advocates seek to safeguard their states' interests by reserving celestial bodies and space itself for the whole community — at least until more is known about what there is in space which may be of value on Earth. However, the kinds of activities which are being conducted in space generally have not been perceived as threats to either the economic or security interests of the subadjacent states. Most of the activities have been peaceful and scientific in character. Of course, perceptions may be expected to change when and if the character of activities change. Reconnaissance satellites are an obvious exception to the peaceful and scientific character now; but reconnaissance has been an issue primarily between only the Soviet Union and the United States and apparently a tacit agreement now has been reached between these two nation-states.

As for economic interests, communications and weather satellites increasingly have economic applications; however, these advantages generally, if unequally, are being shared.[43] Furthermore, few states possess the resources for competing individually in space communications or weather programs.

With the exception of agreements on communication satellites, the only rules affecting economic interests which have been agreed to are rules which deal with bodies or areas so distant from Earth that there is little prospect of most states gaining any individual advantage; that is, the states now exploring or capable of exploring outer space have perceived it to be to their advantage to reject sovereign claims in space. Article II of the 1966 Space Law Treaty is, therefore, an explicit recognition of the inclusive character of states' economic interests in outer space.

On the other hand, decision-makers seem to have adopted a "go slow" approach to accepting rules establishing a boundary or regulating space activities which take place relatively close to Earth, close enough that is to suggest relatively direct economic and security interests in the activities. As the discussion above indicates, it is precisely to these kinds of activities that the air and sea law analogies are most comparable and to which, therefore, they will be most useful as guidelines in seeking solutions.

RESOURCES

Accessibility and location are among the measures of the value of any resource. Natural resources which might be found in outer space are largely inaccessible to Earthlings and are poorly located for use on Earth. For example, no element listed on the periodic table can now be returned economically from outer space.[44] However, those natural resources which are reasonably accessible and which can be used in space *can be* valuable assets in the exploration of outer space.

It can be expected that prospecting for resources such as water, oxygen, building materials, and rocket fuels will be priority projects when men reach the moon. Moon explorers will require about one to one and one-half pounds of oxygen and about one to two pounds of water each day.[45] If moon bases are to be built, it obviously will be to the advantage of the builders to find satisfactory building materials on the moon rather than to transport them from Earth, And, of course, it will be a great advantage to space exploration if fuel sources can be found.

The major advantage to be gained by finding these resources on the moon — or in the more distant future on some other celestial body — is that it will eliminate the extremely expensive task of transporting these necessities from Earth. The Earth is not an economical base from which to explore outer space since the maximum intensity of force and the total energy required to launch spacecraft from Earth is much greater than it would be from the moon and celestial bodies which have less mass and surface gravity. Mars, for example, has only one-third the Earth's surface gravity and a mass roughly only one-tenth that of Earth's.[46] Therefore, it will be much more economical to transport materials from either the moon or Mars than it will be to transport them from Earth.

Although comparatively little is known about natural resources in outer space, geoscientists do speculate about what resources might be found. Jack Green, a geoscientist employed by McDonnel-Douglas, lists the sources of water on the moon in the order of their probability of occurrence as: ". . . (1) chemically bound water (H_2O+) present in volcanic extrusives; (2) ice in permanently shadowed zones in volcanic fractures and fissures; (3) water of crystallization in volcanic sublimates; (4) permafrost in dust basins; and (5) water in carbonaceous chondrites and other rock types."[47] It is not clear what the probabilities are. Apparently, however, the evidence gathered by Surveyor I, Lunar Orbiters, and the Apollo astronauts increasingly supports the notion of lunar volcanic activity in the past.[48] In turn, this would seem to increase the likelihood of finding water since the three most probable lunar water sources are related to past volcanic activity on the moon.[49]

As for building materials, sulfur is one of the most common minerals found in volcanic areas. And Jack Green indicates sulfur can be a useful building material in space.

> Mixing sulfur with volcanic ash makes for a waterless cement that could be used on the Moon to seal fractures . . . . Sulfur and volcanic ash may also be molded into structural forms and insulation. Briquettes made from 15% sulfur and 85% volcanic ash have rather high crushing strengths of 350 g/cm2. On the Moon, these briquettes could sustain a mass that would exert 210 g/cm2.[50]

It seems probable, then, that natural resources of some value will be found in space, on the moon if not on other celestial bodies. However, for the foreseeable future, primarily because of their location, these resources will be of immediate value only to those who can use them in space. This in some ways is quite unlike the situation with regard to resources in and under the sea. In Chapter 2 it was determined that claims to specific breadths of territorial sea, contiguous zones, and the continental shelf were essentially primarily exclusive claims based largely on states' economic interests in the natural resources located in these areas. Some of the claims go beyond the ability of the claiming state to exploit the resources. For example, claims to the continental shelf greatly exceed the technological capabilities of states to exploit the shelf's resources. That is, by including a phrase setting the limit of the shelf at a depth permitting exploitation, the sole limiting factors are the ingenuity of technicians and their ability to produce machines or devices capable of extracting resources at great depths.

Of course, some states have no or only a very limited capability to exploit resources in their adjacent sea and shelf areas. As the analysis in Chapter 3 indicates, this does not prevent these states from asserting claims. In a sense these are conservation claims; that is, claims staked *now* to insure that the adjacent state has something to say about exploitation and a share in benefits and/or to conserve the resources until the adjacent state is itself capable of exploiting them. There is some similarity between these latter claims and the claims which states have made concerning outer space.

The position taken by most governments is that space should be peacefully explored and used for the benefit of all mankind. The United Arab Republic's delegate to the First Committee in 1958, Zaki Kenawi, observed that "his delegation considered [that] the new resources which might be provided by outer space should be used for the welfare of all mankind and that *the interest of the under-developed countries* should be recognized from the very beginning as a basic principle of the international regulation of space."[51] Evangelos Averoff-Tossizza, Greece, contended that "outer space, which . . . [is] in a sense the domain of all the peoples of the world, . . . [belongs] to none of them individually."[52] The Argentine delegate, Mario Amadeo, said:

> A tribute should certainly be paid to the countries which have taken the initiative in exploring outer space, but their privileged position . . . [can] not in any circumstances prejudice the legitimate right of other States to use outer space. It . . . [follows] that, without prejudging the legal status of outer space, the Assembly should affirm at once that all States . . . [have] absolutely equal rights with regard to the use of outer space.[53]

Vasco Vieira Garin, Portugal, also supported the principle that all states should benefit from outer space and should have absolute equality in the use of space.[54]

Similar statements have been made in the years since 1958. For example, in 1961, the Brazilian delegate said that

> . . . in the interests of the scientifically less developed countries, it should be established from the very beginning that the exploitation of outer space should be only for the betterment of mankind and to the benefit of all countries, irrespective of the stage of their economic or scientific development.[55]

The 1966 Space Law Treaty largely reiterates these statements. Article I provides that space exploration shall benefit all countries. And numerous provisions of the treaty provide for the regulation of the exploitation and use of outer space (see Table 21 and Appendix A). Since national appropriation is prohibited, outer space seems to be classified a *res communis,* similar to the high seas. The basic claims made concerning the resources in outer space, then, provide that outer space shall benefit all mankind and that the use of space will be open equally to all states. When these uses involve the uses of resources, the resources or the location of the resources cannot be appropriated. The claims concerning resources are, then, essentially conservation claims similar to claims made in adjacent sea and shelf areas except that the primarily inclusive rather than the primarily exclusive character of the claims is stressed.

However, the character of the problem in space differs in at least two important respects from the problems concerning natural resources on Earth. First, there have been relatively few major problems in using the high seas as a *res communis,* particularly as a medium for communications and transportation. Resources in the high seas generally are not concentrated or can not be liberated economically, if at all, given contemporary technological capabilities. One consequence is that peaceful shared usage usually has been possible.[56] Second, it is now clear that a developing technology makes appropriation of the deep sea bed seem likely.

On the other hand, little or nothing is known about where resources are located in outer space. As indicated, several General Assembly resolutions and the 1966 Space Law Treaty provide that the moon and other celestial bodies cannot be appropriated and that outer space, including the moon and other celestial bodies shall be free for exploration and use by all states. But this does not resolve the problems which might arise if, for example, the sources on the moon for water and building materials are concentrated and if difficulties concerning joint usage do arise. If, in fact, resources are concentrated, sea law will be less useful as an applicable analogy.

ACCESS AND PASSAGE

Freedom of the high seas is a universally-recognized general principle of international law. Coastal and landlocked states alike have a right of freedom of access and use.[57] Subject to certain limitations, there also is a right of innocent passage through territorial seas.[58]

The aircraft of all states may fly freely over the high seas.[59] However, innocent passage through territorial airspace is not a general right in international air law. Passage through territorial airspace must be authorized either by a contractual arrangement or by special permission.

In Chapter 5 it was found that national decision-makers seem to accept the principle of the freedom of the high seas primarily to protect or enhance an economic interest. Sharing the high seas for such uses as, for example, communications, transportation, or fishing is functional to both primarily exclusive and inclusive interests of a majority of states. Apparently the same finding applies in general to the airspace above the high seas.[60]

It is clear, on the basis of the discussions of sovereignty and delimitation and resources in this chapter, that national decision-makers perceive an inclusive interest in outer space similar to that perceived in the high seas and the airspace over the high seas. A number of statements have been cited in which outer space, at least by implication, is characterized as a *res communis*. In fact, the 1966 Space Law Treaty, and several of the General Assembly resolutions which it in effect supersedes, provide for free access and joint usage of outer space and celestial bodies.[61]

Recognition of an inclusive interest in the right of access and usage came almost with the orbiting of the first satellites. The widespread acceptance of this principle is emphasized by the failure of states to protect peaceful activities being conducted in space. In 1958, Antonio Ambrosini, an Italian delegate in the First Committee, stated that in his opinion the lack of protest by overflown states amounted to a "tacit and unanimous agreement."[62] The Yugoslavian delegate, Dobrivoje Vidic, in discussing freedom of access and movement in outer space, observed that

> by virtue of its very nature, and of the fact that penetration into it has been brought about by the common efforts and progress of the whole of mankind, no less so than by virtue of the fact that its abuse could be fatal to the whole world, outer space can only be regarded as *res communis*.[63]

And Austria's delegate, Kurt Waldheim, accepted the view that outer space is a common domain, noting that the principle had been corroborated in practice. He added, "this is a very encouraging development, for it proves that the principle of free use of cosmic space has already now, even in the absence of a respective international convention, gained tacit recognition by all states."[64] Costa Rica's Gonzalo Ortiz Martin stated the claim from the viewpoint of the small states: "If our small country had the economic and scientific means to shoot off satellites that might be placed in orbit, no one would dare to deny us the right to do so, as no one has denied the right to do so to those who have led the scientific race."[65]

In August, 1962, John A. Johnson, then general counsel of the National Aeronautics and Space Administration, observed that since Sputnik I was orbited in October, 1957,

> . . . numerous earth-orbiting satellites launched by both the United States and the USSR have repeatedly passed over the land and territorial waters of every nation on earth. No permission was sought in

advance by the launching State, none was expressly given by any State, and not a single protest has been registered by any State.[66]

McDougal, Lasswell, and Vlasic contend that

the factor of decisive importance in shaping this universal acquiescence of states in the conduct of activities 'over' their territories was of course their quick realization of the immense opportunities for the expansion of human knowledge through such activities and their high expectations with respect to the benefits that might be gained by all from the unimpeded use of the space environment.[67]

The brief International Geophysical Year which resulted in a wealth of highly valuable scientific and technological data contributed to states' expectations with respect to the potential benefits of space.[68]

Since the 1966 Space Law Treaty already has been signed by more than a majority of states, including the major space explorers, freedom of access to and use of outer space appear to be universally applicable as general principles. And as noted in a number of statements cited above, there seems to be in practice a widely accepted right of passage. However, as indicated earlier, the boundary question has not been resolved and therefore any right of passage is somewhat ambiguous.

It is evident from this discussion that the high seas and outer space are similiar in many ways concerning freedom of access and use. However, there are some important differences. Perhaps the most important difference is the relationship of states to the environment, in that outer space is "overhead." Earlier statements in this chapter emphasized peaceful uses of space. Also a number of treaty provisions specifically prohibit certain military uses. This is in sharp contrast with what are considered acceptable uses of the high seas where, for example, military maneuvers are conducted and weapons are tested in areas denied, at least temporarily, to other users.

Another important difference is the presence of celestial bodies in the void of outer space. While the 1966 Space Law Treaty provides that these bodies are not subject to national appropriation and limits the kinds of activities that can be conducted on these bodies, it does not resolve a number of potential problems which might arise. For example, as mentioned earlier, there can still be difficulties between states in using resources "for the benefit and interest of all countries." Simply using space itself can create the same kind of problems, such as the doctrinal dispute between the United States and the Soviet Union concerning the establishment and operation of a communications satellite system, and the dissatisfaction of some of the INTELSAT participants with United States control.

In summary, the general problems of access to and shared use of the high seas and outer space are comparable and in general the interests to be protected and enhanced in each environment are the same. However, there are important differences. The high seas and outer space are not comparable in terms of permissible uses since it is clear that an overwhelming majority of states are determined to prohibit the use of outer space for military purposes. Moreover, the problems associated with the shared uses of celestial bodies are not comparable to shared uses of the high seas. Therefore, while it is helpful to know why decision-makers accept rules concerning access and passage in sea law, the situation and circumstances in outer space are sufficiently different to warrant the exercise of great care in applying the sea law analogy to legal problems concerning access and passage problems in outer space.

LIABILITY, NATIONALITY AND REGISTRATION, AND SAFETY

Liability, nationality and registration, and safety were characterized in Chapter 2 as primarily functional problems. That is, in all environments solutions to these kinds of problems are necessary and functional to peaceful and routine inter-state interaction.

Apparently the two fundamental reasons for insisting that ships and planes have a nationality and/or be registered are to assign responsibility and to afford protection. In Chapter 3, it was found that the state of nationality and registration is held responsible for enforcing, for example, safety standards and crew licensing requirements.[69] Claims made concerning liability, nationality and registration, and safety are obviously interrelated. As there is no general enforcement agency, assigning responsibility to the flag state is likely to be the most effective means of enforcing what are essentially the protective rules concerning liability and safety. This same observation seems to apply to spacecraft.

In 1961, the General Assembly adopted Resolution 1721 (XVI) — International Co-operation in the Peaceful Uses of Outer Space — which calls upon states to furnish information on objects launched into space. Since that time the secretary-general has maintained a registry of launchings.[70] The 1966 Space Law Treaty refers to registration and the responsibilities of the registering state in Article V and VII (see Table 21 and the treaty text).[71] And the international responsibility of states for national activities conducted in outer space is provided for in Article VI. In fact, the competence of states to register and attribute nationality to spacecraft has been assumed implicitly since the earliest days of space exploration.[72]

On September 11, 1962, the United States submitted to the Committee on the Peaceful Uses of Outer Space a draft proposal on liability for space vehicles and personnel and for space vehicle accidents.[73] This proposal assigned to the launching state — apparently meaning the state of nationality — or to the launching international organization liability for personal injury and loss of life or property damage caused by space vehicles.[74] Proof of fault was not to be required in such cases.[75] No mention was made of injuries, damages, and losses by private exploiters, the assumption apparently being that states will be internationally responsible regardless of the character of the launcher.

The most important point, however, is that the types of injuries, damages, and losses being protected against are identically the same surface damages concerning which states have made claims and counterclaims in international air law. The only change seems to be the specific vehicle which is being protected against. That is, at its present state of development the spacecraft may warrant treatment as extrahazardous as, for example, did aircraft in the early days of aviation and so do nuclear ships now.

In the analysis in Chapter 3, it was found that there are very detailed rules and regulations concerning the construction, manning, and operation of ships.[76] Safety is, of course, also a concern in spacecraft. Currently this is mainly a concern for surface damages which might result from spacecraft. However, there must increasingly be a concern for personnel safety in manned vehicles, a point emphasized by the unfortunate tragedy in January 1967, involving the flight crew for the first Apollo flight.

Control over spacecraft is a primary concern in connection with surface damages. For example, the use of destruct devices gives launching states a degree of control over the hazards associated with launching a spacecraft. Another type of control is associated with both safety and interference, the ability to recover or destroy spacecraft which have completed their mission and simply clutter space. A more limited kind of control is the ability to free frequencies by "turning off" spacecraft when their mission is completed.[77]

Concern for the safety of personnel in spacecraft has been limited since only highly specialized and well qualified crews have been permitted to man spacecraft. When and if spacecraft come to be used as common carriers, the concern will, of course, become more general and it might be expected that comprehensive rules comparable to those for air and sea common carriers will be agreed upon.

The problems of liability, nationality and registration, and safety, then, are quite comparable to the same problems in the air and sea environments. A smaller number of vehicles is currently involved in space and the hazards are generally greater. Otherwise the interests are basically if not identically the same and even the preliminary and tentative steps toward solution are comparable to those which have proved functional in the other two environments.

SUMMARY

The problems of sovereignty and delimitation in air, sea, and outer space, while not identical, are reasonably comparable. And the fundamental interests which decision-makers perceive in relation to these problems appear to be identical. While particular air and sea rules are not directly applicable, the problems are comparable enough that knowing what the preconditions of rule acceptance are in air and sea law will be helpful in formulating acceptable rules for the space environment.

General principles concerning the appropriation of distant celestial bodies on which sovereign claims offer little prospect of individual advantage seem to be generally accepted now. However, rules have not been agreed to which establish a boundary between airspace and outer space and which regulate potentially economically rewarding or militarily threatening activities closer to earth. The air and sea law analogies seem to be particularly useful in dealing with these kinds of problems.

Claims concerning resources in outer space are essentially conservation claims similar to claims made in adjacent sea and shelf areas. In outer space, however, these claims emphasize the primarily inclusive interests of the international community rather than the primarily exclusive interests of individual states.

There have been relatively few major problems in sharing the use of the resources of the high seas. This may not be the case in outer space since, in contrast to the high seas, resources may well be concentrated and difficult to share.

The general problems of access to and shared use of the high seas and outer space are comparable and in general the interests to be protected and/or enhanced in each environment are the same. There are important differences, however, and care must be exercised when considering possible outer space rules concerning these problems based on the sea law analogy.

Of all problems or problem areas, liability, nationality and registration, and safety are most comparable in the three environments. Solutions to these kinds of problems are necessary and functional to peaceful and routine interaction in all environments. And while there are now far fewer spacecraft than ships and planes, and while the hazards from spacecraft are generally greater, the fundamental interests which decision-makers seek to protect and/or enhance are identical. In fact, the preliminary and tentative steps taken toward solving these problems are comparable to those which have proved successful in the air and sea environments.

NOTES

1.   Outer space had been discussed at the United Nations earlier, but as a part of the disarmament question and not as a separate and distinct international legal and political problem area.

2.   General Assembly Resolution 1348 (XIII): Question of the Peaceful Uses of Outer Space, December 13, 1958.

3.   United Nations, *Report of the Ad Hoc Committee on the Peaceful Uses of Outer Space* (U.N. Doc. No. A/4141) (July 14, 1959). Two subcommittees, one technical, the other legal, were established to facilitate the work of the committee.

4.   General Assembly Resolution 1472 (XIV): International Cooperation in the Peaceful Uses of Outer Space, December 12, 1959.

5.   General Assembly Resolution 1884 (XVIII): Question of General and Complete Disarmament, October 17, 1963.

6.   Since Resolution 1721 was accepted by the General Assembly, the secretary-general has maintained a registry of launchings. Nation-states have reported to him data concerning the objects which they have launched, and the original reports submitted by both the U.S. and the U.S.S.R. included information on the objects which they had launched prior to the passage of Resolution 1721.

7.   Cf. Jenks, op. cit., pp. 184-85. See also the *Report of the Committee on the Peaceful Uses of Outer Space* (Doc. No. A/5549) (November 24, 1963), and Add. 1 (November 27, 1963).

8.   Letter to this writer from H. Rowan Gaither of the Office of the Legal Adviser, United States Department of State, dated November 17, 1966. This statement was made in response to a question concerning the legal status of G.A. Resolution 1962. Recall that the same position was assumed by the United States concerning G.A. Resolution 1721 — which was also adopted by unanimous vote.

9.   General Assembly Resolution 2222 (XXI).

10.   General Assembly Resolution 2345 (XXII). The 1966 treaty has now been ratified or acceded to by 51 nation-states. An additional 51 nation-states have signed it. The 1967 agreement has been ratified or acceded to by 28 nation-states. An additional 57 nation-states have signed the agreement. This information was furnished by the Office of the Legal Advisor, Department of State, in June 1969.

11.   By Article IV of the 1966 treaty, states are prohibited from: (1) orbiting nuclear weapons and other weapons of mass destruction; and (2) testing weap-

ons of any kind on celestial bodies. Testing nuclear weapons in outer space is prohibited by the earlier treaty banning nuclear weapons tests in the atmosphere, in outer space and under water.

The Soviet Union apparently is developing a Fractional Orbital Bombardment System, (FOBS). According to an Associated Press report printed in the Lafayette, Indiana, *Journal and Courier,* 21 February 1969, p. 2, Defense Department officials have concluded that the Soviet Union has decided to deploy a FOBS. Note the interesting questions which arise since the specific prohibition is against orbiting nuclear weapons and other weapons of mass destruction; but note also the pervasiveness of an emphasis in the treaty and in the resolutions on the peaceful uses of outer space.

12. Article IX of the 1966 treaty, the applicable provision, deals only with interference between space experiments.

13. Statement before the First Committee of the United Nations General Assembly on December 4, 1962, *Department of State Bulletin,* 46 (January 29, 1962), p. 180. For a recent provocative and much criticized discussion of territory, boundaries, and the nature of man, see Robert Ardrey, *The Territorial Imperative: A Personal Inquiry Into the Animal Origins of Property and Nations* (New York: Antheneum, 1966). Ardrey boldly extrapolates explanations of human behavior from studies of animal behavior; most critics have questioned the validity of such an extrapolation.

14. See United Nations Conference on the Law of the Sea, *Official Records, 2* op. cit., passim.

15. It should be noted that failure to establish an uniform breadth for the territorial sea apparently has not inhibited the development of a legal regime of the high seas. On the other hand, a case can be made that until comparatively recently there was an uniform rule specifying a three-mile limit and that the customary rule was not challenged until the 1930 Hague codification attempt. See Colombos, op cit., p. 16.

16. Stephan Latchford, advisor on air law to the United States Delegation at the Chicago conference, states that "the delegates at Chicago had difficulties enough trying to reach an accord on controversial air transport problems without attempting to determine the exact meaning of the term "airspace" ("The Bearing of International Air Navigation Conventions on the Use of Outer Space," *Legal Problems of Space Exploration,* op. cit., p. 495). He goes on to say that there seemed to be no reason to establish an upper limit to territorial airspace in 1944 since there had been no serious attempts to use outer space.

17. McDougal, Laswell, and Vlasic, op. cit., p. 244.

18. Cf., for example, ibid., pp. 220-221; Libson and Katzenbach, op. cit., p. 9; Jenks, *Space Law,* op. cit., p. 138; and Haley, *Space Law and Government,* op. cit., pp. 67-70.

19. There is another facet to this problem since in the future certain space-craft may make flat entries and ". . glide at altitudes ranging from about 25 to 60 miles for distances as great as 7,000 to 10,000 miles before landing" — at least this type of entry has been described by John A. Johnson, former general counsel of the National Aeronautics and Space Administration ("The Future of Manned Space Flight, and the 'Freedom' of Outer Space," an address given before the Section of International and Comparative Law, American Bar Association, in San Francisco, California, in August, 1962, cited by McDougal, Lasswell, and Vlasic, p. 245.).

Presumably the DynaSoar was one of the craft referred to by Johnson. The DynaSoar program was cancelled in December, 1962; however, both NASA and the Air Force are now supporting programs developing "lifting bodies." These craft are shaped so that they obtain aerodynamic lift from body contours rather than from conventional wings. See the feature article "'Wingless Wedge' Shaping Up as Versatile Space Vehicle," by Ralph Dighton, Associated Press Science Writer, which appeared in the Arizona *Daily Star,* 12 February 1967, p. 13. See also *Newsweek* of 24 July 1967, p. 53, for a report concerning the Martin X-24A. This "lifting body" is now being flight tested.

20. Cf. McDougal, Lasswell, and Vlasic, op. cit., pp. 244-245.

21. Cf., for example, Donald N. Michael, "Peaceful Uses," *Outer Space*: Prospects for Man and Society (Englewood Cliffs: Prentice-Hall, Inc., 1962), pp. 31-63, especially pp. 53-55.

22. United Nations, *Official Records of the General Assembly, First Committee, Sixteenth Session, 2-September 1961-15 February 1962* (United Nations: United Nations, 1962), p. 245. Not all of these benefits have been realized, but weather forecasters are now using information obtained from satellites. See, for example, Joseph R. Coyne, "Satellites Improve Weather Forecasts," Arizona *Daily Star,* 12 February 1967, p. 4.

23. Indianapolis *Star,* 26 December 1968, p. 34.

24. Idem. See also, Indianapolis *Star,* 28 November 1968, p. 2.

25. Agreement Establishing Interim Arrangements for a Global Commercial Communications Satellite System. The United States also negotiated special agreements with each of the other member nation-states.

26. See the Indianapolis *Star,* 24 February 1969, p. 4.

27. Not all of these activities have to be conducted over a state for its decision-makers to perceive a national economic interest in the activities.

28. On the security interest in space see: Haley, *Space Law and Government,* op. cit., Jenks, *Space Law,* op. cit.; and McDougal, Lasswell, and Vlasic, op. cit.; the *Official Records of the General Assembly, First Committee* for the years 1958

and subsequent; the *Proceedings* of the Space Law Colloquia, specifically: Kenneth B. Keating, "Space Law and the Fourth Dimension of Our Age," *Proceedings of the First Colloquium on the Law of Outer Space* (Wein: Springer-Verlag, 1959), ed. Andrew G. Haley and Welf Heinrich, Prince of Hanover, p. 87; George J. Feldman, "An American View of Jurisdiction in Outer Space," ibid., p. 47; Valdimir Kopal, "Two Problems of Outer Space Control: The delimitation of Outer Space, and the Legal Ground for Outer-Space Flights," *Proceedings of the Third Colloquium on the Law of Outer Space* (Stockholm: The Organizing Committee of the IXth International Astronautical Congress, 1961), ed. Andrew G. Haley and Kurt Grönfors, pp. 108-109; John A. Johnson, "Remarks in Connection with the Report of Working Committee No. 1," *Proceedings of the Fourth Colloquium on the Law of Outer Space* (Norman: University of Oklahoma Research Institute, 1963), ed. Andrew G. Haley and Mortimer D. Schwartz, p. 354; Jacek Machowski, "Certain Aspects of the Right of Innocent Passage of Space Vehicles," ibid., p. 65; and G. A. Osnitzkaya, "Prospects of the Development of Space Law," *Proceedings of the Fifth Colloquium on the Law of Outer Space* (Washington: The International Institute of Space Law of the International Astronautical Federation, 1963), ed. Andrew G. Haley, pp. 2-4.

29. United Nations, *Official Records of the General Assembly, First Committee, 16 September - 13 December, 1958* (United Nations: United Nations, 1958), passim.

30. United Nations, *Official Records of the General Assembly, Plenary Meetings, Thirteenth Session* (United Nations: United Nations, 1958), p. 614.

31. United Nations, *Official Records of the General Assembly, First Committee, 16 September - 13 December, 1958*, op. cit., p. 193.

32. Ibid., p. 195

33. Idem.

34. Ibid., p. 207

35. Ibid., p. 209. The general debate summarized in ibid., pp. 191-232, records many other statements similar to those cited here. It is reasonable to expect security interests to heighten with public discussion of the Soviet FOBS and of such less well-known programs as the U.S. Sky Guardian (a laser equipped satellite).

36. Article IV. See Table 21. See also the text of the treaty in Appendix A.

37. Article XII.

38. See, for example, Robert D. Crane's "Guide to the Study of Communist Views on the Legal Problems of Space Exploration and a Bibliography," op. cit., passim, but particularly G. Zhukov, "Space Espionage Plans and International

Law," pp. 1095-1101, and Jerry Saztucki, "Security of Nations and Cosmic Space," op. cit., p. 4; G. Sibryakov, "Real Aims of U. S. Space Co-operation," *International Affairs* (Moscow) (Nov. 2, 1966), p. 62; Jerry Saztucki "On the So-Called Upper Limit of National Sovereignty," *Proceedings of the Fifth Colloquium on the Law of Outer Space,* op. cit., p. 7; and G. Zolotov, "Space Rights and Obligations," *International Affairs* (Moscow) (N. 7, 1963), p. 93.

For United States' views see: Richard N. Gardner, "Outer Space: Problems of Law and Power," *Department of State Bulletin,* 49 (September 2, 1963), p. 370; Jessup and Taubenfeld, op. cit., pp. 217-218; and John A. Johnson, "Freedom and Control in Outer Space," *Proceedings of the Conference on Space Science and Space Law* (Hackensack: Fred B. Rothman and Co., 1964), ed. Mortimer D. Schwartz, p. 145.

39. Very little information concerning space reconnaissance is available since both the United States and the Soviet Union maintain a tight security control over their programs. According to *Newsweek* of 17 October 1966, "General Electric, which makes the recoverable film capsules for U. S. satellites, was allowed to say in an ad recently that 'in the last eleven years our reliability record shows 121 successful entries from orbit out of 123 opportunities'" (p. 73). This means, then, that the rate of attempted capsule return has been slightly less than one capsule every month over the entire eleven year period.

See also *Newsweek* of 21 April 1969, pp. 61-64. In a story titled "Sky Spies: Nobody Has a Secret Anymore," *Newsweek* describes what is known about the military space programs of both the Soviet Union and the United States.

40. United Nations, *Official Records of the General Assembly, First Committee, Fourteenth Session, 1959* (United Nations: United Nations, 1959), p. 281.

41. McDougal, Lasswell, and Vlasic, op. cit., pp. 323-359.

Numerous legal scholars have dealt with the delimitation question, however, John Cobb Cooper has been most adamant among them in declaring that the demarcation of the boundary between airspace and outer space is *the* fundamental legal problem of outer space. See, for example, his "High Altitude Flight and National Sovereignty," United States Congress, Senate, Committee on Aeronautics and Space Sciences, *Legal Problems of Space Exploration,* op. cit., pp. 1-7. See also Haley, *Space Law and Government,* op. cit., pp. 75-117. The Committee on Peaceful Uses has now undertaken consideration of the boundary problem on a priority basis.

Much more attention has been given to the question of how best to establish a boundary rather than to the significance of the boundary itself. See, for example, ibid., passim. Interest in the boundary as a priority question has apparently decreased as space exploration has proceeded rather spectacularly without a fixed boundary. But as will be noted below, the delay also indicates an unwillingness of decision-makers to act hastily and perhaps rashly in dealing with the problem.

42. Myres S. McDougal called this to my attention when he commented on the manuscript.

43. Weather data obtained from satellites has been widely shared. And it may be recalled that the Soviet Union and the United States have cooperated in meteorological research programs in space.

44. This observation was made by S. R. Titley, associate professor of geology, University of Arizona, in a conversation with this writer in December, 1966. Titley is one of several geologists who assisted NASA in selecting landing sites for the Apollo moon flights.

45. McDougal, Lasswell, and Vlasic, op. cit., p. 758. See further their Chapter 7, "Claims Relating to the Enjoyment and Acquisition of Resources," pp. 749-871.

46. See John W. Campbell, "Natural Resources in Space," *Analog,* 71 (March, 1963), pp. 8-16, 90-94.

47. Jack Green, "Geosciences Applied to Lunar Exploration," *The Moon*: *Symposium No. 14 of the International Astronomical Union* (London and New York: Academic Press, 1962), ed. Zdenek Kopal and Zdenka Kadla Mikhailov, p. 214. Water, of course, also can be used as a source of oxygen.

See also the *Time* article on Green in the 23 February 1968 issue (p. 70). *Time* attributes to Green an assertion that heating hydrous rocks to 500-800 degrees F. will release as much as one gallon of water for each cubic foot of rock. He expects that such rocks will be found since volcanic formations on earth contain them.

48. Colonel Thomas P. Stafford, Apollo 10, is quoted by *Newsweek* of 2 June 1969, as saying while orbiting the moon: "There's no doubt about it." Commander John W. Young is said to have added: "There was one volcano that was all white on the outside and definitely black on top" (p. 27).

49. See also Kenneth F. Weaver, "The Moon: Man's First Goal in Space," *National Geographic,* 135 (February, 1969), pp. 207-232. In the caption of a picture of the Marius Hills, Weaver states: "studying the Marius features, most experts now agree that many of the domes, rising as high as 1,000 feet, are outpourings of lava. They find a parallel on earth in domes such as 500-foot high Howard Mesa . . . in Arizona's San Francisco volcanic field" (p. 220).

50. Green, loc. cit.

51. United Nations, *Official Records of the General Assembly, First Committee, Thirteenth Session,* op. cit., p. 224. Emphasis added.

52. Ibid., p. 228.

53. Ibid., p. 205.

54. Ibid., p. 225.

55. United Nations, *Official Records of the General Assembly, First Committee, Sixteenth Session,* op. cit., p. 269. The statements which have been cited are only a few of the many expressing similar positions. See ibid., p. 245-270, and United Nations, *Official Records of the General Assembly, First Committee, Thirteenth Session,* op. cit., pp. 191-232.

56. Certain fish do concentrate in particular sea areas and action has had to be taken to conserve species and to ensure maximum possible yields. Several states have domestic legislation in which they assert conservation claims, and the 1958 United Nations Conference on the Law of the Sea adopted a Convention on Fishing and Conservation of the Living Resources of the High Seas.

57. See the section on the high seas in Chapter 3.

58. See Chapter 3.

58. See Chapter 3 for an analysis of this right and the limitations such as those concerning warships, submarines, and fishing vessels.

59. Recall that this is one of the provisions of Article 2 of the Convention on the High Seas which had sufficient support at the 1958 conference to be considered a universally recognized principle.

60. While this aspect of air law was not analyzed separately, it was considered briefly in the analysis concerning the high seas. See the preceding footnote.

61. For the treaty provisions see Table 21. The full text is contained in Appendix A. See also Resolution 1721 (XVI): International Co-operation in the Peaceful Uses of Outer Space, December 20, 1961; and Resolution 1962 (XVIII): Declaration of Legal Principles Governing the Activities of States in the Exploration and Use of Outer Space, December 13, 1963.

62. McDougal, Lasswell, and Vlasic, op. cit., p. 207.

63. Cited by McDougal, Lasswell, and Vlasic, idem.

64. Cited by McDougal, Lasswell, and Vlasic, idem.

65. Cited by McDougal, Lasswell, and Vlasic, ibid., p. 206.

66. "The Future of Manned Space Flight, and the 'Freedom' of Outer Space," cited in McDougal, Lasswell, and Vlasic, ibid., p. 200.

67. Ibid., p. 205.

68. Idem.

69. Recall that the "genuine link" provision in the 1958 Convention on the High Seas seems to have been included to insure effective enforcement of such requirements.

70. General Assembly Resolution 1721 (XVI); International Co-operation in the Peaceful Uses of Outer Space, December 20, 1961, Part B, paragraphs 1 and 2. States have reported to the secretary-general data concerning the objects which they have launched into outer space. The original reports by the United States and the U.S.S.R. included data on the objects which they had launched before 1961.

71. See also General Assembly Resolution 1962 (XVIII); Declaration of Legal Principles Governing the Activities of States in the Exploration and Use of Outer Space, December 13, 1963, paragraphs 7 and 9.

72. See, for example, the 1959 Report of the *Ad Hoc* Committee on the Peaceful Uses of Outer Space.

73. Report of the Committee on the Peaceful Uses of Outer Space (Doc. A/5181), *Official Records of the General Assembly, Seventeenth Session, Annexes,* (United Nations: United Nations, 1962) p. 3.

74. Ibid., p. 9.

75. Idem. Recall that a U. S. delegate at Rome in 1952 had argued for a system of liability based on a presumption of fault rather than a system of absolute liability. See again the section on liability in Chapter 5.

76. There are also similar comprehensive regulations concerning aircraft. See the relevant annexes to the 1944 Chicago convention. Annex 2 deals with personnel licensing and Annex 8 with airworthiness of aircraft.

77. See McDougal, Lasswell, and Vlasic, op. cit., pp. 603-605. See also the Report of the *Ad Hoc* Committee on the Peaceful Uses of Outer Space, op. cit.

APPENDIXES

APPENDIX A

TREATY ON PRINCIPLES GOVERNING THE ACTIVITIES OF STATES IN THE EXPLORATION AND USE OF OUTER SPACE, INCLUDING THE MOON AND OTHER CELESTIAL BODIES

The States Parties to this Treaty,

Inspired by the great prospects opening up before mankind as a result of man's entry into outer space,

Recognizing the common interest of all mankind in the progress of the exploration and use of outer space for peaceful purposes,

Believing that the exploration and use of outer space should be carried on for the benefit of all peoples irrespective of the degree of their economic or scientific development,

Desiring to contribute to broad international co-operation in the scientific as well as the legal aspects of the exploration and use of outer space for peaceful purposes,

Believing that such co-operation will contribute to the development of mutual understanding and to the strengthening of friendly relations between States and peoples,

Recalling resolution 1962 (XVIII), entitled "Declaration of Legal Principles Governing the Activities of States in the Exploration and Use of Outer Space", which was adopted unanimously by the United Nations General Assembly on 13 December 1963,

Recalling resolution 1884 (XVIII), calling upon States to refrain from placing in orbit around the earth any objects carrying nuclear weapons or any other kinds of weapons of mass destruction or from installing such weapons on celestial bodies, which was adopted unanimously by the United Nations General Assembly on 17 October 1963,

Taking account of United Nations General Assembly resolution 110 (II) of 3 November 1947, which condemned propaganda designed or likely to provoke or encourage any threat to the peace, breach of the peace or act of aggression, and considering that the aforementioned resolution is applicable to outer space,

Convinced that a Treaty on Principles Governing the Activities of States in the Exploration and Use of Outer Space, including the Moon and Other Celestial Bodies, will further the Purposes and Principles of the Charter of the United Nations,

Have agreed on the following:

ARTICLE I

The exploration and use of outer space, including the moon and other celestial bodies, shall be carried out for the benefit and in the interest of all countries, irrespective of their degree of economic or scientific development, and shall be the province of all mankind.

Outer space, including the moon and other celestial bodies, shall be free for exploration and use by all States without discrimination of any kind, on a basis of equality and in accordance with international law, and there shall be free access to all areas of celestial bodies.

There shall be freedom of scientific investigation in outer space, including the moon and other celestial bodies, and States shall facilitate and encourage international co-operation in such investigation.

ARTICLE II

Outer space, including the moon and other celestial bodies, is not subject to national appropriation by claim of sovereignty, by means of use or occupation, or by any other means.

ARTICLE III

States Parties to the Treaty shall carry on activities in the exploration and use of outer space, including the moon and other celestial bodies, in accordance with international law, including the Charter of the United Nations, in the interest of maintaining international peace and security and promoting international co-operation and understanding.

ARTICLE IV

States Parties to the Treaty undertake not to place in orbit around the earth any objects carrying nuclear weapons or any other kinds of weapons of mass destruction, install such weapons on celestial bodies, or station such weapons in outer space in any other manner.

The moon and other celestial bodies shall be used by all States Parties to the Treaty exclusively for peaceful purposes. The establishment of military bases, installations and fortifications, the testing of any type of weapons and the conduct of military manoeuvres on celestial bodies shall be forbidden. The use of military personnel for scientific research or for any other peaceful purposes shall not be prohibited. The use of any equipment or facility necessary for peaceful exploration of the moon and other celestial bodies shall also not be prohibited.

ARTICLE V

States Parties to the Treaty shall regard astronauts as envoys of mankind in outer space and shall render to them all possible assistance in the event of accident, distress, or emergency landing on the territory of another State Party or on the high seas. When astronauts make such a landing, they shall be safely and promptly returned to the State of registry of their space vehicle.

In carrying on activities in outer space and on celestial bodies, the astronauts of one State Party shall render all possible assistance to the astronauts of other States Parties.

States Parties to the Treaty shall immediately inform the other States Parties to the Treaty or the Secretary-General of the United Nations of any phenomena they discover in outer space, including the moon and other celestial bodies, which could constitute a danger to the life or health of astronauts.

ARTICLE VI

States Parties to the Treaty shall bear international responsibility for national activities in outer space, including the moon and other celestial bodies, whether such activities are carried on by governmental agencies or by non-governmental entities, and for assuring that national activities are carried out in conformity with the provisions set forth in the present Treaty. The activities of non-governmental entities in outer space, including the moon and other celestial bodies, shall require authorization and continuing supervision by the State concerned. When activities are carried on in outer space, including the moon and other celestial bodies, by an international organization, responsibility for compliance with this Treaty shall be borne both by the international organization and by the States Parties to the Treaty participating in such organization.

ARTICLE VII

Each State Party to the Treaty that launches or procures the launching of an object into outer space, including the moon and other celestial bodies, and each State Party from whose territory or facility an object is launched, is internationally liable for damage to another State Party to the Treaty or to its natural or juridical persons by such object or its component parts on the Earth, in air space or in outer space, including the moon and other celestial bodies.

ARTICLE VIII

A State Party to the Treaty on whose registry an object launched into outer space is carried shall retain jurisdiction and control over such object, and over any personnel thereof, while in outer space or on a celestial body. Ownership of objects launched into outer space, including objects landed or constructed on a celestial body, and of their component parts, is not affected by their presence in outer space or on a celestial body or by their return to the Earth. Such objects or component parts found beyond the limits of the State Party to the Treaty on whose registry they are carried shall be returned to that State, which shall, upon request, furnish identifying data prior to their return.

ARTICLE IX

In the exploration and use of outer space, including the moon and other celestial bodies, States Parties to the Treaty shall be guided by the principle of co-operation and mutual assistance and shall conduct all their activities in outer space, including the moon and other celestial bodies, with due regard to the corresponding interests of all other States Parties to the Treaty. States Parties to the Treaty shall pursue studies of outer space, including the moon and other celestial bodies, and conduct exploration of them so as to avoid their harmful contamination and also adverse changes in the environment of the Earth resulting from the introduction of extraterrestrial matter and, where necessary, shall adopt appropriate measures for this purpose. If a State Party to the Treaty has reason to believe that an activity or experiment planned by it or its nationals in outer space, including the moon and other celestial bodies, would cause potentially harmful interference with activities of other States Parties in the peaceful exploration and use of outer space, including the moon and other celestial bodies, it shall undertake appropriate international consultations before proceeding with any such activity or experiment. A State Party to the Treaty which has reason to believe that an activity or experiment planned by another State Party in outer space, including the moon and other celestial bodies, would cause potentially harmful interference with activities in the peaceful exploration and use of outer space, including the moon and other celestial bodies, may request consultation concerning the activity or experiment.

ARTICLE X

In order to promote international co-operation in the exploration and use of outer space, including the moon and other celestial bodies, in conformity with the purposes of this Treaty, the States Parties to the Treaty shall consider on a basis of equality any requests by other States Parties to the Treaty to be afforded an opportunity to observe the flight of space objects launched by those States.

The nature of such an opportunity for observation and the conditions under which it could be afforded shall be determined by agreement between the States concerned.

ARTICLE XI

In order to promote international co-operation in the peaceful exploration and use of outer space, States Parties to the Treaty conducting activities in outer space, including the moon and other celestial bodies, agree to inform the Secretary-General of the United Nations as well as the public and the international scientific community, to the greatest extent feasible and practicable, of the nature, conduct, locations and results of such activities. On receiving the said information, the Secretary-General of the United Nations should be prepared to disseminate it immediately and effectively.

ARTICLE XII

All stations, installations, equipment and space vehicles on the moon and other celestial bodies shall be open to representatives of other States Parties to the Treaty on a basis of reciprocity. Such representatives shall give reasonable advance notice of a projected visit, in order that appropriate consultations may be held and that maximum precautions may be taken to assure safety and to avoid interference with normal operations in the facility to be visited.

ARTICLE XIII

The provisions of this Treaty shall apply to the activities of States Parties to the Treaty in the exploration and use of outer space, including the moon and other celestial bodies, whether such activities are carried on by a single State Party to the Treaty or jointly with other States, including cases where they are carried on within the framework of international inter-governmental organizations.

Any practical questions arising in connection with activities carried on by international inter-governmental organizations in the exploration and use of outer space, including the moon and other celestial bodies, shall be resolved by the States Parties to the Treaty either with the appropriate international organization or with one or more States members of that international organization, which are Parties to this Treaty.

ARTICLE XIV

1. This Treaty shall be open to all States for signature. Any State which does not sign this Treaty before its entry into force in accordance with paragraph 3 of this article may accede to it at any time.

2. This Treaty shall be subject to ratification by signatory States. Instruments of ratification and instruments of accession shall be deposited with the Governments of the Union of Soviet Socialist Republics, the United Kingdom of Great Britain and Northern Ireland and the United States of America, which are hereby designated the Depositary Governments.

3. This Treaty shall enter into force upon the deposit of instruments of ratification by five Governments including the Governments designated as Depositary Governments under this Treaty.

4. For States whose instruments of ratification or accession are deposited subsequent to the entry into force of this Treaty, it shall enter into force on the date of the deposit of their instruments of ratificiaion or accession.

5. The Depositary Governments shall promptly inform all signatory and acceding States of the date of each signature, the date of deposit of each instrument of ratification of and accession to this Treaty, the date of its entry into force and other notices.

6. This Treaty shall be registered by the Depositary Governments pursuant to Article 102 of the Charter of the United Nations.

ARTICLE XV

Any State Party to the Treaty may propose amendments to this Treaty. Amendments shall enter into force for each State Party to the Treaty accepting the amendments upon their acceptance by a majority of the State Parties to the Treaty on the date of acceptance by it.

ARTICLE XVI

Any State Party to the Treaty may give notice of its withdrawal from the Treaty one year after its entry into force by written notification to the Depositary Governments. Such withdrawal shall take effect one year from the date of receipt of this notification.

ARTICLE XVII

This Treaty, of which the Chinese, English, French, Russian and Spanish texts are equally authentic, shall be deposited in the archives of the Depositary Governments. Duly certified copies of this Treaty shall be transmitted by the Depositary Governments to the Governments of the signatory and acceding States.

IN WITNESS WHEREOF the undersigned, duly authorized, have signed this Treaty.

DONE in ...., at the cities of London, Moscow, and Washington, the .... day of one thousand nine hundred and ....
....

APPENDIX B

AGREEMENT ON THE RESCUE OF ASTRONAUTS, THE RETURN OF ASTRONAUTS AND THE RETURN OF OBJECTS LAUNCHED INTO OUTER SPACE

The Contracting Parties,

Noting the great importance of the Treaty on Principles Governing the Activities of States in the Exploration and Use of Outer Space, including the Moon and Other Celestial Bodies, which calls for the rendering of all possible assistance to astronauts in the event of accident, distress or emergency landing the prompt and safe return of astronauts, and the return of objects launched into outer space,

Desiring to develop and give further concrete expression to these duties,

Wishing to promote international cooperation in the peaceful exploration and use of outer space,

Prompted by sentiments of humanity,

Have agreed on the following:

ARTICLE 1

Each Contracting Party which receives information or discovers that the personnel of a spacecraft have suffered accident or are experiencing conditions of distress or have made an emergency or unintended landing in territory under its jurisdiction or on the high seas or in any other place not under the jurisdiction of any State shall immediately:

(a) Notify the launching authority or, if it cannot identify and immediately communicate with the launching authority, immediately make a public announcement by all appropriate means of communication at its disposal; and

(b) Notify the Secretary-General of the United Nations who should disseminate the information without delay by all appropriate means of communication at his disposal.

ARTICLE 2

If, owing to accident, distress, emergency or unintended landing, the personnel of a spacecraft land in territory under the jurisdiction of a Contracting Party, it shall immediately take all possible steps to rescue them and render them all necessary assistance. It shall inform the launching authority and also the Secretary-General of the United Nations of the steps it is taking and of their progress. If assistance by the launching authority would help to effect a prompt rescue or would contribute substantially to the effectiveness of search and rescue operations, the launching authority shall cooperate with the Contracting Party with a view to the effective conduct of search and rescue operations. Such operations shall be subject to the direction and control of the Contracting Party, which shall act in close and continuing consultation with the launching authority.

ARTICLE 3

If information is received or it is discovered that the personnel of a spacecraft have alighted on the high seas or in any other place not under the jurisdiction of any State, those Contracting Parties which are in a position to do so shall, if necessary, extend assistance in search and rescue operations for such personnel to assure their speedy rescue. They shall inform the launching authority and the Secretary-General of the United Nations of the steps they are taking and of their progress.

ARTICLE 4

If, owing to accident, distress, emergency or unintended landing, the personnel of a spacecraft land in territory under the jurisdiction of a Contracting Party or have been found on the high seas or in any other place not under the jurisdiction of any State, they shall be safely and promptly returned to representatives of the launching authority.

ARTICLE 5

1. Each Contracting Party which receives information or discovers that a space object or its component parts has returned to Earth in territory under its jurisdiction or on the high seas or in any other place not under the jurisdiction of any State, shall notify the launching authority and the Secretary-General of the United Nations.

2. Each Contracting Party having jurisdiction over the territory on which a space object or its component parts have been discovered shall, upon the request of the launching authority and with assistance from that authority if requested, take such steps as it finds practicable to recover the object or component parts.

3. Upon request of the launching authority, objects launched into outer

space or their component parts found beyond the territorial limits of the launching authority shall be returned to or held at the disposal of representatives of the launching authority, which shall, upon request, furnish identifying data prior to their return.

4. Notwithstanding paragraphs 2 and 3 of this article, a Contracting Party which has reason to believe that a space object or its component parts discovered in territory under its jurisdiction, or recovered by it elsewhere, is of a hazardous or deleterious nature may so notify the launching authority which shall immediately take effective steps, under the direction and control of the said Contracting Party to eliminate possible danger or harm.

5. Expenses incurred in fulfilling obligations to recover and return a space object or its component parts under paragraphs 2 and 3 of this article shall be borne by the launching authority.

ARTICLE 6

For the purposes of this Agreement, the term "launching authority" shall refer to the State responsible for launching, or, where an international intergovernmental organization is responsible for launching, that organization provided that that organization declares its acceptance of the rights and obligations provided for in this Agreement and a majority of the States members of that organization are Contracting Parties to this Agreement and to the Treaty on Principles Governing the Activities of States in the Exploration and Use of Outer Space, Including the Moon and Other Celestial Bodies.

ARTICLE 7

1. This Agreement shall be open to all States for signatures. Any State which does not sign this Agreement before its entry into force in accordance with paragraph 3 of this article may accede to it at any time.

2. This Agreement shall be subject to ratification by signatory States. Instruments of ratification and instruments of accession shall be deposited with the Governments of the United States of America, the United Kingdom of Great Britain and Northern Ireland and the Union of Soviet Socialist Republics, which are hereby designated the Depositary Governments.

3. This Agreement shall enter into force upon the deposit of instruments of ratification by five Governments including the Governments designated as Depositary Governments under this Agreement.

4. For States whose instruments of ratification or accession are deposited

subsequent to the entry into force of this Agreement, it shall enter into force on the date of the deposit of their instruments of ratification or accession.

5. The Depositary Governments shall promptly inform all signatory and acceding States of the date of each signature, the date of deposit of each instrument of ratification of and accession to this Agreement, the date of its entry into force and other notices.

6. This Agreement shall be registered by the Depositary Governments pursuant to Article 102 of the Charter of the United Nations.

ARTICLE 8

Any State Party to the Agreement may propose amendments to this Agreement. Amendments shall enter into force for each State Party to the Agreement accepting the amendments upon their acceptance by a majority of the States Parties to the Agreement and thereafter for each remaining State Party to the Agreement of the date of acceptance by it.

ARTICLE 9

Any State Party to the Agreement may give notice of its withdrawal from the Agreement one year after its entry into force by written notification to the Depositary Governments. Such withdrawal shall take effect one year from the date of receipt of this notification.

ARTICLE 10

This Agreement, of which the English, Russian, French, Spanish and Chinese texts are equally authentic, shall be deposited in the archives of the Depositary Governments. Duly certified copies of this Agreement shall be transmitted by the Depositary Governments to the Governments of the signatory and acceding States.

IN WITNESS WHEREOF the undersigned, duly authorized, have signed this Treaty.

APPENDIX C

STATE CLAIMS TO TERRITORIAL SEA

State	Claim
Afghanistan	landlocked
Albania	10
Algeria	12
Argentina	3
Australia	3
Austria	landlocked
Belgium	3
Bolivia	landlocked
Brazil	3
Bulgaria	12
Burma	12
Burundi	landlocked
Cambodia	5
Cameroon	6
Canada	3
Central African Republic	landlocked
Ceylon	6
Chad	landlocked
Chile	200[a]
China (Republic of)	3
China (People's Republic of)	12
Colombia	6
Congo (Brazzaville)	3
Congo (Leopoldville)	3

Costa Rica	200[a]
Cuba	3
Cyprus	12
Czechoslovakia	landlocked
Dahomey	3
Denmark	3
Dominican Republic	3
Ecuador	200[a]
El Salvador	200[a]
Ethiopia	12
Finland	4
France	3
Gabon	3
Germany (Democratic Republic)	3
Germany (Federal Republic)	3
Ghana	12
Greece	6
Guatemala	12
Guinea	130
Haiti	6
Honduras	200[a]
Hungary	landlocked
Iceland	12
India	12
Indonesia	12
Iran	12
Iraq	12
Ireland	3
Israel	6

Italy	6
Ivory Coast	12
Jamaica	3
Japan	3
Jordan	3
Kenya	3
Korea (People's Democratic Republic)	12
Korea (Republic of)	12
Kuwait	6
Laos	landlocked
Lebanon	6
Liberia	3
Libya	12
Luxembourg	landlocked
Malagasy Republic	12
Malawi	landlocked
Malaysia	3
Mali	landlocked
Malta	3
Mauritania	3
Mexico	9
Mongolia	landlocked
Morocco	12
Nepal	landlocked
Netherlands	3
New Zealand	3
Nicaragua	3
Niger	landlocked

Nigeria	3
Norway	4
Pakistan	3
Panama	12
Paraguay	landlocked
Peru	200[a]
Philippines	archipelago[b]
Poland	3
Portugal	3
Romania	12
Rwanda	landlocked
Saudi Arabia	12
Senegal	6
Sierra Leone	12
Somalia	3-6
South Africa	6
Spain	6
Sudan	12
Sweden	4
Switzerland	landlocked
Syria	12
Tanzania	12
Thailand	6
Togo	12
Trinidad and Tobago	3
Tunisia	6
Turkey	6
Uganda	landlocked

USSR	12
United Arab Republic	12
United Kingdom	3
United States	3
Upper Volta	landlocked
Uruguay	6
Venezuela	12
Vietnam (Democratic Republic of)	12
Vietnam (Republic of)	3
Yemen	12
Yugoslavia	6
Zambia	landlocked

SOURCE: Based on "Synoptical Table Concerning the Breadth and Juridicial Status of the Territorial Sea and Adjacent Zones," (U.N. Doc. A/Conf. 19/4) (1960), in Second United Nations Conference on the Law of the Sea, *Official Records, Summary of Plenary Meetings and Meetings of the Committee of the Whole* (U.N. Doc. Conf. 19/8) (1960), pp. 157-164; and *Sovereignty of the Sea, Geographic Bulletin* No. 3 (April, 1965) (Washington: Department of State, 1965), pp. 26-27. In case of conflict, the Department of State data are accepted although the claims listed in the *Sovereignty of the Sea* are not necessarily official. Cf. Lewis M. Alexander, "Breaths of Territorial Sea and Other Official Zones," 1968, *Proceedings of the Law of the Sea Institute*, pp. 313-318.

NOTE: Claims are given in nautical miles.

a   Although these claims are not always specifically made as claims to this breadth of territorial sea, in each instance sovereignty or comprehensive jurisdiction over superjacent waters is claimed.

b   See *Yearbook of the International Law Commission*, 1956, 2 (United Nations: United Nations, 1956), pp. 69-70, for the Philippines' special claim as an archipelago.

APPENDIX D

TABLE 22

STATES, ASSOCIATIONS, AND ORGANIZATIONS
REPRESENTED BY IDENTIFIERS OF OUTER SPACE
LEGAL PROBLEMS, 1958-64

Problem Category	1958 Legal Scholars	1959 Legal Scholars	1960 Legal Scholars	1961 Legal Scholars	1962 Legal Scholars	1963 Legal Scholars	1964 Legal Scholars
I General Problems	Brazil	Brazil	Austria	Argentina	Austria	Austria	Belgium
	Canada	Canada	Belgium	Austria	Belgium	Belgium	Bulgaria
	Czecho-slovakia	Czecho-slovakia	Canada	Belgium	Bulgaria	Canada	West Germany
	West Germany	West Germany	Czecho-slovakia	Bulgaria	Czecho-slovakia	West Germany	France
	France	France	Hungary	Canada	West Germany	Hungary	Greece
	Poland	India	ILO	Czecho-slovakia	France	Israel	Hungary
	USSR	Nether-lands	USSR	West Germany	East Germany	Italy	Italy
	US	USSR	US	France	Hungary	USSR	Poland
	Yugoslavia	US		Nether-lands	UK	US	Romania
		Yugoslavia		US	USSR	Yugoslavia	Spain
				Yugoslavia	US		USSR
					Yugoslavia		US
							Yugoslavia

Government Personnel	All Others	Documents
Chile, Czechoslovakia, West Germany, Italy, Sweden, USSR, US	UK, UN, US	USSR, US
Netherlands, UK, US	USSR	International Astronautical Federation, UN
Brazil, Canada, US		Bar Association of New York City, International Law Association, US, Western Disarmament Proposal
France, Iran, Poland, US	UN, US	USSR, US, Joint US/India Statement
Poland, US	UK, UN, US	UK, UN, USSR, US, Joint US/UK Proposal, Joint US/USSR Proposal
Argentina, US	UK, UN, US	Davies Institute Draft Code, Institute of International Law, UN
Argentina, US	US	US

II Functional Problems

	Legal Scholars	Legal Scholars	Legal Scholars	Legal Scholars	Legal Scholars	Legal Scholars	Legal Scholars
Legal Scholars	West Germany France East Germany Nether-lands Poland USSR US Yugoslavia	Brazil Canada West Germany France India Portugal USSR US Yugoslavia	Belgium Canada Czecho-slovakia ILO US Yugoslavia	Argentina Bulgaria Canada West Germany France Nether-lands US	Austria Belgium Czecho-slovakia West Germany France East Germany Hungary Nether-lands USSR UK US	Belgium Canada West Germany Greece Hungary Nether-lands USSR US Yugoslavia	West Germany Greece Poland Romania Spain USSR US Yugoslavia

	Government Personnel	Government Personnel	Government Personnel	Government Personnel	Government Personnel	Government Personnel	Government Personnel
Government Personnel	West Germany	US	Brazil Canada US	Iran San Marino US	US	Argentina US	US

	All Others	All Others	All Others	All Others	All Others	All Others	All Others
All Others	UK				UK UN US	UK UN US	

III Primarily Political Problems	1	2	3	4	5	6	7
Legal Scholars	Brazil Canada Czecho-slovakia West Germany France East Germany Poland USSR US Yugoslavia	Brazil Canada Czecho-slovakia West Germany France India Nether-lands Portugal USSR US Yugoslavia	Austria Canada Czecho-slovakia Hungary ILO USSR US Yugoslavia	Argentina Austria Belgium Canada West Germany US Yugoslavia	Austria Bulgaria Czecho-slovakia France East Germany Hungary USSR US Yugoslavia	Austria Canada Hungary USSR US Yugoslavia	Austria Bulgaria West Germany Greece Hungary Italy Poland USSR US Yugoslavia
Documents	USSR	Inter-national Astro-nautical Federa-tion	Bar Asso-ciation of New York City US Western Dis-armament Proposal		UAR USSR UN US	Davies Institute Draft Code Institute of Inter-national Law UN	Davies Institute Draft Code UN

Government Personnel	Government Personnel	Government Personnel	Government Personnel	Government Personnel	Government Personnel	Government Personnel
Argentina Chile West Germany Italy Peru US	Netherlands US	Brazil Canada US	Iran Poland San Marino US	Argentina Hungary Poland US	Argentina US	Argentina US
All Others	**All Others**	**All Others**	**All Others**	**All Others**	**All Others**	**All Others**
Poland UK UN	USSR		UN US	UK UN US	UN	US
Documents	**Documents**	**Documents**	**Documents**	**Documents**	**Documents**	**Documents**
	International Astronautical Federation	Bar Association of New York City USSR US Western Disarmament Proposal	US	UAR UK UN USSR US Joint US/USSR Proposal	Davies Institute Draft Code Institute of International Law UN	Davies Institute Draft Code UN

APPENDIX E

TABLE 23

STATES INCLUDED IN THE 1964 INTERNATIONAL
POLITICAL SYSTEM WHICH HAVE A SPECIAL
INTEREST IN THE LAW OF THE SEA NOT
REPRESENTED AT THE 1958 AND 1960 GENEVA
CONFERENCES ON THE LAW OF THE SEA

State	Merchant Marine Fleet[a]	Port Activity[b]	Fishing Activity[c]	Naval Forces[d] Large and Small Combatants
		Basis of Special Interest		
Algeria		2		
China (Red)		9[e]	1	3
Gabon		3		
Ivory Coast		3		
Jamaica		3		
Kenya		3		
Nigeria		3		
Senegal		3		
Syria		3		
Tanzania		3		
Trinidad and Tobago		2		
Total	0	10	1	1

[a] Based on data furnished by the American Bureau of Shipping for seagoing steam and motor vessels of 1,000 gross tons and over as of December 31, 1964, and supplemented where necessary by data obtained from the United Nations, *Statistical Yearbook, 1965* (United Nations: United Nations, 1966). Codes: (1) Very Large (more than 10% of the world total); (2) Large (4-10% of the world total); and (3) Medium (2-3% of the world total).

[b] Based on data contained in the United Nations, *Statistical Yearbook, 1965,* ibid., for thousand gross registered tons vessels entering and clearing ports, excluding vessels in ballast. Codes (1) Very Active (more than 55,000); (2) Active (20-55,000); and (3) Moderately Active (6-19,999).

[c] Based on data reported in Food and Agriculture Organization, *Yearbook of Fishery Statistics, 1964* (Rome: Food and Agriculture Organization, 1965).

Codes: (1) Very Active (more than 10% of world total fishing catch); (2) Active (2-10% of world total fishing catch); and (3) Moderately Active (1-1.9% of world total fishing catch).

d   Based on data reported by Raymond V. B. Blackman, ed., *Jane's Fighting Ships 1965-66* (Great Missenden Bucks: Jane's Fighting Ships, 1966), and supplemented with data obtained in S. H. Steinberg, ed. *The Statesman's Year Book 1965-66* (New York: St. Martin's Press, 1965). Codes: (1) Very Large (more than 1,000 large and/or small combatants); (2) Large (70-1,000 large and/or small combatants); and (3) Medium (25-69 large or small combatants).

e   Not ascertained.

APPENDIX F

CODE BOOK

N = 121

DECK 1

ACCEPTANCE AND REJECTION OF RULES OR PRINCIPLES

Column Number	N	Code
01-05		Study Number (W5951)
06		Deck Number (1)
07-09		State Code Number
10-18		State Name
19-20		Breadth of Territorial Sea Favored at 1960 Conference

19   1. Supported 18-Power Proposal (12 mile territorial sea or combination territorial sea and contiguous zone of up to 12 miles).

	N	
	34	1. Yes
	37	2. No
	12	3. Abstained
	38	8. Not Applicable

Source: Records of the 1960 Conference on the Law of the Sea

20   2. Supported US-Canadian Proposal in Plenary (6/6)

	N	
	51	1. Yes
	26	2. No
	5	3. Abstained
	39	8. Not Applicable

Source: Records of 1960 Conference on the Law of the Sea

21   Contiguous Zone (Sea)

3. Either has signed, ratified or otherwise adhered to

1958 Convention on the Territorial Sea and the
Contiguous Zone and/or has made a unilateral claim
to one or more contiguous zones.

78   1. Yes
9   2. No
12   8. Not Applicable
22   9. Not Ascertained

Source: Information furnished by the Treaty Sec-
tion, The Legal Division, United Nations
Secretariat in June, 1966, and from
"Synoptical Table concerning the Breadth
and Juridical Status of the Territorial Sea
and Adjacent Zones," (U.N. Doc. A Conf.
19/4) (1960), in Second United Nations
Conference on the Law of the Sea, *Official
Records, Summary of Plenary Meetings and
Meetings of the Committee of the Whole*
(U.N. Doc. No. 19/8) (1960), pp. 157-
164.

22   Continental Shelf

4. Either has signed, ratified or otherwise adhered to
1958 Convention on the Continental Shelf and/or
has made a unilateral claim to the shelf.

70   1. Yes
38   2. No
13   8. Not Applicable
0   9. Not Ascertained

Source: Information furnished by the Treaty Sec-
tion, The Legal Division, United Nations
Secretariat in June, 1966, and from Shigeru
Oda, *International Control of Sea Resources*
(Leyden: A. W. Sythoff, 1963), pp. 148-
150.

23-24   High Seas

23   5. Supported Articles 1 and 2 in Plenary Session of
1958 Conference (High Seas Convention)

81   1. Yes
40   8. Not Applicable

Source: Records of 1958 Conference on the Law of the Sea.

24

6. Either has signed, ratified or otherwise adhered to 1958 Convention on the High Seas.

60   1. Yes
61   2. No

Source: Information furnished by the Treaty Section, The Legal Division, United Nations Secretariat in June, 1966.

25

Nationality and Registration of Ships

7. Either has signed, ratified or otherwise adhered to 1958 Convention on the High Seas and/or has domestic legislation on nationality and/or registration.

81   1. Yes
0   2. No
10   8. Not Applicable
30   9. Not Ascertained

Source: Information furnished by the Treaty Section, The Legal Division, United Nations Secretariat in June, 1966, United Nations Legislative Series, *Laws Concerning the Nationality of Ships* (St/Leg/Ser. B/5) (United Nations: United Nations, 1955), and United Nations Legislative Series, *Supplement to Laws and Regulations on the Regime of the High Seas (Volumes I and II) and Laws Concerning the Nationality of Ships* (St/Leg/Ser. B/8) (United Nations: United Nations, 1959).

26-27

Safety at Sea

26

8. Either has signed, ratified or otherwise adhered to 1948 and/or 1960 Safety of Life at Sea Convention.
75   1. Yes
46   2. No

Source: Department of State, *Treaties in Force: A List of Treaties and Other International*

Agreements in Force on January 1, 1966
(Washington: Government Printing Office,
1966).

27   9. Either has signed, ratified or otherwise adhered to
1929 Load Line Convention as modified in 1938
and 1957.

73   1. Yes
48   2. No

Source: Department of State, *Treaties in Force: A
List of Treaties and Other International
Agreements in Force on January 1, 1966*
(Washington: Government Printing Of-
fice, 1966).

28   Innocent Passage in Territorial Waters

10. Either has signed, ratified or otherwise adhered to
1958 Convention on the Territorial Sea and the
Contiguous Zone.

53   1. Yes
68   2. No

Source: Information furnished by the Treaty Section, The Legal Division, United Nations
Secretariat in June, 1966.

29   Sovereignty or Comprehensive Jurisdiction in Territorial
Airspace

11. Either has signed, ratified or otherwise adhered to
1944 Chicago Convention on Civil Aviation and/or
has domestic legislation which asserts a claim either
to comprehensive jurisdiction or sovereignty over
superjacent airspace.

117   1. Yes
4   9. Not Ascertained

Source: Department of State, *Treaties in Force: A
List of Treaties and Other International
Agreements in Force on January 1, 1966*
(Washington: Government Printing Of-
fice, 1966), and United States Congress,
Senate, Committee on Commerce. *Air*

Laws and Treaties of the World, 89th Cong. 1st Sess., 1965.

30   Nationality and Registration of Civil Aircraft

12. Either has signed, ratified or otherwise adhered to 1944 Chicago Convention on Civil Aviation and/or has domestic legislation providing for registration and/or nationality.

115   1. Yes

6   9. Not Ascertained

Source: Department of State, *Treaties in Force: A List of Treaties and Other International Agreements in Force on January 1, 1966* (Washington: Government Printing Office, 1966), and United States Congress, Senate, *Committee on Commerce, Air Laws and Treaties of the World,* 89th Cong. 1st Sess., 1965.

31-32   Liability in Civil Aviation

31   13. Either has signed, ratified or otherwise adhered to the 1929 Warsaw Convention as modified by the 1955 Hague Protocol.

86   1. Yes

35   2. No

Source: Department of State, *Treaties in Force: A List of Treaties and Other International Agreements in Force on January 1, 1966* (Washington: Government Printing Office, 1966).

32   14. Either has signed, ratified or otherwise adhered to the 1952 Rome Convention on Damage Caused by Foreign Aircraft to Third Parties on the Surface.

38   1. Yes

83   2. No

Source: Information furnished by the ICAO in September, 1966.

33-34   Innocent Passage in Territorial Airspace

33

15. Either has signed, ratified or otherwise adhered to the 1944 Chicago Convention on Civil Aviation.

109 1. Yes
12   2. No

Source: Department of State, *Treaties in Force: A List of Treaties and Other International Agreements in Force on January 1, 1966* (Washington: Government Printing Office, 1966).

34

16. Either has signed, ratified or otherwise adhered to the International Air Services Transit Agreement.

70   1. Yes
51   2. No

Source: Department of State, *Treaties in Force: A List of Treaties and Other International Agreements in Force on January 1, 1966* (Washington: Government Printing Office, 1966).

35-36

Indications of Acceptance of International Regulations in Sea Environment

35

17. Either has signed, ratified or otherwise adhered to Brussels Convention for Unification of Certain Rules with Respect to Assistance and Salvage at Sea.

44   1. Yes
77   2. No

Source: Department of State, *Treaties in Force: A List of Treaties and Other International Agreements in Force on January 1, 1966* (Washington: Government Printing Office, 1966).

36

18. Either has signed, ratified or otherwise adhered to Convention for the Prevention of Pollution of the Sea by Oil, London, 1954.

29   1. Yes
92   2. No

Source: Information furnished by the Treaty Section, The Legal Division, United Nations Secretariat in June, 1966.

37   Acceptance of International Sanitary Regulations in Air and Sea Environments

19. Either has signed, ratified or otherwise adhered to Additional Regulations Amending the International Sanitary Regulations with Respect to Disinfecting Ships and Aircraft and Appendices 3 and 4, etc., Geneva, May 12, 1965 (WHO Regs).

113   1. Yes
8   2. No

Source: Department of State, *Treaties in Force: A List of Treaties and Other International Agreements in Force on January 1, 1966* (Washington: Government Printing Office, 1966).

38-41   Indications of Acceptance of International Regulations in Air Environment

38   20. Either has signed, ratified or otherwise adhered to Convention on the International Recognition of Rights in Aircraft, Geneva, 1948.

38   1. Yes
83   2. No

Source: Information supplied by ICAO in September, 1966.

39   21. Either has signed, ratified or otherwise adhered to Convention on Offences and Certain Other Acts Committed on Board Aircraft, Tokyo, 1963.

25   1. Yes
96   2. No

Source: Information supplied by ICAO in September, 1966.

40   22. Either has signed, ratified or otherwise adhered to Multilateral Agreement on Commercial Rights of Non-scheduled Air Services in Europe, Paris, 1956.

18   1. Yes

10   2. No

93   8. Not Applicable

    Source: Information supplied by ICAO in September, 1966.

41   23. Either has signed, ratified or otherwise adhered to Convention for the Unification of Certain Rules Relating to the Precautionary Attachment of Aircraft, Rome, 1933.

19   1. Yes

102   2. No

    Source: J. P. Honig, *The Legal Status of Aircraft* (The Hague: Martinus Nijhoff, 1956), p. 117.

42-45   Indications of Acceptance of Miscellaneous International Conventions or Regulations

42   24. Either has signed, ratified or otherwise adhered to the Nuclear Test Ban Treaty, Moscow, 1963.

87   1. Yes

34   2. No

    Source: Department of State, *Treaties in Force: A List of Treaties and Other International Agreements in Force on January 1, 1966* (Washington: Government Printing Office, 1966).

43   25. Either has signed, ratified or otherwise adhered to Agreement Establishing Interim Arrangements for a Global Commercial Communications Satellite System, Washington, 1964.

45   1. Yes

76   2. No

    Source: Department of State, *Treaties in Force: A List of Treaties and Other International Agreements in Force on January 1, 1966* (Washington: Government Printing Office, 1966).

44   26. Either has signed, ratified or otherwise adhered to

Radio Regulations, with Appendices, Annexed to the International Telecommunications Convention, 1959, and Additional Protocol, Geneva, 1959.

62   1. Yes
59   2. No

Source: Department of State, *Treaties in Force: A List of Treaties and Other International Agreements in Force on January 1, 1966* (Washington: Government Printing Office, 1966).

45   27. Supported General Assembly Resolution 1962 (XVIII), a Declaration of Legal Principles Governing the Activities of States in the Exploration and Use of Outer Space

109   1. Yes
12   8. Not Applicable

Source: United Nations, *Official Records of the General Assembly, Eighteenth Session, Plenary Meetings, Verbatim Records of Meetings,* 3 (United Nations: United Nations, 1965).

APPENDIX G

CODE BOOK

N = 121

DECK 2

ECONOMIC, POLITICAL, AND SOCIAL INDICATORS

Column Number	N	Code
01-05		Study Number (W5951)
06		Deck Number (2)
07-09		State Code Number
10-18		State Name
19-20		1. Areal Grouping
	2	01. Australasia
	4	02. Caribbean
	8	03. Central America
	30	04. Central and South Africa
	6	05. East Asia
	9	06. East Europe
	12	07. Middle East
	4	08. North Africa
	3	09. North America
	5	10. Scandinavia
	11	11. South America
	4	12. South Asia
	9	13. Southeast Asia
	14	14. West Europe

Source: Arthur S. Banks and Robert B. Textor, *A Cross-Polity Survey* (Cambridge: The M.I.T. Press, 1963), and *New Cosmopolitan World Atlas* (Enlarged Global View Edition; Chicago, New York and San Francisco, 1966).

21   2. Land Size

     6   1. Very Large (2 million square miles and above)
     26   2. Large (300,000-1.9 million square miles)
     39   3. Medium (75,000-299,000 square miles)
     50   4. Small (below 75,000 square miles)

Source: Arthur S. Banks and Robert B. Textor, *A Cross-Polity Survey* (Cambridge: The M.I.T. Press, 1963), and United Nations, *Statistical Yearbook, 1965* (United Nations: United Nations, 1966).

22   3. Population Size

     4   1. Very Large (100 million and above)
     23   2. Large (17-99.9 million)
     36   3. Medium (6-16.9 million)
     58   4. Small (under 6 million)

Source: Arthur S. Banks and Robert B. Textor, *A Cross-Polity Survey* (Cambridge: The M.I.T. Press, 1963), and United Nations, *Statistical Yearbook, 1965* (United Nations: United Nations, 1966).

23   4. Population Density

     5   1. Very High (600 per square mile and above)
     13   2. High (300-599 per square mile)
     30   3. Medium (100-299 per square mile)
     73   4. Low (below 100 per square mile)

Source: Arthur S. Banks and Robert B. Textor, *A Cross-Polity Survey* (Cambridge: The M.I.T. Press, 1963), and United Nations, *Statistical Yearbook, 1965* (United Nations: United Nations, 1966).

24   5. Population Growth Rate

     70   1. High (2 percent or above)
     50   2. Low (less than 2 percent)
     1   3. Not Ascertained

Source: Arthur S. Banks and Robert B. Textor, *A Cross-Polity Survey* (Cambridge: The

M.I.T. Press, 1963), and United Nations, *Statistical Yearbook, 1965* (United Nations: United Nations, 1966).

25   6. Level of Urbanization

56   1. High (20 percent or more of population in cities of 20,000 or more and 12.5 percent or more of population in cities of 100,000 or more)

49   2. Low (less than 20 percent of population in cities of 20,000 or more and less than 12.5 percent of population in cities of 100,000 or more)

5   8. Ambiguous
11   9. Not Ascertained

Source: Arthur S. Banks and Robert B. Textor, *A Cross-Polity Survey* (Cambridge: The M.I.T. Press, 1963).

26   7. Agricultural Population as Percent of Total Population

57   1. High (over 66 percent)
33   2. Medium (34-66 percent)
17   3. Low (16-33 percent)
7   4. Very Low (under 16 percent)
7   9. Not Ascertained

Source: Arthur S. Banks and Robert B. Textor, *A Cross-Polity Survey* (Cambridge: The M.I.T. Press, 1963), and *The F.A.O. Yearbook, 1964* (Rome: The Food and Agriculture Organization, 1965).

27   8. Gross National Product

2   1. Very High ($125 billion and above)
8   2. High ($25-124.9 billion)
21   3. Medium ($5-24.9 billion)
34   4. Low ($1-4.9 billion)
56   5. Very Low (under $1 billion)
0   9. Not Ascertained

Source: Arthur S. Banks and Robert B. Textor,
          A Cross-Polity Survey (Cambridge: The
          M.I.T. Press, 1963), United Nations,
          Statistical Yearbook, 1965 (United Na-
          tions: United Nations, 1966), and Bruce
          M. Russett, et al., *World Handbook of
          Political and Social Indicators* (New
          Haven: Yale University Press, 1964).

28

9. Per Capita Gross National Product

15   1. Very High ($1200 and above)
13   2. High ($600-1199)
18   3. Medium ($300-599)
22   4. Low ($150-299)
53   5. Very Low (under $150)
0   9. Not Ascertained

Source: Arthur S. Banks and Robert B. Textor,
          A Cross-Polity Survey (Cambridge: The
          M.I.T. Press, 1963), United Nations,
          Statistical Yearbook, 1965 (United Na-
          tions: United Nations, 1966), and Bruce
          M. Russett, et al., *World Handbook of
          Political and Social Indicators* (New
          Haven: Yale University Press, 1964).

29

10. International Financial Status

2   1. Very High (UN assessment of 10 percent or
            more)
9   2. High (UN assessment of 1.50-9.99 percent)
28   3. Medium (UN assessment of 0.25-1.49 percent)
34   4. Low (UN assessment of 0.05-0.24 percent)
42   5. Very Low (minimum UN assessment of 0.04
            percent)
6   9. Not Ascertained

Source: Arthur S. Banks and Robert B. Textor,
          A Cross-Polity Survey (Cambridge: The
          M.I.T. Press, 1963) and General Assem-
          bly Resolution 1691 (XVI), Scale of As-
          sessments for the Apportionment of the
          Expenses of the United Nations.

30   11. Status of Economic Development

18   1. Developed (self-sustaining economic growth. GNP per capita over $600)

18   2. Intermediate (sustained and near self-sustaining economic growth)

15   3. Underdeveloped (reasonable prospect of attaining sustained economic growth by mid-1970's)

61   4. Very Underdeveloped (little or no prospect of attaining sustained economic growth within the foreseeable future)

6   8. Ambiguous

3   9. Not Ascertained

Source: Arthur S. Banks and Robert B. Textor, *A Cross-Polity Survey* (Cambridge: The M.I.T. Press, 1963), and column 27.

31   12. Religious Homogeneity

57   1. Homogeneous (country Protestant, Catholic, East Orthodox, Hindu, Buddhist, Muslim, or Jewish)

46   2. Heterogeneous (mixed Christian; mixed literate non-Christian; mixed: Christian; non-literate; mixed: literate non-Christian, non-literate; Christian, literate non-Christian, non-literate)

3   8. Ambiguous

15   9. Not Ascertained

Source: Arthur S. Banks and Robert B. Textor, *A Cross-Polity Survey* (Cambridge: The M.I.T. Press, 1963), and S. H. Steinberg, ed *The Statesman's Yearbook 1965-1966* (New York: St. Martin's Press, 1965)

32   13. Racial Homogeneity

82   1. Homogeneous (90 percent or more of one race)

25   2. Heterogeneous (less than 90 percent of one race)

3   8. Ambiguous

15   9. Not Ascertained

Source: Arthur S. Banks and Robert B. Textor, *A Cross-Polity Survey* (Cambridge: The

M.I.T. Press, 1963), and S. H. Steinberg, ed., *The Statesman's Yearbook 1965-1966* (New York: St. Martin's Press, 1965).

33   14. Linguistic Homogeneity

52   1. Homogeneous (majority of 85 percent or more; no significant single minority)

12   2. Weakly Heterogeneous (majority of 85 percent or more; significant minority of 15 percent or less)

49   3. Strongly Heterogeneous (no single group of 85 percent or more)

1   8. Ambiguous

7   9. Not Ascertained

Source: Arthur S. Banks and Robert B. Textor, *A Cross-Polity Survey* (Cambridge: The M.I.T. Press, 1963), and S. H. Steinberg, ed., *The Statesman's Yearbook 1965-1966* (New York: St. Martin's Press, 1965).

34   15. Date of Independence

22   1. Before the 19th century
31   2. 1800-1913
13   3. 1914-1945
51   4. After 1945
4   8. Ambiguous

Source: Arthur S. Banks and Robert B. Textor, *A Cross-Polity Survey* (Cambridge: The M.I.T. Press, 1963), and S. H. Steinberg, ed., *The Statesman's Yearbook 1965-1966* (New York: St. Martin's Press, 1965).

35   16. Westernization

22   1. Historically western nation
8   2. Significantly westernized (no colonial relationship)
28   3. Significantly westernized (colonial relationship)
7   4. Partially westernized (no colonial relationship)
41   5. Partially westernized (colonial relationship)
2   6. Non-westernized (no colonial relationship. Little or no visible westernization)

2	8. Ambiguous
11	9. Not Ascertained

Source: Arthur S. Banks and Robert B. Textor, *A Cross-Polity Survey* (Cambridge: The M.I.T. Press, 1963).

36   17. Former Colonial Ruler

28	1. Britain
25	2. France
18	3. Spain
9	4. Other
41	5. Irrelevant

Source: Arthur S. Banks and Robert B. Textor, *A Cross-Polity Survey* (Cambridge: The M.I.T. Press, 1963), and S. H. Steinberg, ed., *The Statesman's Yearbook 1965-1966* (New York: St. Martin's Press, 1965).

37   18. Political Modernization. Historical Type.

13	1. Early European or early European derived (early modernizing European society or off-shoot)
40	2. Later European or later European derived (later modernizing European society or off-shoot)
10	3. Non-European Autochthonous (self-modernizing extra-European society)
29	4. Developed Tutelary (developed society modernizing under tutelage)
23	5. Undeveloped Tutelary (undeveloped society modernizing under tutelage)
0	8. Ambiguous
6	9. Not Ascertained

Source: Arthur S. Banks and Robert B. Textor, *A Cross-Polity Survey* (Cambridge: The M.I.T. Press, 1963).

38   19. Political Modernization. Periodization.

61	1. Advanced (transitional phase completed)
16	2. Mid-transitional (entered transitional phase prior to 1945)

36   3.   Early Transitional (entered transitional phase 1945 or later)

1   4.   Pre-Transitional (not yet in transitional phase)

0   8.   Ambiguous

7   9.   Not Ascertained

Source: Arthur S. Banks and Robert B. Textor, *A Cross-Polity Survey* (Cambridge: The M.I.T. Press, 1963).

39   20.   Ideological Orientation

13   1.   Doctrinal

29   2.   Developmental

5   3.   Situational

33   4.   Conventional

5   5.   Traditional

0   7.   Unascertainable

25   8.   Ambiguous

11   9.   Not Ascertained

Source: Arthur S. Banks and Robert B. Textor, *A Cross-Polity Survey* (Cambridge: The M.I.T. Press, 1963).

40   21.   System Style

22   1.   Mobilizational

12   2.   Limited Mobilizational

75   3.   Non-Mobilizational

2   7.   Unascertainable

2   8.   Ambiguous

8   9.   Not Ascertained

Source: Arthur S. Banks and Robert B. Textor, *A Cross-Polity Survey* (Cambridge: The M.I.T. Press, 1963).

41   22.   Constitutional Status of Current Regime

52   1.   Constitutional (Government conducted with reference to recognized constitutional norms)

24   2.   Authoritarian (no effective constitutional limitation, or fairly regular recourse to extra-constitutional powers. Arbitrary exercise of power confined largely to the political sector)

17   3.   Totalitarian (no effective constitutional limita-

tion. Broad exercise of power by the regime in both political and social spheres)

8   7. Unascertainable
6   8. Ambiguous
14   9. Not Ascertained

Source: Arthur S. Banks and Robert B. Textor, *A Cross-Polity Survey* (Cambridge: The M.I.T. Press, 1963), S. H. Steinberg, ed., *The Statesman's Yearbook 1965-1966* (New York: St. Martin's Press, 1965), and various books and articles on particular states.

42   23. Governmental Stability

22   1. Government generally stable since World War I or major inter-war constitutional change
31   2. Government generally stable since World War II or major post-war constitutional change
11   3. Government moderately stable since World War II or major post-war constitutional change
33   4. Government unstable since World War II or major post-war constitutional change
18   7. Unascertainable
3   8. Ambiguous
3   9. Not Ascertained

Source: Arthur S. Banks and Robert B. Textor, *A Cross-Polity Survey* (Cambridge: The M.I.T. Press, 1963), S. H. Steinberg, ed., *The Statesman's Yearbook 1965-1966* (New York: St. Martin's Press, 1965), and various books and articles on particular states.

43   24. Political Leadership

30   1. Elitist (recruitment confined to a particular racial, social, or ideological stratum)
16   2. Moderate elitist (recruitment largely but not wholly confined to a particular racial, social, or ideological stratum)
48   3. Non-elitist (recruitment largely on the basis of achievement criteria only)

7   7. Unascertained
11   8. Ambiguous
9   9. Not Ascertained

Source: Arthur S. Banks and Robert B. Textor, *A Cross-Polity Survey* (Cambridge: The M.I.T. Press, 1963).

44   25. Political Participation by the Military

26   1. Interventive (presently exercises or has recently exercised direct power)

31   2. Supportive (performs para-political role in support of traditionalist, authoritarian, totalitarian, or modernizing regime)

51   3. Neutral (a-political or of minor political importance)

6   8. Ambiguous
7   9. Not Ascertained

Source: Arthur S. Banks and Robert B. Textor, *A Cross-Polity Survey* (Cambridge: The M.I.T. Press, 1963), S. H. Steinberg, ed., *The Statesman's Yearbook 1965-1966* (New York: St. Martin's Press, 1965), and various books and articles on particular states.

45   26. Role of Police

67   1. Politically significant (important continuing or intermittent political function in addition to law-enforcement)

32   2. Not politically significant (role confined to law-enforcement only)

0   7. Unascertainable
22   9. Not Ascertained

Source: Arthur S. Banks and Robert B. Textor, *A Cross-Polity Survey* (Cambridge: The M.I.T. Press, 1963), S. H. Steinberg, ed., *The Statesman's Yearbook 1965-1966* (New York: St. Martin's Press, 1965), and various books and articles on particular states.

46-47   27. Character of Legal System

33   01. Civil Law
11   02. Mixed Civil-Indigenous
6   03. Common Law
2   04. Mixed Common-Indigenous
2   05. Mixed Civil-Common
1   06. Mixed Civil-Common-Indigenous
2   07. Muslim
8   08. Mixed Civil-Muslim
2   09. Mixed Civil-Muslim-Indigenous
8   10. Mixed Civil-Muslim-Indigenous
4   11. Mixed Common-Muslim-Indigenous
5   12. Scandinavian
13   13. Communist
12   14. Other
0   15. Unascertainable
2   16. Ambiguous
10   00. Not Ascertained

Source: Arthur S. Banks and Robert B. Textor, *A Cross-Polity Survey* (Cambridge: The M.I.T. Press, 1963).

48   28. Bloc Alignment

14   1. Communist
0   2. Quasi-Communist
104   3. Non-Communist
0   8. Ambiguous
3   9. Not Ascertained

Source: Arthur S. Banks and Robert B. Textor, *A Cross-Polity Survey* (Cambridge: The M.I.T. Press, 1963), S. H. Steinberg, ed., *The Statesman's Yearbook 1965-1966* (New York: St. Martin's Press, 1965), and various books and articles on particular states.

49   29. Merchant Marine Fleet (Seagoing steam and motor vessels of 1,000 gross tons and over)

3   1. Very Large (more than 10 percent of world merchant fleet)

4	2. Large (4-10 percent of world merchant fleet)
6	3. Medium (2-3.9 percent of world merchant fleet)
6	4. Small (.75-1.9 percent of world merchant fleet)
61	5. Very Small (less than .75 percent of world merchant fleet)
41	6. None
0	9. Not Ascertained

Source: Information furnished by the American Bureau of Shipping, and supplemented by data from the United Nations, *Statistical Yearbook, 1965* (United Nations: United Nations, 1966).

50

30. Port Activity (thousand gross registered tons vessels entered)

11	1. Very Active (more than 55,000)
10	2. Active (20,000-55,000)
23	3. Moderately Active (6,000-19,999)
30	4. Inactive (2,000-5,999)
8	5. Very Inactive (less than 2,000)
18	6. Landlocked or no major seaport
21	9. Not Ascertained

Source: United Nations, *Statistical Yearbook, 1965* (United Nations: United Nations, 1966).

51

31. Total Scheduled Civil Aviation Services (coded to highest category)

2	1. Very Active (more than 200 million kilometers flown and/or more than 50 billion passenger kilometers)
21	2. Active (20-200 million kilometers flown and/or 1-50 billion passenger kilometers)
16	3. Moderately Active (10-19.9 million kilometers flown and/or 300-999.9 million passenger kilometers)
30	4. Inactive (1-9.9 million kilometers flown and/or 100-299.9 million passenger kilometers)
2	5. Very Inactive (less than 1 million kilometers flown and/or less than 100 million passenger kilometers)
0	6. None
50	9. Not Ascertained

Source: United Nations, *Statistical Yearbook, 1965*
(United Nations: United Nations, 1966).

52   32. International Civil Aviation Activity

  1   1. Very Active (more than 200 million kilometers flown and/or more than 50 billion passenger kilometers)

14   2. Active (20-200 million kilometers flown and/or 1-50 billion passenger kilometers)

18   3. Moderately Active (10-19.9 million kilometers flown and/or 300-999.9 million passenger kilometers)

30   4. Inactive (1-9.9 million kilometers flown and/or 100-299.9 million passenger kilometers)

  5   5. Very Inactive (less than 1 million kilometers flown and/or less than 100 million passenger kilometers)

  0   6. None

53   9. Not Ascertained

Source: United Nations, *Statistical Yearbook, 1965*
(United Nations: United Nations, 1966).

53   33. Summary of Balance Payments

  1   1. Very Large Deficit (in excess of $500 million)

19   2. Large Deficit ($20-500 million)

29   3. Small Deficit ($0-19.9 million)

18   4. Small Surplus ($0-20 million)

  6   5. Large Surplus (more than $20 million)

48   9. Not Ascertained

Source: United Nations, *Statistical Yearbook, 1965*
(United Nations: United Nations, 1966),
and *Yearbook of International Trade
Statistics, 1964* (United Nations: United
Nations, 1965).

54   34. Fishing Activity

  3   1. Very Active (more than 10 percent of world fishing catch)

  7   2. Active (2-10 percent of world fishing catch)

11   3. Moderately Active (1-1.9 percent of world fishing catch)

19   4. Inactive (.25-.99 percent of world fishing catch)

64   5. Very Inactive (less than .25 percent of world fishing catch)

7   6. No Fishing Activity

10   9. Not Ascertained

Source: Food and Agriculture Organization, *Yearbook of Fishery Statistics, 1964* (Rome: Food and Agriculture Organization, 1965).

55   35. Fishery Products: Canned

5   1. Large Producer (more than 5 percent of world total canned fish)

6   2. Medium Producer (2-4.9 percent of world total canned fish)

16   3. Small Producer (less than 2 percent of world total canned fish)

93   4. Non-Producer

1   9. Not Ascertained

Source: United Nations, *Statistical Yearbook, 1965* (United Nations: United Nations, 1966).

56   36. Fishery Products: Salted

3   1. Large Producer (more than 3.5 percent of world total salted fish)

10   2. Medium Producer (1-3.4 percent of world total salted fish)

11   3. Small Producer (less than 1 percent of world total salted fish)

96   4. Non-Producer

1   9. Not Ascertained

Source: United Nations, *Statistical Yearbook, 1965* (United Nations: United Nations, 1966).

57   37. Fishery Products: Fish Meals and Solubles

2   1. Very Large Producer (more than 20 percent of world total fish meals and solubles)

3   2. Large Producer (5-19.9 percent of world total fish meals and solubles)

6   3. Medium Producer (5-19.9 percent of world total fish meals and solubles)

8   4. Small Producer (less than 2 percent of world total fish meal and solubles)

102   5. Non-Producer

0   9. Not Ascertained

Source: United Nations, *Statistical Yearbook, 1965* (United Nations: United Nations, 1966).

58   38. Fishery Products: Whale Meals, Liver Meals, and Solubles

2   1. Very Large Producer (more than 15 percent of world total whale meals, liver meals, and solubles)

2   2. Large Producer (4-14.9 percent of world total whale meals, liver meals, and solubles)

3   3. Medium Producer (2-3.9 percent of world total whale meals, liver meals, and solubles)

2   4. Small Producer (less than 2 percent of world total whale meals, liver meals, and solubles)

111   5. Non-Producer

1   9. Not-Ascertained

Source: United Nations, *Statistical Yearbook, 1965* (United Nations: United Nations, 1966).

59   39. Net Food Supplies

24   1. Adequate (over 2700 calories per capita per day and over 30 grams of animal protein per capita per day)

10   2. Marginal (2200-2700 calories per capita and over 15 and under 30 grams of animal protein per capita per day)

18   3. Inadequate (below 2200 calories per capita per day and 15 and under grams of animal protein per capita per day)

22   4. Adequate or marginal in calories, animal protein marginal or inadequate or not ascertained)

3   5. Adequate or marginal in animal protein, calories marginal or inadequate or not ascertained)

44   9. Not Ascertained

Source: United Nations, *Statistical Yearbook, 1965 tics of Hunger* (Rome: Food and Agriculture Organization, 1962), and United States Congress, Senate, *World Population and Food Crisis,* Hearing Before the Consultative Subcommittee on Economic and Social Affairs of the Committee on Foreign Relations, 89th Cong., 1st Sess.

60   40. Mineral Production: Fertilizers

2   1. Phosphates, potash, and sulfur
13   2. At least two of the fertilizer group
28   3. At least one of the fertilizer group
1   4. None of the fertilizer group
77   9. Not Ascertained

Source: United Nations, *Statistical Yearbook, 1965* (United Nations: United Nations, 1966).

61   41. Mineral Production: Fuels

15   1. Coal, lignite, crude petroleum, and natural gas
21   2. At least three of the fuel group
16   3. At least two of the fuel group
21   4. At least one of the fuel group
48   5. None of the fuel group
0   9. Not Ascertained

Source: United Nations, *Statistical Yearbook, 1965* (United Nations: United Nations, 1966).

62   42. Mineral Production: Iron

1   1. Very Large Producer (more than 20 percent of world total)
4   2. Large Producer (4-20 percent of world total)
5   3. Medium Producer (1.5-3.9 percent of world total)
11   4. Small Producer (.4-1.4 percent of world total)
32   5. Very Small Producer (less than .4 percent of world total)
67   6. Non-Producer or negligible
1   9. Not Ascertained

Source: United Nations, *Statistical Yearbook, 1965*
(United Nations: United Nations, 1966).

63   43.   Mineral Production: Basic Manufacturing Metals

1   1.   Copper, Lead, Zinc, Tin, and Aluminum
(Bauxite)
17   2.   At least four of this group
15   3.   At least three of this group
15   4.   At least two of this group
17   5.   At least one of this group
53   6.   None of this group
3   9.   Not Ascertained

Source: United Nations, *Statistical Yearbook, 1965*
(United Nations: United Nations, 1966).

64   44.   Mineral Production: Iron Alloys

0   1.   Manganese, Magnesite, Chromium, Molybden-
um, Nickel, Aluminum, and Tungsten
1   2.   At least six of this group
3   3.   At least five of this group
7   4.   At least four of this group
8   5.   At least three of this group
17   6.   At least two of this group
18   7.   At least one of this group
7   8.   Non-Producer
60   9.   Not Ascertained

Source: United Nations, *Statistical Yearbook, 1965*
(United Nations: United Nations, 1966).

65   45.   Mineral Production: Salt

69   1.   Producer
52   2.   Non-Producer
0   9.   Not Ascertained

Source: United Nations, *Statistical Yearbook, 1965*
(United Nations: United Nations, 1966).

66   46.   Mineral Production: Gold, Silver, and Diamonds

4   1.   Gold, Silver, and Diamonds
27   2.   At least two of this group
24   3.   At least one of this group
64   4.   Non-Producer or negligible

2   9. Not Ascertained

Source: United Nations, *Statistical Yearbook, 1965* (United Nations: United Nations, 1966).

67-68   47. Mineral Production: Now producing some mineral from the sea

0   01. Crude petroleum and other petroleum products

1   02. Diamonds

1   03. Tin Concentrates

0   04. Iron

0   05. Magnesium

0   06. Bromine

0   07. Sulfur

0   08. Gold

2   09. Salt

1   10. Coal

3   11. More than one of these mineral or mining products

111   12. None

2   99. Not Ascertained

Source: H. D. Hess, "The Ocean: Mining's New Frontier," Part IV of Engineering and Mining Journal's Undersea Mining Series, *Engineering and Mining Journal,* CLXVI (August, 1965), pp. 79-96, and John L. Mero, "Fourth Session," *Proceedings of the Mineral and Chemical Industry Seminar Series,* 1963-64, collated by J. D. Forrester and R. M. Edwards (Tucson: University of Arizona Press, 1964), pp. 85-125.

69   48. Claims to Territorial Sea

36   1. 3 miles

23   2. More than 3 miles but not more than 6 miles

34   3. More than 6 miles but not more than 12 miles

6   4. More than 12 miles

21   8. Not Applicable

1   9. Not Ascertained

Source: "Synoptical Table Concerning the Breadth and Juridicial Status of the Territorial Sea and Adjacent Zones," (U.N. Doc. A Conf. 19/4) (1960), in Second United Nations Conference on the Law of the Sea, *Official Records, Summary of Plenary Meetings and Meetings of the Committee of the Whole* (U.N. Doc. No. A/Conf. 19/8) (1960), and *Sovereignty of the Sea, Geographic Bulletin* No. 3 (April, 1965) (Washington: Department of State, 1965), pp. 26-27.

70-71   49. Miles of Sea Coast

9	01.	Less than 100 miles
39	02.	100-499 miles
17	03.	500-999 miles
12	04.	1,000-1,499 miles
6	05.	1,500-1,999 miles
3	06.	2,000-2,499 miles
4	07.	2,500-2,999 miles
1	08.	3,000-3,499 miles
9	09.	3,500 or more miles
21	10.	No sea coast
	00.	Not Ascertained

Source: *Sovereignty of the Sea, Geographic Bulletin* No. 3 (April, 1965) (Washington: Department of State, 1965), pp. 26-27.

72   50. Security Forces: Army (total personnel)

2	1.	Very Large (more than 1 million)
17	2.	Large (200,000-1,000,000)
18	3.	Medium (50,000-199,999)
22	4.	Small (10,000-49,999)
25	5.	Very Small (less than 10,000)
1	6.	None
36	9.	Not Ascertained

Source: *The Military Balance 1963-64* (London: The Institute for Strategic Studies, 1963), *The Military Balance 1965-1966* (London: The Institute for Strategic Studies, 1965), Helen Kitchen, ed., *A Handbook of African Affairs* (New York: Frederick A. Praeger for the African-American Institute, 1964), and S. H. Steinberg, ed., *The Statesman's Yearbook 1965-66* (New York: St. Martin's Press, 1965).

73   51. Security Forces: Navy (total vessels)

2	1. Very Large (more than 2,000)
11	2. Large (200-2,000)
13	3. Medium (90-199)
25	4. Small (20-89)
69	5. Very Small (less than 20) or none
0	6. None
1	9. Not Ascertained

Source: S. H. Steinberg, ed., *The Statesman's Yearbook 1965-66* (New York: St. Martin's Press, 1965), and Raymond V. B. Blackman, ed., *Jane's Fighting Ships 1965-66* (Great Missenden Bucks: Jane's Fighting Ships, 1966).

74   52. Security Forces: Navy (large and small combatants)

1	1. Very Large (more than 1,000)
3	2. Large (70-1,000)
11	3. Medium (25-69)
16	4. Small (10-24)
88	5. Very Small (less than 10) or none
1	6. None
1	9. Not Ascertained

Source: S. H. Steinberg, ed., *The Statesman's Yearbook 1965-66* (New York: St. Martin's Press, 1965), and Raymond V. B. Blackman, ed., *Jane's Fighting Ships 1965-66* (Great Missenden Bucks: Jane's Fighting Ships, 1966).

75   53. Security Forces: Air Force (front line combat a/c)

3	1. Very Large (more than 2,000)
5	2. Large (750-2,000)
12	3. Medium (300-749)
18	4. Small (100-299)
23	5. Very Small (less than 100)
2	6. None
58	9. Not Ascertained

Source: *The Military Balance 1963-64* (London: The Institute for Strategic Studies, 1963), *The Military Balance 1965-66* (London: The Institute for Strategic Studies, 1965), and S. H. Steinberg, ed., *The Statesman's Yearbook 1965-66* (New York: St. Martin's Press, 1965).

76   54. Military Personnel as a Percentage of Total Population

1	1. Very High (more than 4 percent of total population)
22	2. High (1.10-4 percent)
36	3. Medium (.35-1.09 percent)
28	4. Low (.05-.34 percent)
21	5. Very Low (less than .05 percent)
13	9. Not Ascertained

Source: Bruce M. Russett, et al., *World Handbook of Political and Social Indicators* (New Haven: Yale University Press, 1964), and calculated from populations obtained from United Nations, *Statistical Yearbook, 1965* (United Nations: United Nations, 1966), and military force figures obtained from *The Military Balance 1963-64* (London: The Institute for Strategic Studies, 1963), and *The Military Balance 1965-66* (London: The Institute for Strategic Studies, 1965), and Helen Kitchen, ed., *A Handbook of African Affairs* (New York: Frederick A. Praeger for the African-American Institute, 1964).

77   55. Expenditures on Defense as a Percentage of Gross National Product

1	1. Very High (more than 20 percent)
13	2. High (6-20 percent)
30	3. Medium (3-5.9 percent)
34	4. Low (1-2.9 percent)
10	5. Very Low (less than 1 percent)
33	9. Not Ascertained

Source: Bruce M. Russett, et al., *World Handbook of Political and Social Indicators* (New Haven: Yale University Press, 1964) *The Military Balance 1963-64* (London: The Institute for Strategic Studies, 1963), and *The Military Balance 1965-66* (London: The Institute for Strategic Studies, 1965).

78   56. Major Maritime Power (Special interest in sea law)

52	1. Yes
69	2. No

Source: Chapter 3 of this study

79   57. Major Air Power (Special interest in air law)

33	1. Yes
88	2. No.

Source: Chapter 4 of this study

SELECTED BIBLIOGRAPHY

1. AIR

ARTICLES

Brown, Elizabeth Gaspar. "The Rome Conventions of 1933 and 1952: Do they Point A Moral?" *Journal of Air Law and Commerce* 28 (Autumn 1961-62), 418-443.

Cabranes, Jose A. "Limitations of Liability in International Air Law: The Warsaw and Rome Conventions Reconsidered." *International and Comparative Law Quarterly* 15 (July 1966), 660-689.

Carroz, Jean. "International Legislation on Air Navigation Over the High Seas." *Journal of Air Law and Commerce* 26 (Spring 1959), 158-172.

Kreindler, Lee S. "The Denunciation of the Warsaw Convention." *Journal of Air Law and Commerce* 31 (Autumn 1965), 291-303.

Latchford, Stephen. "Freedom of the Air — Early Theories: Freedom; Zone; Sovereignty." *Documents and State Papers* 1. Washington: Department of State, (August 1948), 303-322.

_____. "The Right of Innocent Passage in International Civil Air Navigation Agreements." *Department of State Bulletin* 11 (2 July 1944), 19-24.

Lissitzyn, Oliver J. "Some Legal Implications of the U-2 and RB-47 Incidents." *American Journal of International Law* 56 (January 1962), 135-142.

_____. "The Treatment of Aerial Intruders in Recent Practice and International Law." *American Journal of International Law* 47 (October 1953), 559-588.

Moon, Albert I., Jr. "A Look at Airspace Sovereignty." *Journal of Air Law and Commerce* 29 (Autumn 1963), 328-345.

Rinck, Gerd. "Damage Caused by Foreign Aircraft to Third Parties." *Journal of Air Law and Commerce* 28 (Autumn 1961-62), 405-417.

Sand, Peter H. "Air Carriers' Limitation of Liability and Air Passengers' Accident Compensation Under the Warsaw Convention." *Journal of Air Law and Commerce* 28 (Summer 1961-62), 260-284.

BOOKS

Billyou, De Forest. *Air Law*. New York: Ad Press, Ltd., 1963.

Cooper, John C. *The Right to Fly*. New York: Henry Holt and Co., 1947.

Honig, J. P. *The Legal Status of Aircraft*. The Hague: Martinus Nijhoff, 1956.

Johnson, D. H. N. *Rights in Air Space*. Manchester: Manchester University Press, 1965.

McNair, Lord Arnold D. *The Law of the Air*. 2nd ed. London: Kerr and MacCrindle, 1953.

Rhyne, Charles S. *Aviation Accident Law*. Washington: Columbia Law Book Co., 1947.

Sand, Peter H. et al. *An Historical Survey of the Law of Flight*. Montreal: Institute of Air and Space Law, McGill University, 1961.

Shawcross, C. N. and K. M. Beaumont. *Air Law*. 2nd ed. London: Butterworth, 1951.

Verplaetse, Julian G. *International Law in Vertical Space: Air, Outer Space, Ether*. South Hackensack: Fred B. Rothman and Co., 1960.

Wassenbergh, H. A. *Post-War International Civil Aviation Policy and the Law of the Air*. 2nd rev. ed. The Hague: Martinus Nijhoff, 1962.

II. SEA

ARTICLES

Allen, Edward W. "Territorial Waters and Extraterritorial Rights." *American Journal of International Law* 47 (July 1953), 478-480.

Boggs, S. Whitmore. "Delimitation of Seaward Areas Under National Jurisdiction." *American Journal of International Law* 45 (April 1951), 240-266.

Briggs, Herbert W. "Jurisdiction Over the Sea Bed and Subsoil Beyond Territorial Waters." *American Journal of International Law* 45 (April 1951), 338-342.

Dean, Arthur H. "The Geneva Conference on the Law of the Sea: What was Accomplished." *American Journal of International Law* 52 (October 1958), 607-628.

_____. "The Second Geneva Conference on the Law of the Sea." *American Journal of International Law* 54 (October 1960), 751-789.

Goddu, L. W., Jr. "IMCO, An Assistance to the American Merchant Marine." *United States Naval Institute Proceedings* 93 (December 1966), 70-83.

Gross, Leo. "Geneva Conference on the Law of the Sea and the Right of Innocent Passage Through the Gulf of Aqaba." *American Journal of International Law* 53 (July 1959), 564-594.

Gutteridge, J. A. C. "The Regime of the Continental Shelf." *Transactions of the Grotius Society* 44 (1957), 77-89.

Jessup, Philip C. "The Law of the Sea Around Us." *American Journal of International Law* 55 (January 1961), 104-109.

Kunz, Josef L. "Continental Shelf and International Law: Confusion and Abuse." *American Journal of International Law* 50 (October 1956), 828-853.

McDougal, Myres S., William T. Burke, and Ivan A. Vlasic. "Maintenance of Public Order at Sea and the Nationality of Ships." *American Journal of International Law* 54 (January 1960), 25-116.

Menchaca, Andres A. Aramburu. "Character and Scope of the Rights Declared and Practiced Over the Continental Sea and Shelf." *American Journal of International Law* 47 (January 1953), 120-123.

Sorensen, Max. "The Law of the Sea." *International Conciliation* 520 (1958).

Waldock, C. H. M. "The Legal Basis of Claims to the Continental Shelf." *Transactions of the Grotius Society* 36 (1950), 115-148.

Whiteman, Marjorie M. "Conference on the Law of the Sea: Convention on the Continental Shelf." *American Journal of International Law* 52 (October 1958), 629-659.

Young, Richard. "The Geneva Convention on the Continental Shelf: A First Impression." *American Journal of International Law* 52 (October 1958), 733-738.

_____. "Sedentary Fisheries and the Convention on the Continental Shelf." *American Journal of International Law* 55 (April 1961), 359-373.

BOOKS

Colombos, C. John. *The International Law of the Sea.* 5th rev. ed. London: Longmans, Green and Co., Ltd., 1962.

Johnson, Douglas M. *The International Law of Fisheries: A Framework for Policy-Oriented Inquiries.* New Haven and London: Yale University Press, 1965.

McDougal, Myres S. and William T. Burke. *The Public Order of the Oceans: A Contemporary Law of the Sea.* New Haven and London: Yale University Press, 1962.

Oda, Shigeru. *International Control of Sea Resources.* Leyden: A. W. Sythoff, 1963.

Reiff, Henry. *The United States and the Treaty Law of the Sea.* Minneapolis: University of Minnesota Press, 1959.

Research in International Law of the Harvard Law School. *The Law of Territorial Waters. American Journal of International Law, Supplement* 23 (April 1929).

Smith, H. A. *The Law and Custom of the Sea.* 2nd ed. New York: Frederick A. Praeger, 1950.

III. SPACE*

ARTICLES

Becker, Loftus. "Major Aspects of the Problems of Outer Space." *Department of State Bulletin* 38 (9 June 1958), 962-967.

————. "The Control of Space." *Department of State Bulletin* 39 (15 September 1958), 416-420.

————. "United States Foreign Policy and the Development of Law for Outer Space." *The JAG Journal* (February 1959), 4-7, 28-31.

Beresford, Spencer M. "Surveillance Aircraft and Satellites: A Problem of International Law." *Journal of Air Law and Commerce* 27 (Spring 1960), 107-118.

---

* For a comprehensive bibliography on outer space see Irvin L. White, Clifton E. Wilson, and John A. Vosburgh, *Law and Politics in Outer Space: A Bibliography,* forthcoming in 1970 from the Institute of Government Research, University of Arizona.

Berkner, Lloyd V. "Earth Satellites and Foreign Policy." *Foreign Affairs* 36 (January 1958), 221-231.

Campbell, John W. "Natural Resources in Space." *Analog* 71 (March 1963), 8-16, 90-94.

Cheng, Bin. "International Law and High Altitude Flight: Balloons, Rockets, and Man-Made Satellites." *International and Comparative Law Quarterly* 6 (July 1957), 487-505.

Cheprov, I. "Global or American Space Communications System?" *International Affairs* (Moscow) No. 12 (1964), 69-74.

Cooper, John Cobb. "Flight Space and the Satellites." *International and Comparative Law Quarterly* 7 (1958), 82-91.

_____. "Legal Problems of Upper Space." *Journal of Air Law and Commerce* 23 (Summer 1956), 308-316.

_____. "Missiles and Satellites — The Law and Our National Policy." *American Bar Association Journal* 44 (April 1958), 317-321.

_____. "The Russian Satellite — Legal and Political Problems." *Journal of Air Law and Commerce* 24 (Autumn 1957), 379-383.

_____. "Space above the Seas." *The JAG Journal* (February 1959), 8-9, 31-34.

Craig, D. Broward. "National Sovereignty at High Altitudes. *Journal of Air Law and Commerce* 24 (Autumn 1957), 384-397.

Crane, Robert D. "The Beginnings of Marxists Space Jurisprudence." *American Journal of International Law* 57 (July 1963), 615-625.

_____. "Soviet Attitude Toward International Space Law." *American Journal of International Law* 56 (July 1962), 685-723.

Draper, Delbert M. "Satellites and Sovereignty." *The JAG Journal* (September-October 1956), 23-24.

Gardner, Richard N. "Outer Space: Problems of Law and Power." *Department of State Bulletin* 49 (2 September 1963), 367-371.

Jacobini, H. B. "Effective Control as Related to the Extension of Sovereignty in Space." *Journal of Public Law* 7 (Spring 1958), 97-119.

Jaffe, Morton S. "International Law and Space Exploration." *Saint Louis University Law Journal* 6 (Spring 1960), 68-80.

—————. "Some Considerations in the International Law and Politics of Space." *Saint Louis University Law Journal* 5 (Spring 1959), 375-384.

Jenks, C. Wilfred. "International Law and Activities in Space." *International and Comparative Law Quarterly* 5 (1956), 99-114.

Jessup, Philip C. and Howard J. Taubenfeld. "The United Nations *Ad Hoc* Committee on the Peaceful Uses of Outer Space." *American Journal of International Law* 53 (October 1959), 877-881.

Knorr, Klaus. "On the International Implications of Outer Space Activities." *World Politics* 12 (July 1960), 564-584.

Korvin, E. "International Status of Cosmic Space." *International Affairs* (Moscow) no. 1 (1959), 53-59.

Larionov, V. "The Doctrine of Military Domination in Outer Space." *International Affairs* (Moscow) no. 10 (1964), 25-30.

Lissitzyn, Oliver J. "The American Position on Outer Space and Antarctica." *American Journal of International Law* 53 (January 1959), 126-131.

McDougal, Myres S. "Artificial Satellites: A Modest Proposal." *American Journal of International Law* 51 (January 1957), 74-77.

————— and Leon Lipson. "Perspectives for a Law of Outer Space." *American Journal of International Law* 52 (July 1958), 407-431.

McMahon, J. F. "Legal Aspects of Outer Space." *British Yearbook of International Law* 38 (1962), 339-399.

Merchant, Livingston. "Importance of the Space Program in International Relations." *Department of State Bulletin* 42 (8 February 1960), 213-217.

Milstein, M. "The U.S.A. Plans Military Use of Outer Space." *International Affairs* (Moscow) no. 5 (1959), 44-49.

Niholayev, A. "International Co-operation for the Peaceful Uses of Outer Space." *International Affairs* (Moscow) no. 5 (1950), 76-80.

Perchorkin, V. "The Pentagon Theoreticians and the Cosmos." *International Affairs* (Moscow) no. 3 (1961), 32-36.

Quigg, Philip. "Open Skies and Open Space." *Foreign Affairs* 37 (October 1958), 95-106.

Schick, F. B. "A Functional Approach to the Problems of Space Law." *Utah Law Review* 7 (Spring 1961), 322-341.

Sibryakov, G. "Real Aims of U.S. Space Co-operation." *International Affairs* (Moscow) no. 2 (1966), 62-65.

Weinmann, Eric. "The Law of Space." *Foreign Service Journal* 35 (April 1958), 22-25.

Winthrop, H. "The Space Sciences and Social Change." *Journal of Human Relations* 12:1 (1964), 127-141.

Yeager, Philip B. and John R. Stark. "Decatur's Doctrine: A Code for Outer Space." *United States Naval Institute Proceedings* 83 (September 1957), 931-937.

Zolotov, G. "Space Rights and Obligations." *International Affairs* (Moscow) no. 7 (1963), 92-93.

BOOKS

Christol, Carl Q. *The International Law of Outer Space*. Naval War College, International Law Studies 1962. Washington: U.S. Government Printing Office, 1966.

Cohen, Maxwell (ed.). *Law and Politics in Space: Specific and Urgent Problems in the Law of Outer Space*. Montreal: McGill University Press, 1964.

Fawcett, J. E. S. *Outer Space and International Order*. Annual David Davies Memorial Lecture, March 1964. London: The David Davies Memorial Institute of International Studies, 1964.

Goldsen, Joseph M. (ed.). *Outer Space in World Politics*. New York: Frederick A. Praeger, 1963.

Golovine, M. N. *Conflict in Space: A Pattern of War in a New Dimension*. New York: St. Martin's Press, 1962.

Haley, Andrew G. *Space Law and Government*. New York: Appleton-Century-Crofts, 1963.

Hall, R. Cargill. *The International Legal Problems in Space Exploration, An Analytical Review*. Sunnyvale: Lockheed Missiles and Space Co., 1964.

Jenks, C. Wilfred. *Space Law*. New York and Washington: Frederick A. Praeger, 1965.

Jessup, Philip C. and Howard J. Taubenfeld. *Controls for Outer Space and the Antarctic Analogy.* New York: Columbia University Press, 1959.

Lipson, Leon and Nicholas deB. Katzenback. *Report to the National Aeronautics and Space Administration on the Law of Outer Space.* Chicago: American Bar Foundation, 1961.

McDougal, Myres S., Harold D. Lasswell, and Ivan A. Vlasic. *Law and Public Order in Space.* New Haven and London: Yale University Press, 1963.

Schick, F. B. *Who Rules the Skies: Some Political and Legal Problems of the Space Age.* Salt Lake City: Institute of International Studies, University of Utah, 1961.

Schwartz, Leonard E. *International Organizations and Space Co-operation.* Durham: World Rule at Law Center, Duke University, 1962.

Taubenfeld, Howard J. (ed.). *Space and Society: Studies for the Seminar on Problems of Outer Space Sponsored by the Carnegie Endowment for International Peace.* Dobbs Ferry: Oceana Publications, Inc., 1964.

Vasquez, Modesto Seara. *Cosmic International Law.* Translated by Elaine Malley. Detroit: Wayne University Press, 1965.

INDEX

Decision-Making for Space was printed by the letterpress process on 60 pound Chatfield Sixty-Eight Opaque paper. The typeface chosen for the text was Granjon, and Optima Roman was used for headings. The printing of the book and the binding in Interlaken Pallium Linen bookcloth were carried out by the Benton Review Publishing, Company, Fowler, Indiana. The dust jacket was printed by offset lithography by Owen Litho Service, Spencer, Indiana, and features a photograph of the earth provided by the National Aeronautics and Space Administration Manned Spacecraft Center, Houstin, Texas. Designwork was by Larry Stultz, Purdue University graphics designer, and editorial and production supervision were by Diane Dubiel, assistant university editor at Purdue.